IMAGES of America

LINCOLN

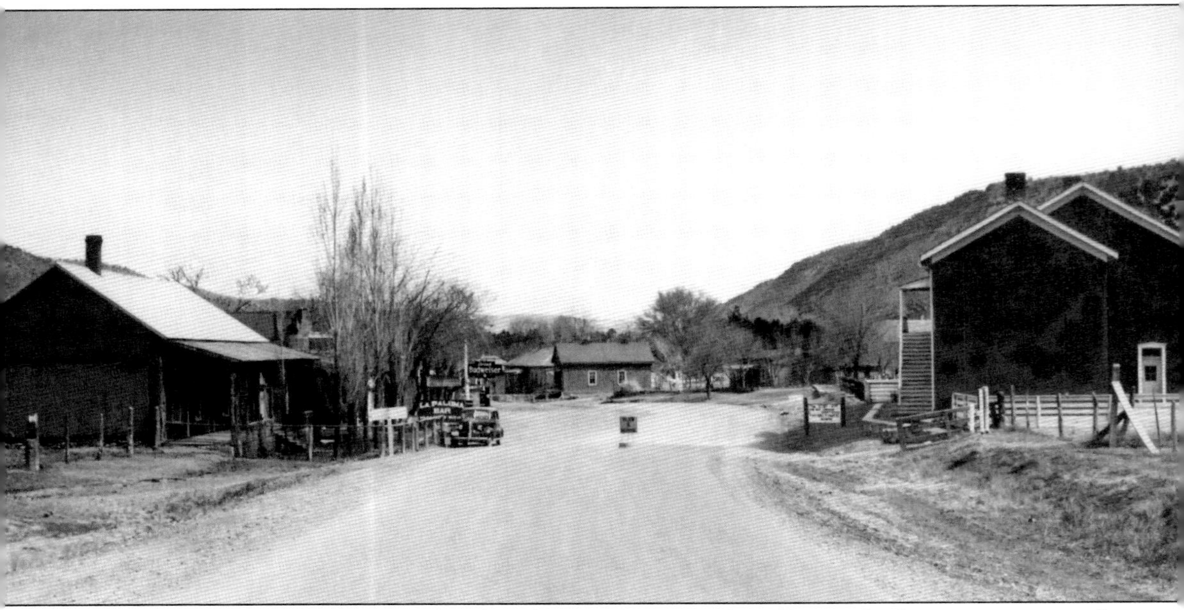

Lincoln County at the time of its founding on January 16, 1869, was the largest county in the United States. The town of Lincoln, originally called La Placita del Río Bonito by the Spanish, was settled in the 1840s and became the county seat. This photograph of the peaceful main street of Lincoln in the 1940s belies its turbulent history. Pres. Rutherford B. Hayes called it "the most dangerous street in America." The likes of Billy the Kid, Sheriff Pat F. Garrett, and other notables kicked up the dust in Lincoln as they rode into the pages of history.

On the Cover: The La Paloma Museum Gift Shop and Bar was a popular tourist attraction in Lincoln.

IMAGES
of America

LINCOLN

Ray John de Aragón

ARCADIA
PUBLISHING

ISBN 978-1-4671-3056-1

Published by Arcadia Publishing
Charleston, South Carolina

Printed in the United States of America

Library of Congress Control Number: 2013948886

For all general information, please contact Arcadia Publishing:
Telephone 843-853-2070
Fax 843-853-0044
E-mail sales@arcadiapublishing.com
For customer service and orders:
Toll-Free 1-888-313-2665

Visit us on the Internet at www.arcadiapublishing.com

This book is dedicated to my father, Maximo de Aragón, who introduced me to Billy the Kid and the Lincoln County War as a boy.

Contents

Acknowledgments

First, I would like to acknowledge my father, Maximo de Aragón, who piqued my interest in Billy the Kid and all of his aficionados. Later influences included S. Omar Barker in my hometown of Las Vegas, New Mexico, and Tom McGrath, who was a living legend. My father and McGrath knew some of the participants in the famous Lincoln County War and shared precious memories concerning this episode in New Mexico history with anyone who would listen. My great-grandmother, Doña Catalina Mondragon de Valdez, treated Billy the Kid when she was a medicine woman and was personally acquainted with and cared for many who would make a mark in New Mexico history in the late 19th century and early 20th century. I would like to recognize Don Lavash, Leon Metz, Marc Simmons, Bob Utley, Howard Bryan, Will Kelleher (whom my father knew), Luis Branch, Dr. Lynn Perrigo, and Nora Henn, who steered me in the right direction. My wife, Rosa María Calles, is deeply appreciated; without her guiding influence and hard work, these people would never have been brought back to life. All of those Lincoln forebears who passed on a rich legacy in history for generations are remembered in memoriam with this book.

I would also like to thank Las Vegas, New Mexico, historian Marcus Gottschalk; Susan Berry, researcher at the Silver City Museum; Robin Gilliam, former member of the Lincoln County Heritage Trust Photograph Analysis Project; and Robert Stahl, historian from Arizona, for their invaluable help. Assistance from Arthur Olivas and Richard Rudisill, from the Photo Archives at the Museum of New Mexico, is also deeply appreciated. Additionally, Dianne Stein, with the New Mexico Historical Society; Lawrence O. Ealy, great-grandson of Taylor Ealy; Janice Maxwell, of the Pete Maxwell family; Fred N. Kimmel, author of *The Lincoln County Trilogy*; Grant B. Romer, of the George Eastman House at the International Museum of Photography and Film; Sharon Long; Susan Mathews, former assistant archivist at the University of Arizona; Norman J. Bender; Beth Schneider of the J. Evetts Haley History Center; Dr. Thomas G. Kyle; and J.W. Grassham, of the Center for Southwest Research, are respectfully acknowledged for their gracious assistance.

Unless otherwise noted, all images in this volume appear courtesy of the author.

INTRODUCTION

Few other towns in the Old West have captured the public imagination as much as Lincoln, New Mexico. The area the town sits on was first the home of the Piros Indians. Next, Hispanic sheepherders from as far away as Socorro, Belen, Mesilla, and other parts of New Mexico grazed their large flocks of sheep on the lush green fields near the Río Bonito and other nearby waterways. The sheepherders erected *jacales*—temporary seasonal dwellings meant to provide shelter during inclement weather. Sometime in the 1840s, Hispanic ranchers and their families decided to build permanent homes in a spot they called La Placita del Río Bonito de San Juan Bautista, "the little town of the beautiful river of St. John the Baptist." The town flourished through the years with the building of a church, school, and general stores. The principal methods of construction in the town included adobe (mud bricks made with a dirt and straw mixture) and *vigas* (pine wood beams transported from northern New Mexico forests and used to create roofs). Fields were planted, cattle and other farm animals were brought in, and the area thrived.

After New Mexico became a US territory in 1850, Fort Stanton was erected about 10 miles west of Lincoln in 1855 to protect settlers along the Río Bonito from warring Indians. Soldiers stationed at Fort Stanton bought beef, grain, and other necessary items such as soap and candles at the settlement. In 1869, Saturnino Baca, a leading member of the community and a member of the New Mexico territorial legislature, sponsored a bill to create a new county that would incorporate the settlement of La Placita del Río Bonito. On January 16, 1869, the county of Lincoln was created and named after Pres. Abraham Lincoln. La Placita was renamed Lincoln, and the town became the county seat. Trade increased between Lincoln and Fort Stanton, so Emil Fritz, a former officer at the fort, partnered with Maj. Lawrence G. Murphy to operate a business on the grounds of the fort called L.G. Murphy and Company. Murphy secured government contracts to provide beef, vegetables, and other staples to the fort and the nearby Mescalero Apache Indian Reservation agency. The staples were purchased from the residents at Lincoln and nearby farms and ranches. Murphy was an unscrupulous businessman who never thought twice about price gouging and selling stolen items to his customers. He hired another ex-soldier named James J. Dolan as a store clerk. Dolan, in a dispute, attempted to murder Capt. James Randlett, and after this incident, they were all evicted from the fort.

Murphy managed to keep the government contracts, so he decided to build a massive two-story building in Lincoln as the home base of L.G. Murphy and Company. The business—often called "The House"—was extremely profitable; in fact, it was so profitable that the company monopolized the region's economy. Major Murphy allied himself with the Santa Fe Ring, and with this political powerhouse on his side, he could engage in land theft, cattle rustling, and other illegal activities with impunity from the law. After Fritz left the area because of health issues and Murphy began to deal with his own serious health problems, he sold the business to Dolan, who took on John H. Riley as his partner. The business then became known as James J. Dolan and Company. Dolan kept hired gunmen, first employed by Murphy, to intimidate the local populace, and he continued previous tactics of lawlessness to maintain economic control of the region. In 1879, an Englishman named John H. Tunstall moved to Lincoln and began a partnership with Alexander McSween, a lawyer who had built his home and law office in Lincoln. Tunstall established a rival business named J.H. Tunstall and Company and purchased supplies and merchandise for his store from Otero, Sellers, and Company and Brown and Manzanres Company, wholesale distributing companies located in Las Vegas, New Mexico. Tunstall's business grew rapidly, and it did not take long for a feud to erupt between the two factions. This became known as the Lincoln County War, which began in 1878 and proceeded off and on until 1881. Both Tunstall and McSween became victims of the war along with several of their followers. Dolan had the support of the military at Fort Stanton, so his side—which included corrupt lawmen and politicians—succeeded in getting rid of the competition.

After the Lincoln County War, the town of Lincoln grew and prospered. With nearly 1,000 families residing in the area by 1884, Lincoln had its own newspaper, resident photographer, blacksmith, several mercantile stores, an undertaker, and, eventually, its own baseball team. However, since Lincoln was far removed from rail centers, it was only a matter of time before the town would decline. The town still lives on in history due to one of its most famous residents, Billy the Kid, and the famous clash between its merchants and gunfighters.

One

Lincoln, Land of Opportunity

Lincoln County and the town of Lincoln attracted many newcomers who saw the area as a great land of opportunity. New arrivals included Union and Confederate veterans of the Civil War, plus some Southern sympathizers. Prominent among the former Confederates was Capt. Joseph Calloway Lea, who had distinguished himself as a member of William Clarke Quantrill's Confederate guerilla raiders. For the most part, the armed men felt the only way to a bright future was through appropriation and enforcing claims with weapons. They also captured and branded horses and cattle and fenced in land and water holes with barbed wire. The resulting range wars pitted Hispanic free-range ranchers and farmers against those who sought to ignore the rights of civilians. Lawyers with dubious credentials and other opportunists vied against each other for advantage, so vigilante justice prevailed.

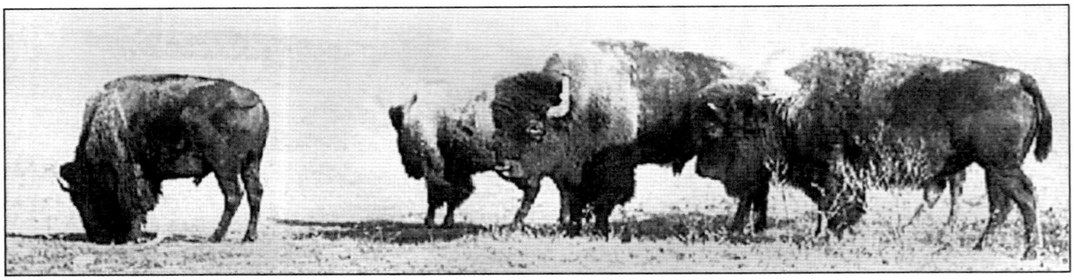

Buffalo and other wildlife grazed on the lands of Lincoln.

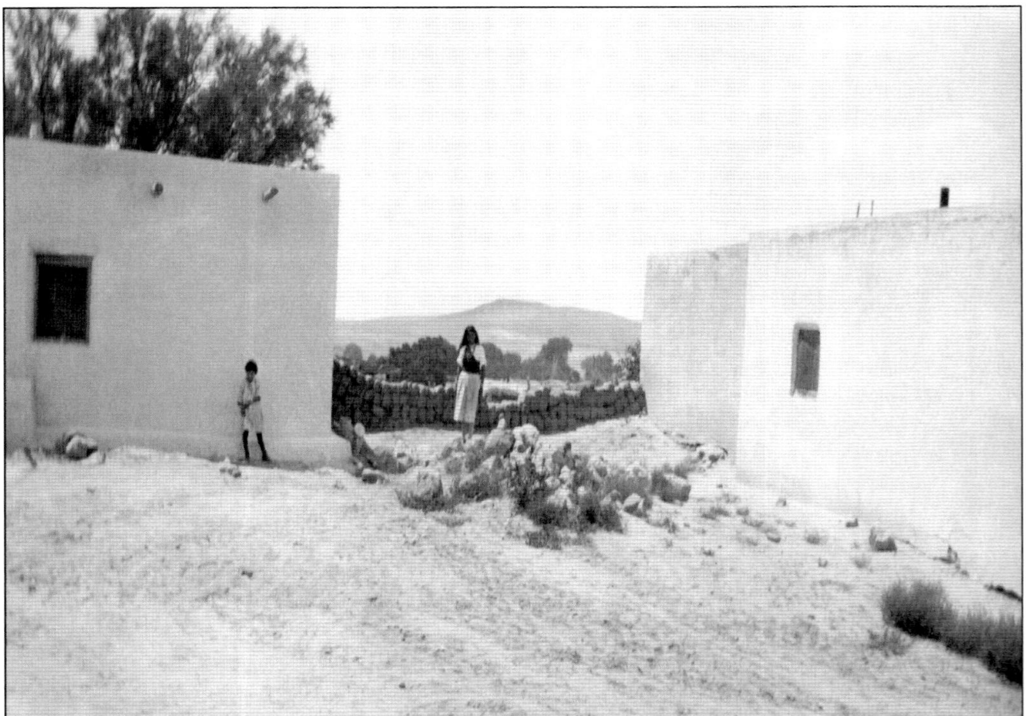

Various Native American tribes claimed the area of Lincoln, including the Piros, Jicarilla, and Mescalero Indian tribes. The Apaches and other tribes traveled the area hunting for wild game. The Spanish had policies to protect and conserve the environment so that buffalo (bison) and other species could continue to thrive. After the white settlers arrived, fur traders, the railroad, and sportsmen nearly decimated the buffalo, and a major food source for the Indians disappeared.

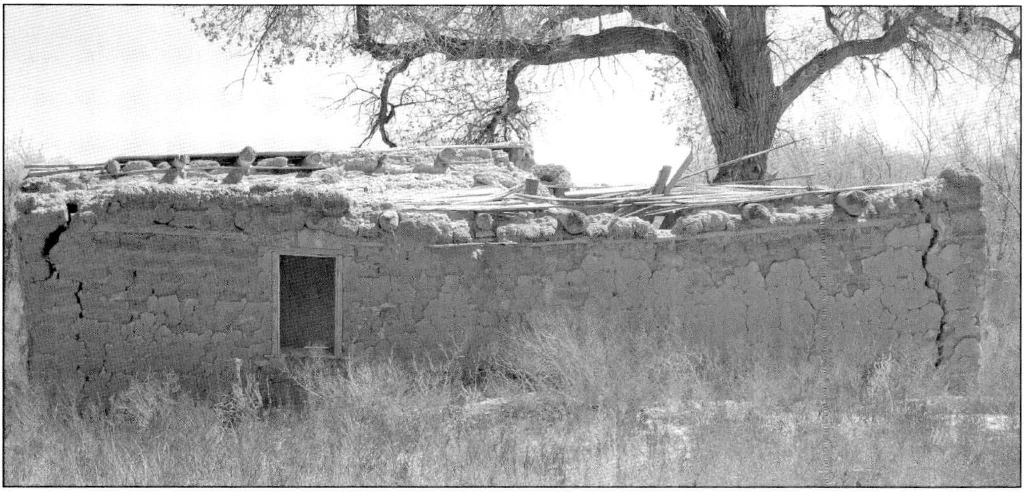

Hispanic sheep herders from various communities in New Mexico moved into the area of Lincoln to graze their sheep. They built temporary shelters called jacales (shacks) like the one pictured. Some of the sheep herders decided to live in the area, so they built more permanent dwellings for themselves and their families. (Photograph by Santiago de Aragón.)

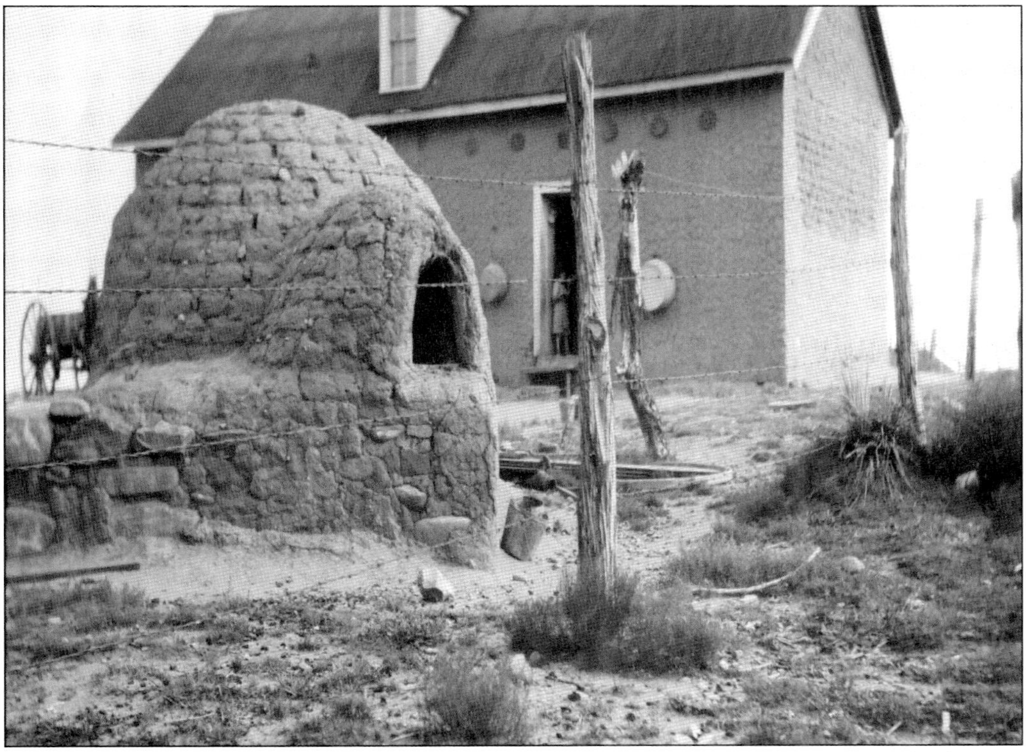

Permanent homes resembled the one pictured here. These often included a *horno*, which was a beehive-shaped oven used to bake bread. The horno was of Moorish and Spanish Colonial origin. Pueblo Indians readily adapted the horno to their culture and built many at their dwellings.

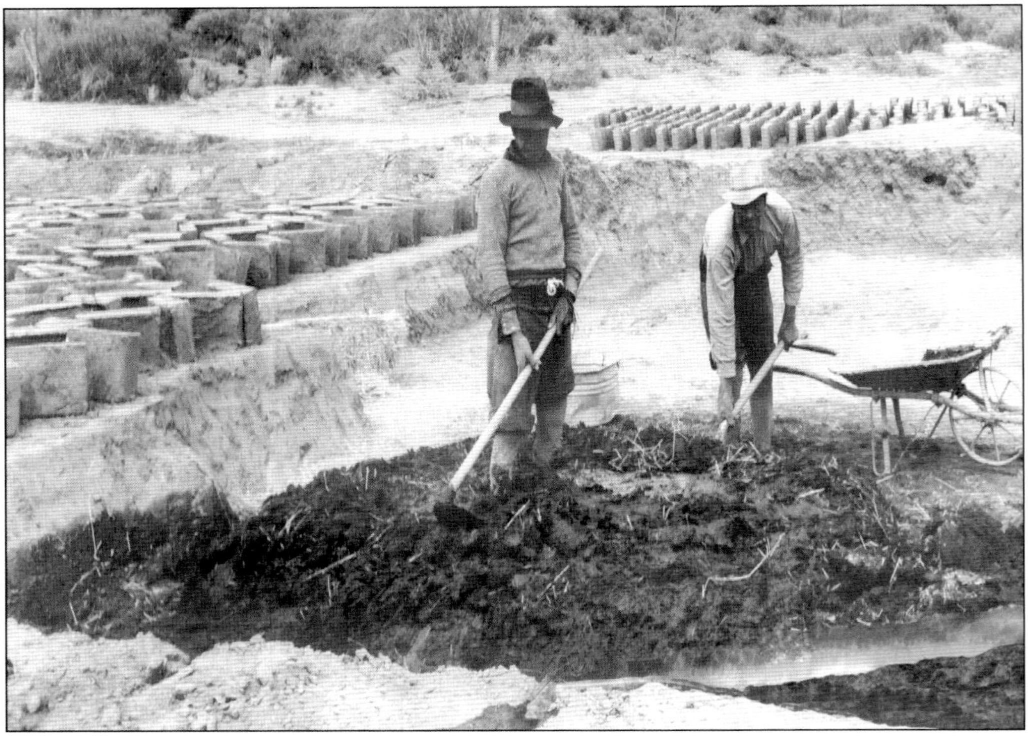

Hispanic settlers used adobe bricks made from mud and straw for construction (above). The *torreon* (fortified tower) pictured in the image below was used for protection, and the horno was built with adobe.

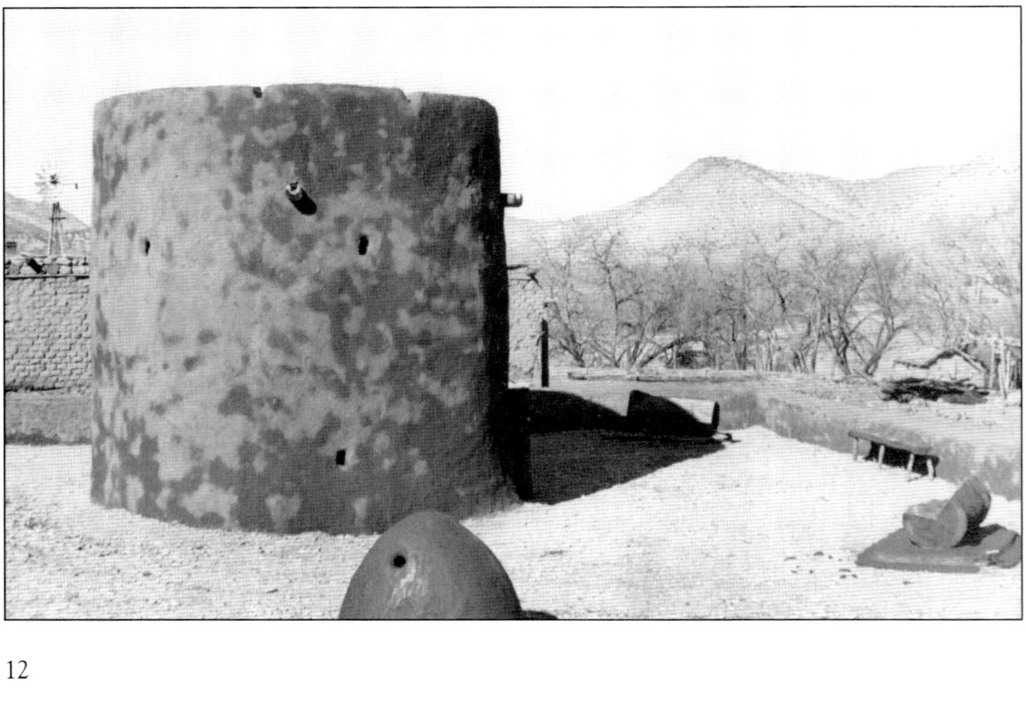

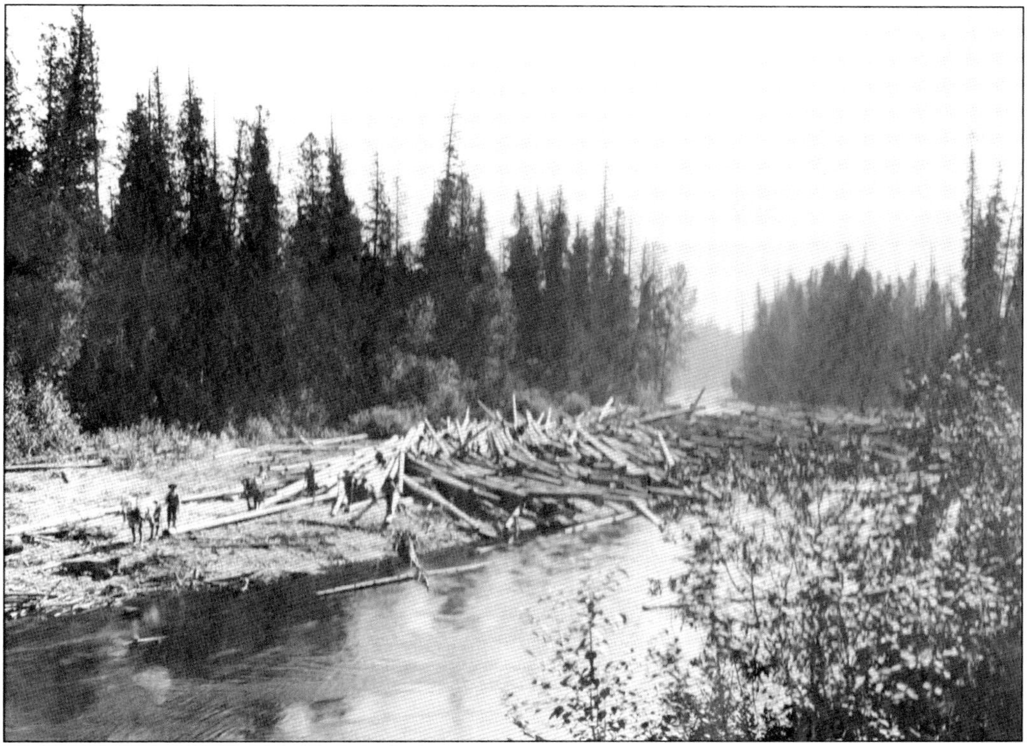

Loggers working in northern New Mexico forests shipped pine vigas (beams for roofs) and milled lumber. The lumber was used for construction on many farms and ranches, like the Anderson Ranch pictured below, and in towns including Lincoln.

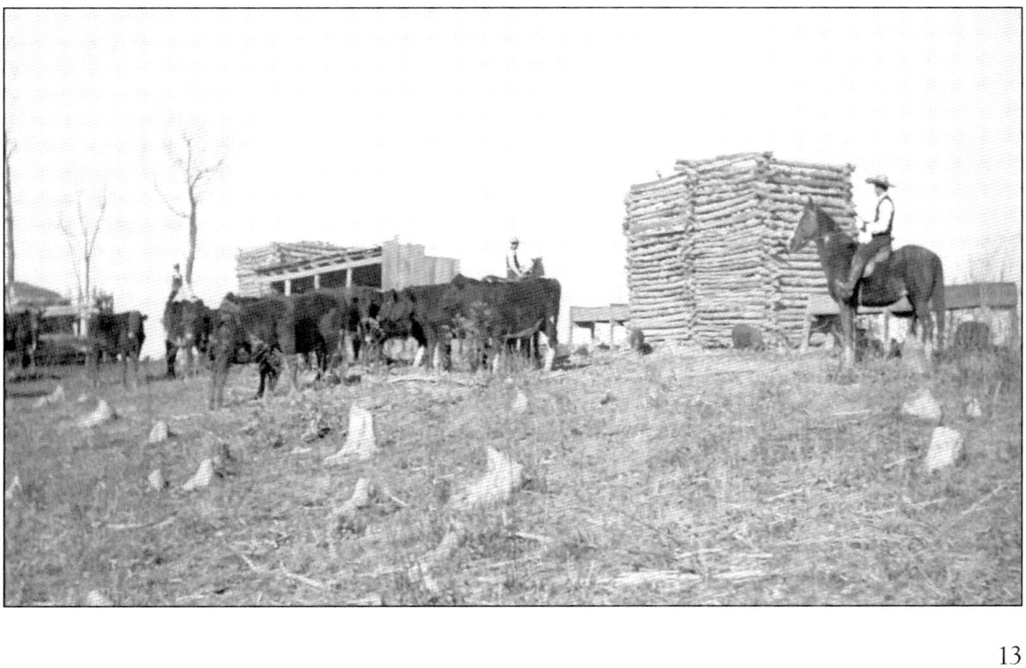

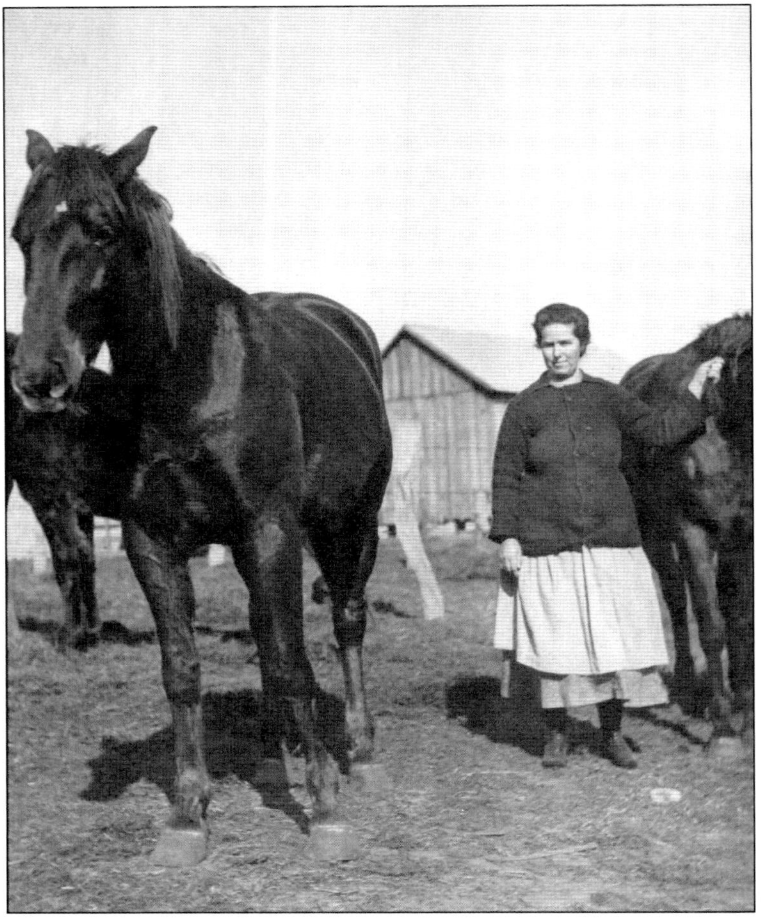

Women participated in all activities of the farms and ranches around Lincoln, including feeding the horses and cows and taking care of the children. They also had vegetable gardens and fruit trees and sewed and cooked. Life was hard, as women washed clothes and carried water from the wells or rivers like the Río Bonito—which flowed near Lincoln—to their homes.

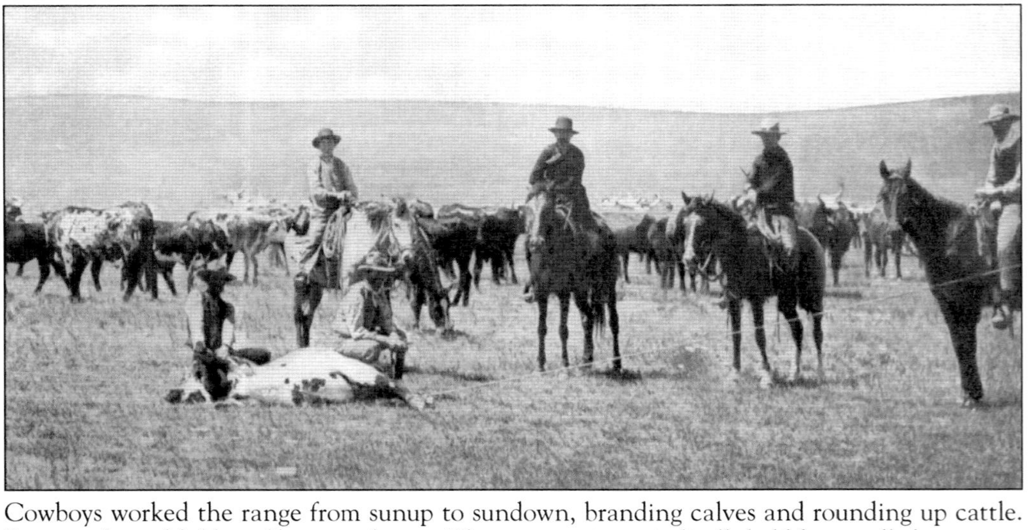

Cowboys worked the range from sunup to sundown, branding calves and rounding up cattle. Farmers planted fields and harvested crops. The community periodically held feasts called *matanzas*, wherein fattened pigs were slaughtered and barbequed, and all shared the meat.

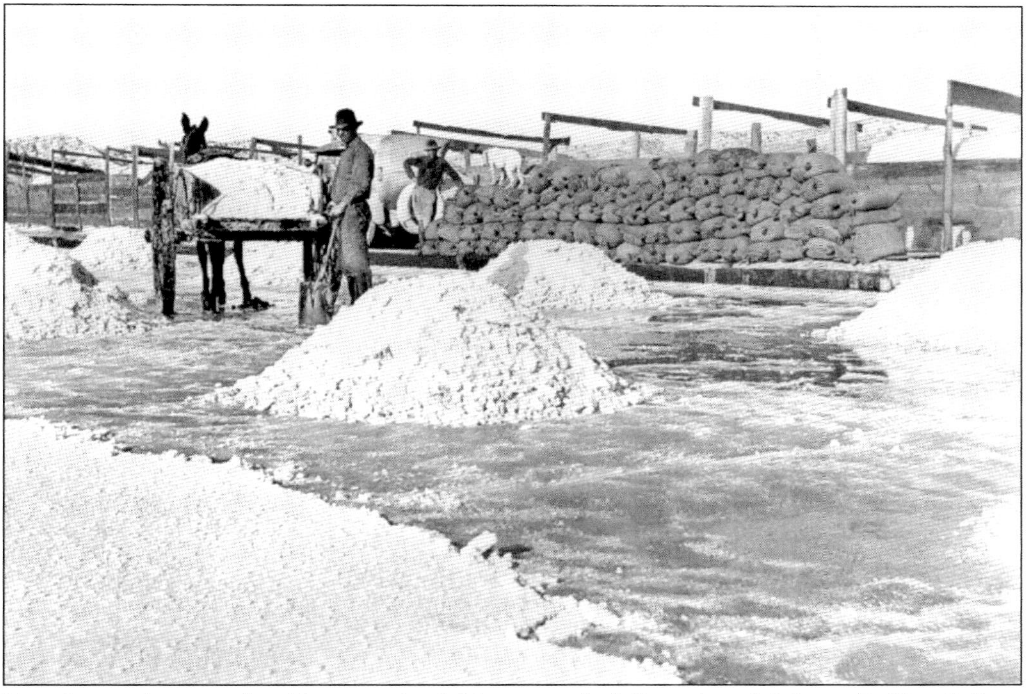

Lincoln merchants and residents received shipments of salt from the salt lakes called Las Salinas that were located near Willard, New Mexico.

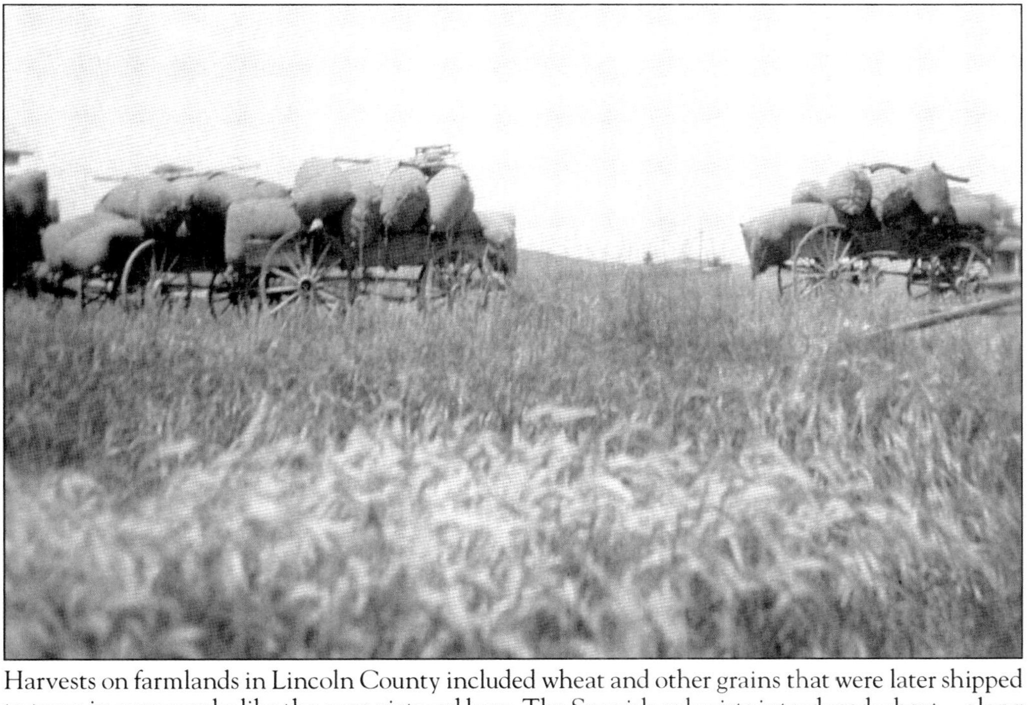

Harvests on farmlands in Lincoln County included wheat and other grains that were later shipped to town in gunnysacks like the ones pictured here. The Spanish colonists introduced wheat—along with horses, cattle, swine, and chickens—into New Mexico in the late 16th century.

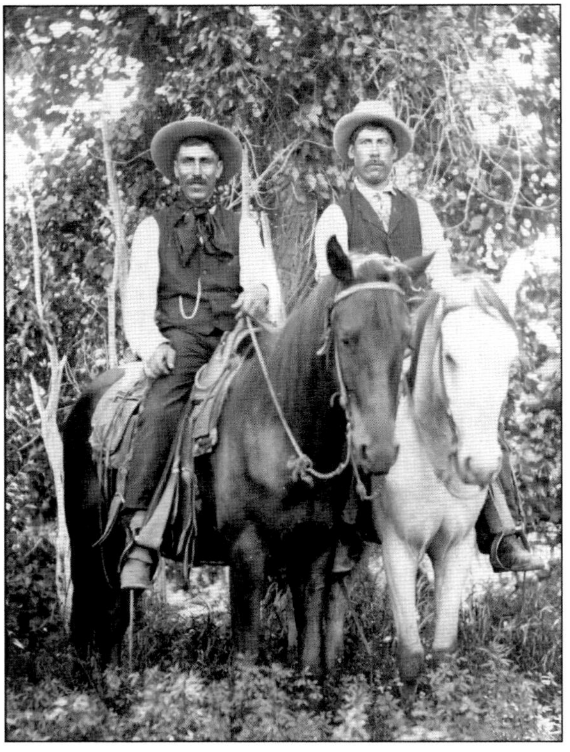

José Valdez (left) was involved in the Lincoln County War and was well known in Lincoln. The other man in the photograph is Ilizardo Maestas.

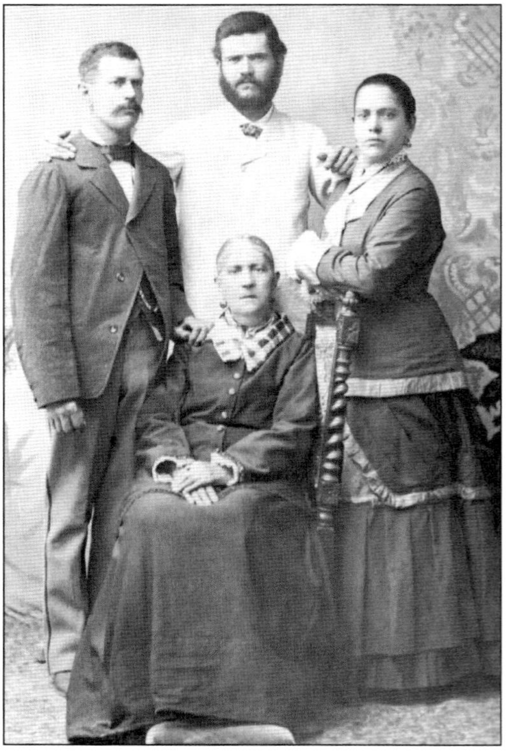

Pictured here are Calletano Hernandez, J.M. Hernandez, Librada Hernandez, and Mariana Hernandez. This photograph was taken on April 13, 1881.

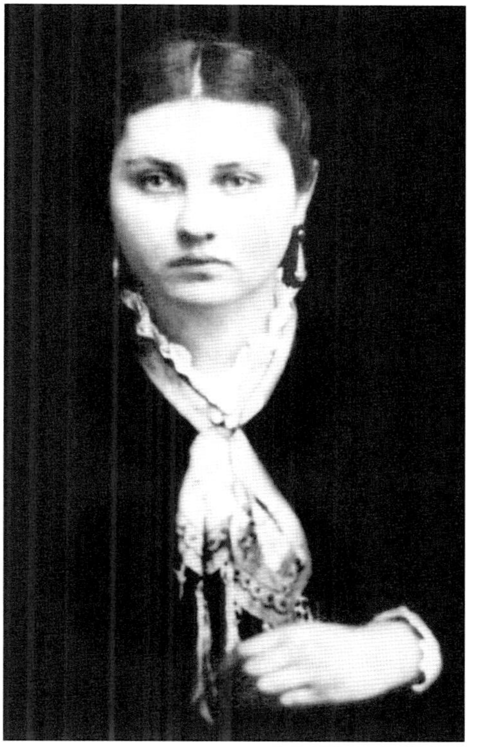

Hispanic women picked the crops in Lincoln. They dried and canned fruit and vegetables, which was then a tradition unknown in the eastern United States. They made beef jerky and hardtack biscuits for the men who shepherded or drove cattle. The women also created wool weavings and other items they sold or traded. Hispanic women were important figures in Lincoln. They served as role models and sometimes fought along with their husbands during Indian attacks. The women pictured in these 1870s tintypes offer a representation of the hair and dress styles that were popular in Lincoln.

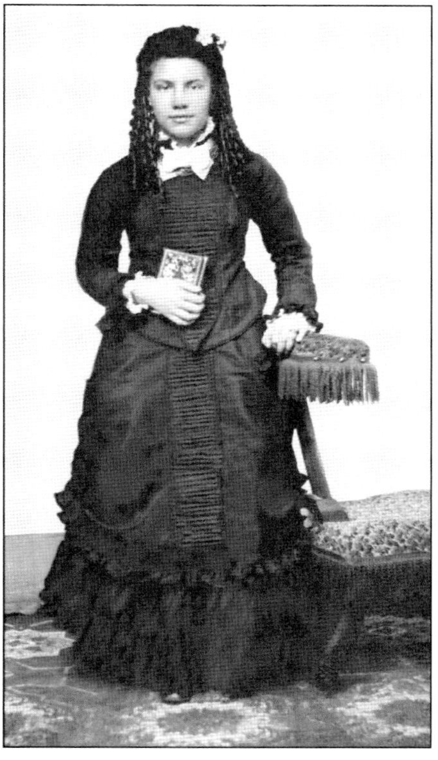

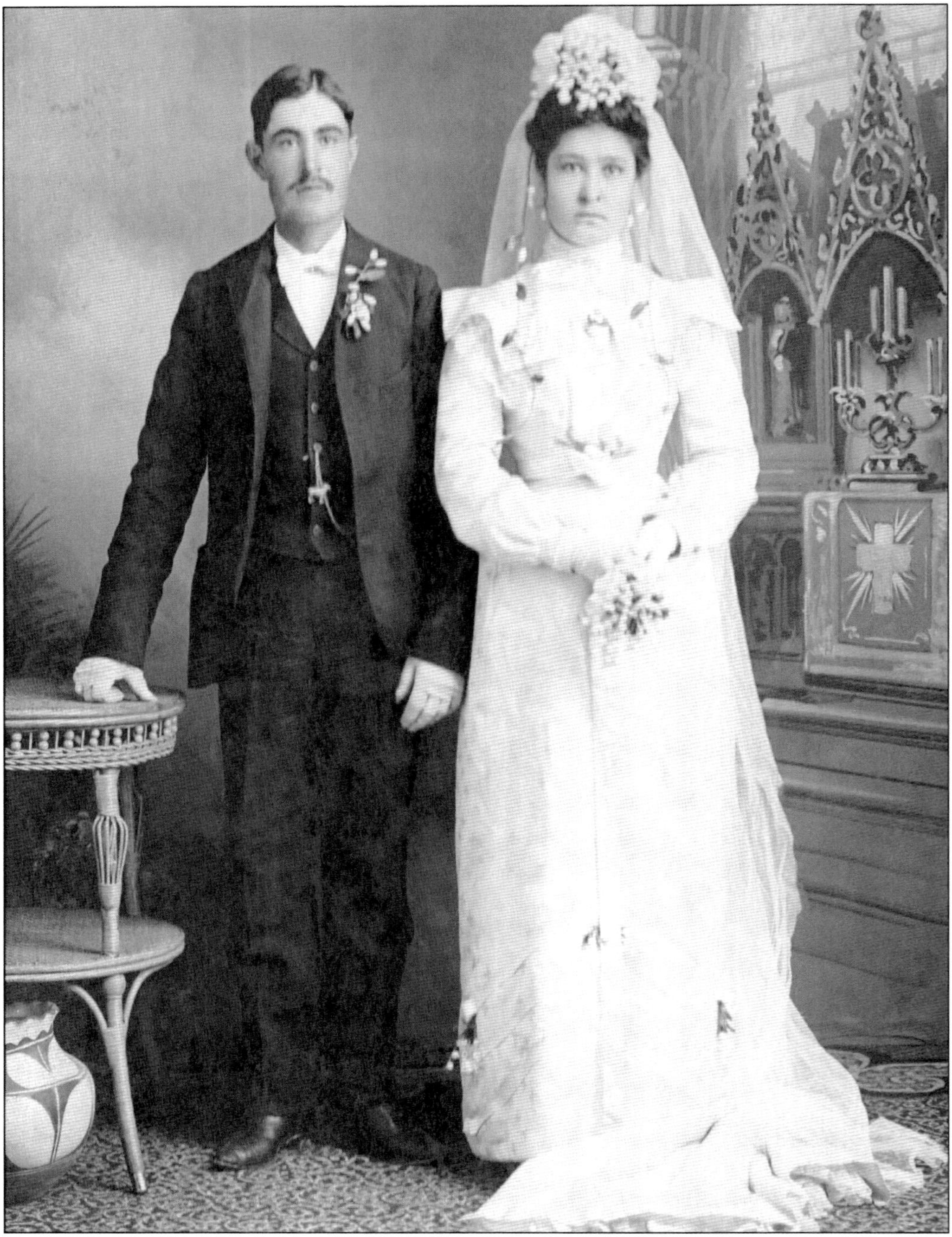

At the San Juan Bautista Catholic Church, important celebrations included feast days, baptisms, and weddings. The settlement of La Placita revolved around activities at the church. The year the church was first erected is not recorded, but notations do exist that show that it served the residents of Lincoln for many funerals during the Lincoln County War (which began in the 1870s). The church of San Juan Bautista at Lincoln currently serves as a mission of the parish of Santa Rita at Carrizozo, New Mexico.

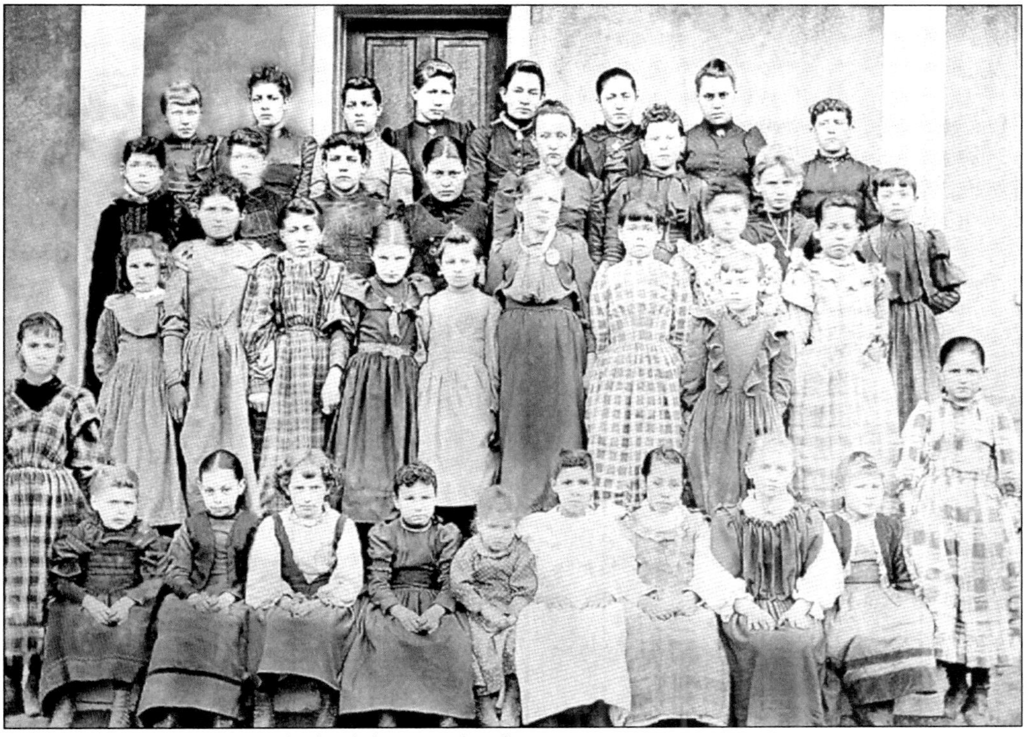

Education was important for both boys and girls in Lincoln. Throughout New Mexico, teachers were hired from other places to educate students at schools in rural areas. The early Spanish Franciscan friars were the first ones to introduce education in the territory. Many of the children did not go to school during harvest time. Children learned how to read and write in Spanish and were taught music and the arts. Girls, such as the ones shown in the image at right, also learned the skills of horseback riding. Adults learned trades such as weaving, dying, and ceramics, or were trained in ironwork, carpentry, and masonry. Children worked many hours at farms and ranches feeding and caring for the animals and looking after the gardens.

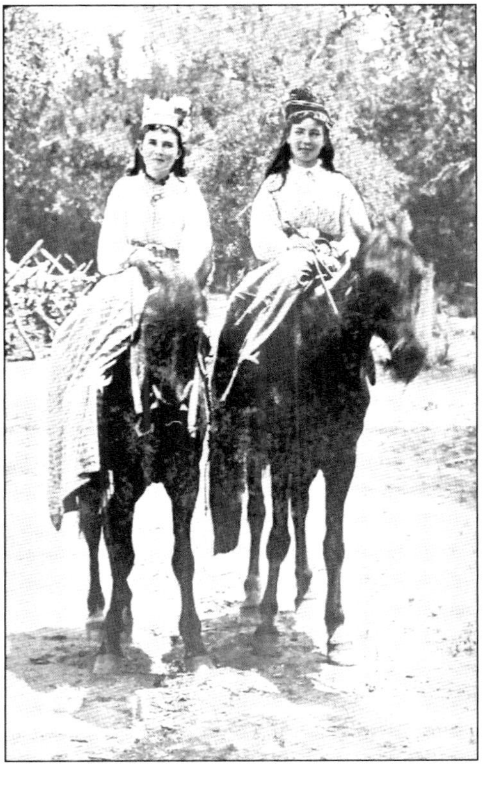

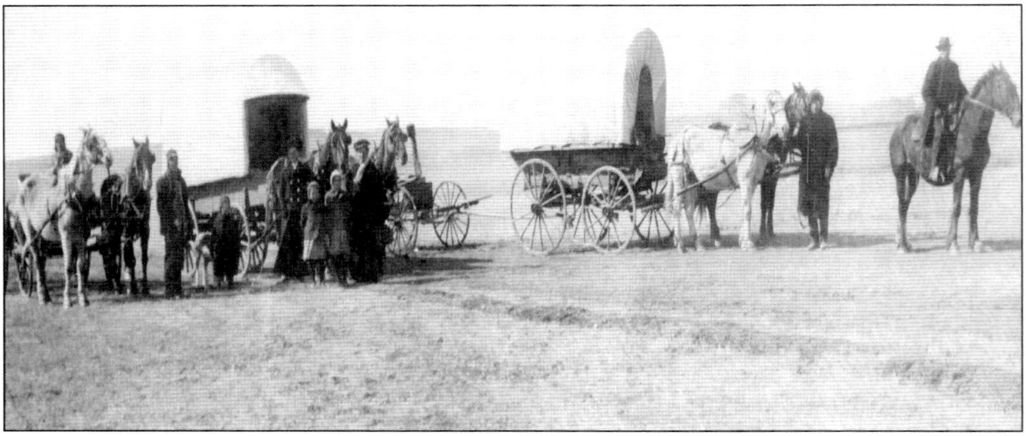

After New Mexico became a territory of the United States in 1850, many American settlers traveled on the Santa Fe Trail searching for a new life. In the 1870s, Lincoln was touted as a booming town, so many headed in that direction.

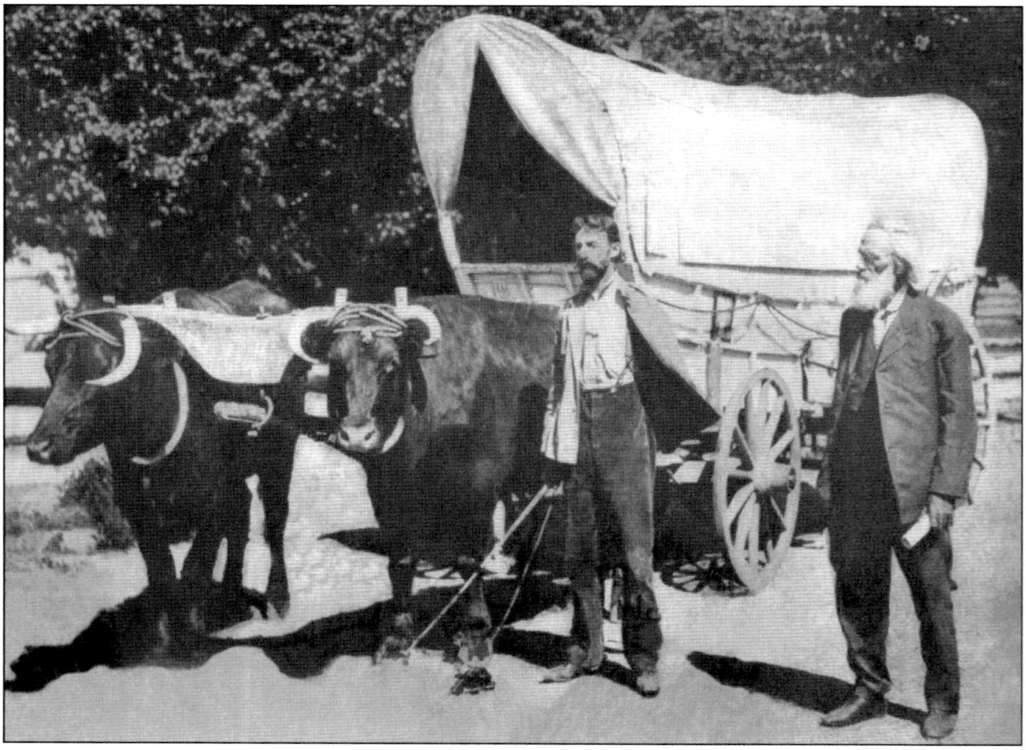

Among the American settlers, like those pictured here, who flocked to New Mexico and its fledgling towns were fur traders, merchants, snake oil peddlers, lawyers, miners, and farmers.

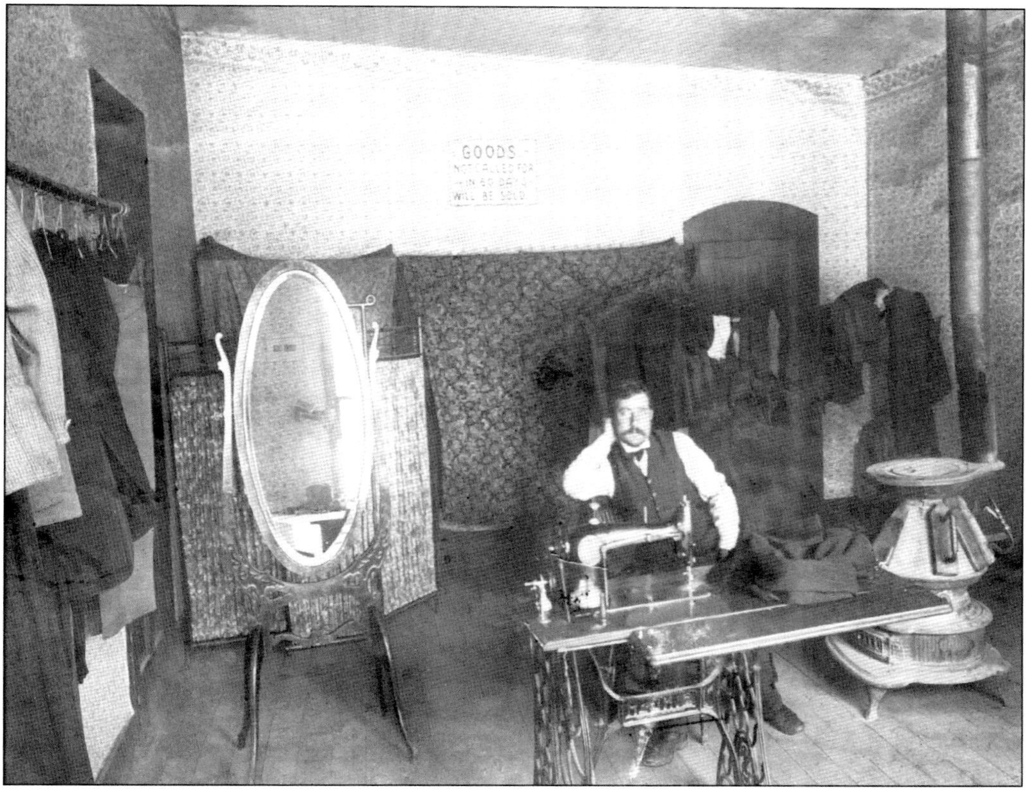

Tailor Pedro Cidio (pictured) was kept busy fashioning clothes for locals and newcomers.

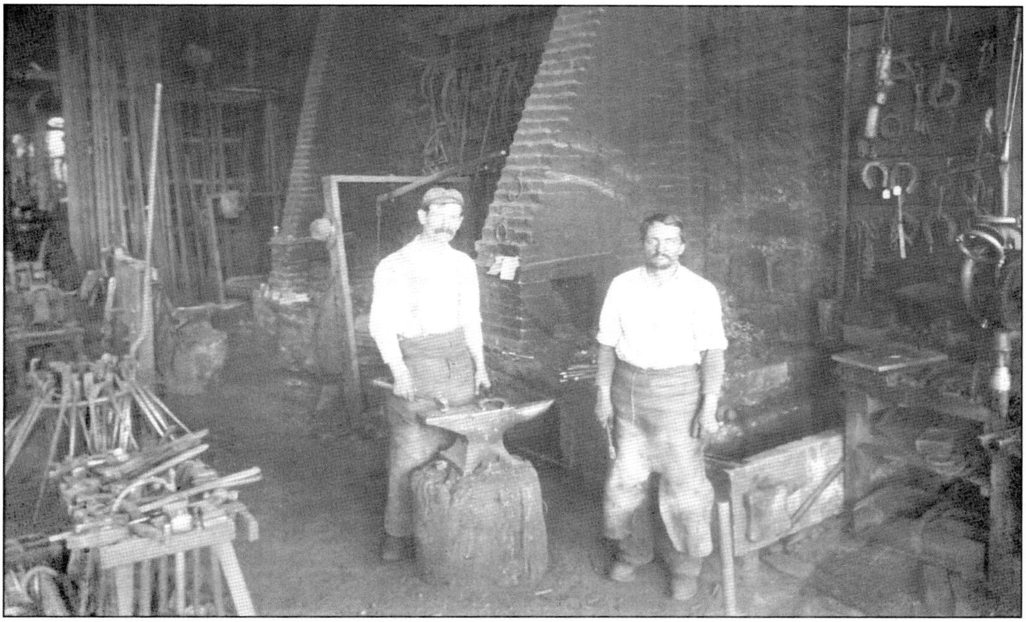
C.S. Rogers (left) and Epimenio Valerio repaired wagon wheels and produced horseshoes, as well as doing other ironwork that was in demand, including creating nails and iron implements.

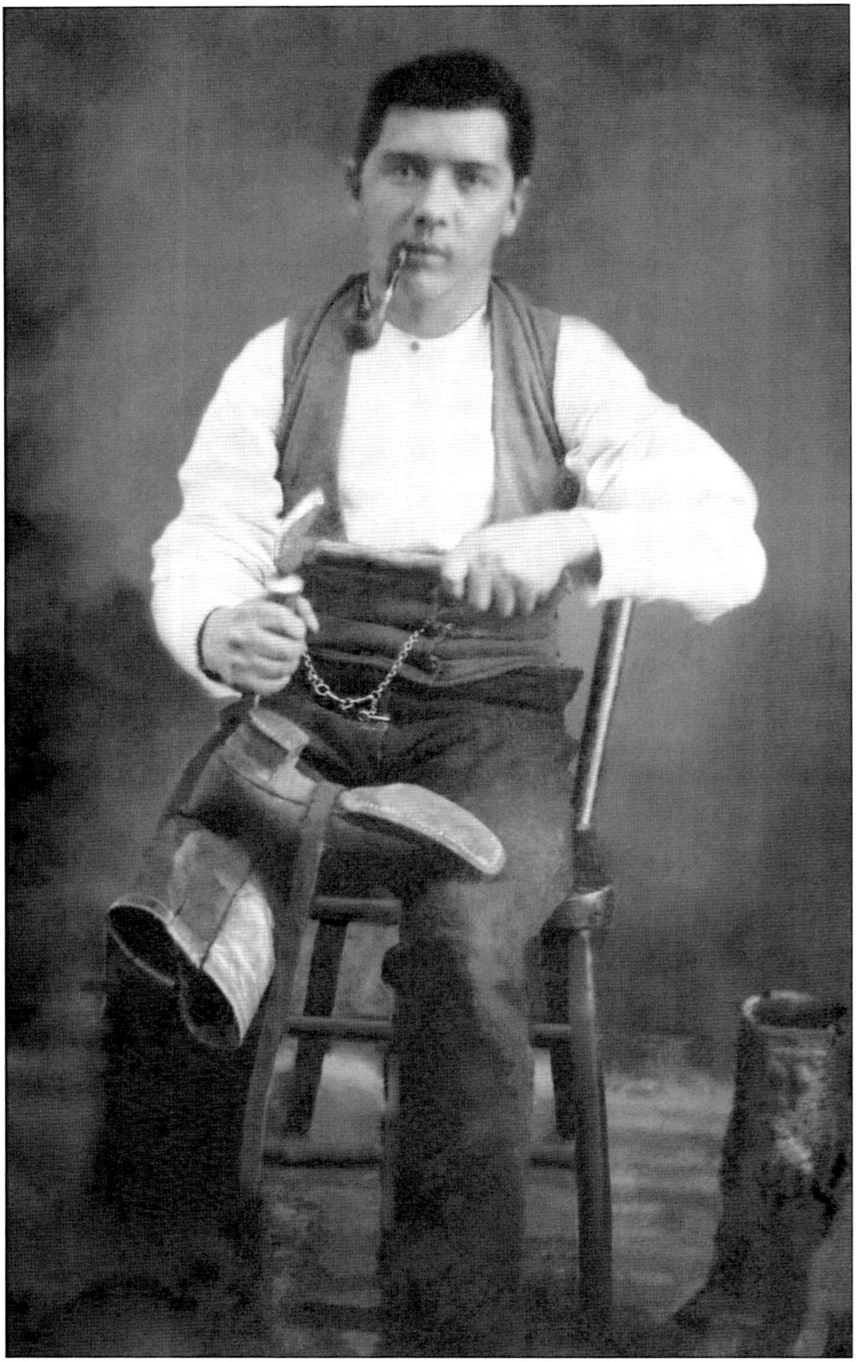

Bootmaker Pedro Mondragon maintained a thriving business by producing handmade cowhide boots for ranchers and cowboys in and around Lincoln. His boots featured either walking or riding heels and went from square-toe shapes in the 1870s to round-toe in the 1880s. Mondragon boots were suited for horseback riding and cattle drives. Area blacksmiths manufactured iron spurs that complemented the footwear.

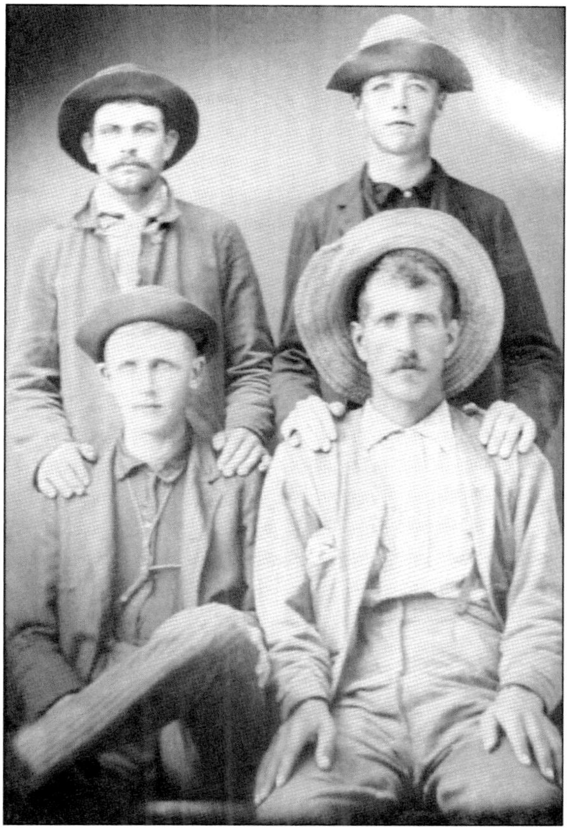

A stage line opened up between Lincoln, White Oaks, and Nogal in New Mexico. White Oaks was a mining town that attracted miners (like those pictured at right) and other fortune-seekers from distant communities. In 1880, the Old Abe, the South Homestake, and the North were the main gold mines in and around White Oaks; outside of Lincoln, it was the best-known town in Lincoln County. Large amounts of gold were discovered in the area, and enterprising citizens from Lincoln made White Oaks a second center for their businesses. Those traveling to and from White Oaks to Lincoln included Billy the Kid, John Chisum, Pat Garrett, and many miners, like those pictured below.

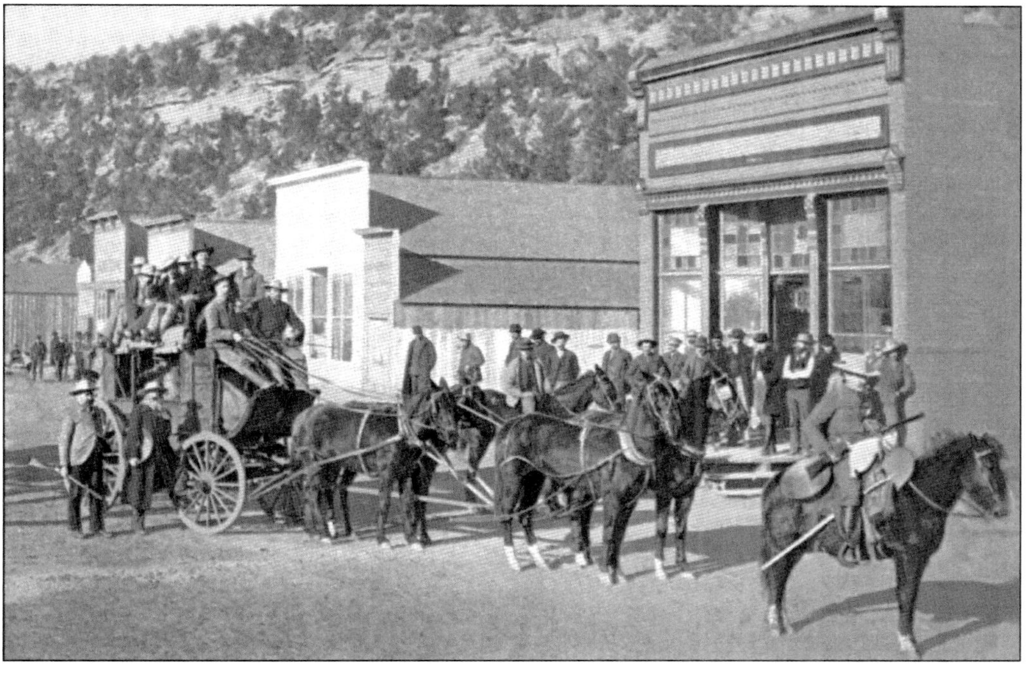

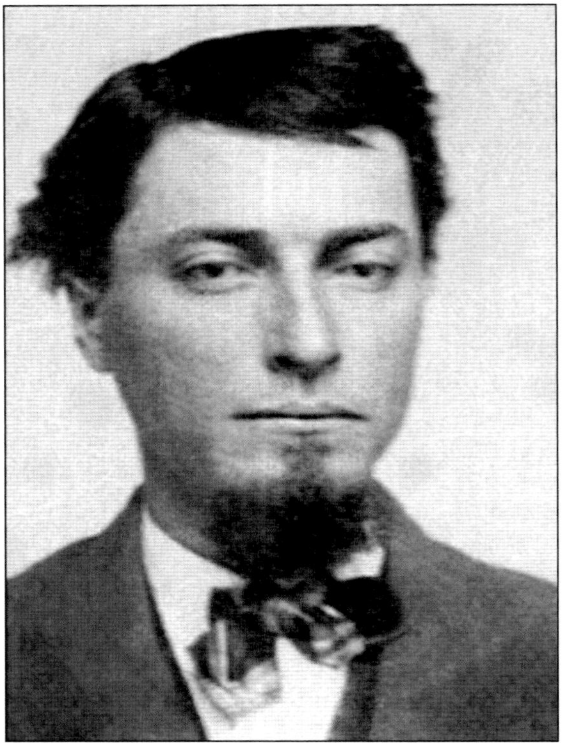

David Pugh Shield (left); his wife, Elizabeth (below); and their children, George H., David Curtis, and Mary M., arrived in Lincoln in July 1877. David Shield sought a promising new career in Lincoln, which he thought would provide a brighter future for himself and his wife. He was Alexander McSween's brother-in-law and partner in a new law firm. Elizabeth Shield was Sue McSween's sister, so she and her children moved into the McSween home. The Shields' sons worked in the Tunstall Store, while David's legal work sometimes took him out of town. While David was on a trip to Santa Fe, Elizabeth and Sue were in the McSween house when Sheriff George Peppin, his posse, and the James Dolan faction set their house on fire. During the Lincoln County troubles, David Shield decided to return to Las Vegas to establish a new law practice.

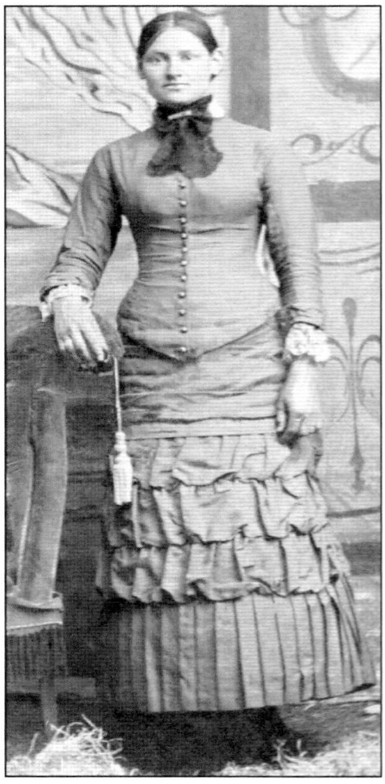

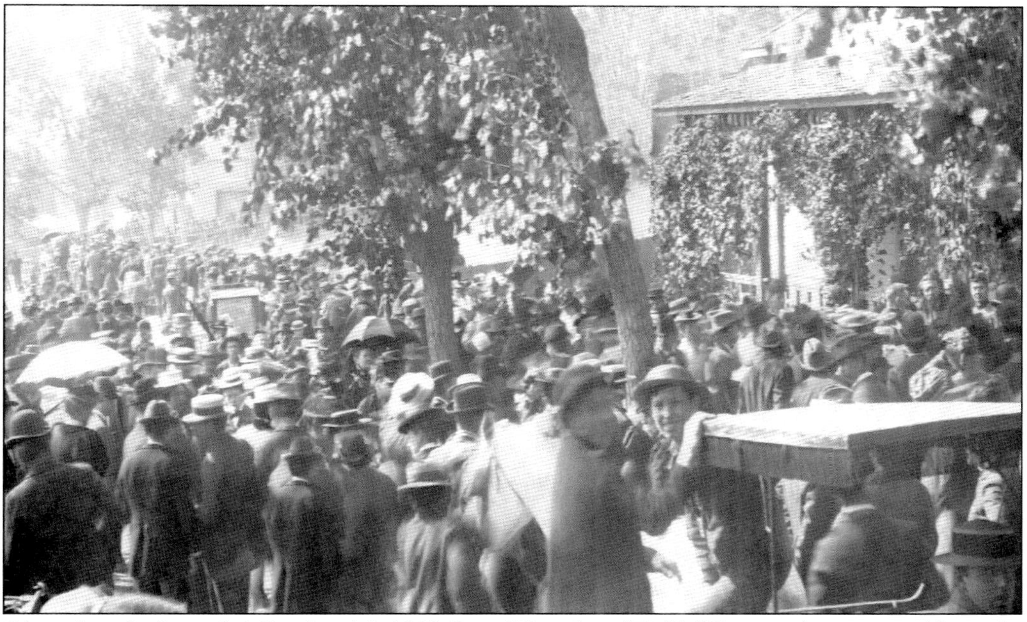

Glory days for Lincoln! On April 1, 1907, Pres. Theodore "Teddy" Roosevelt appointed Lincoln resident George Curry as governor of the New Mexico Territory. Curry had served as sheriff of Lincoln County and in other political posts and had distinguished himself as an officer in Roosevelt's Rough Riders during the Spanish-American War. During his days in Lincoln, Curry had captained a baseball team that competed against teams from White Oaks, Fort Stanton, and Roswell. In this 1908 photograph, Lincoln citizens celebrate a visit from Governor Curry.

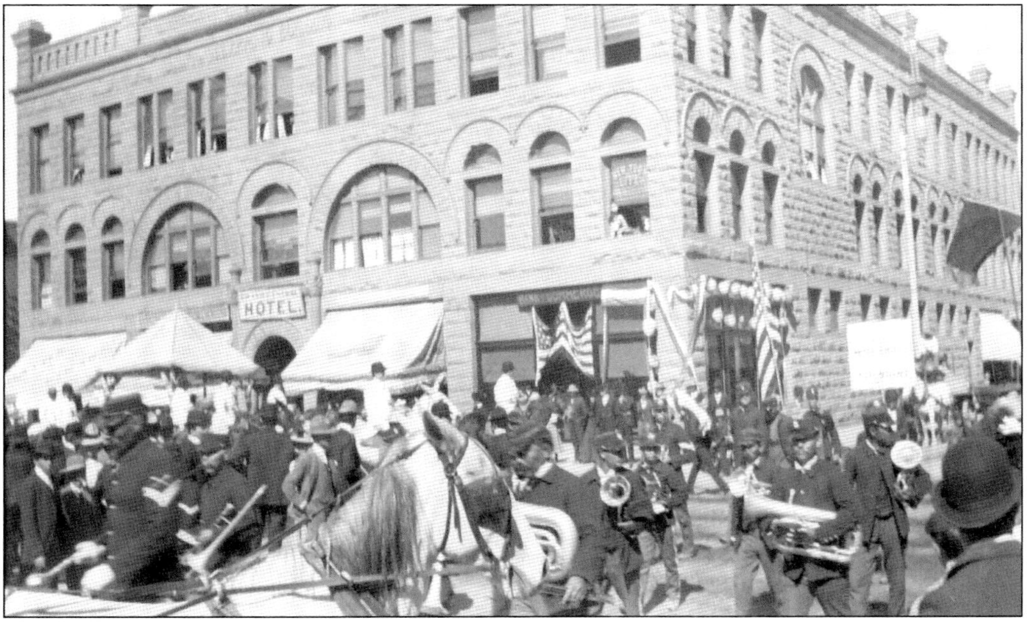

On January 6, 1912, New Mexico was admitted as the 47th state. A grand statehood celebration was held in Albuquerque, pictured here. People traveled from Lincoln and other towns to Albuquerque and the capitol city of Santa Fe to celebrate.

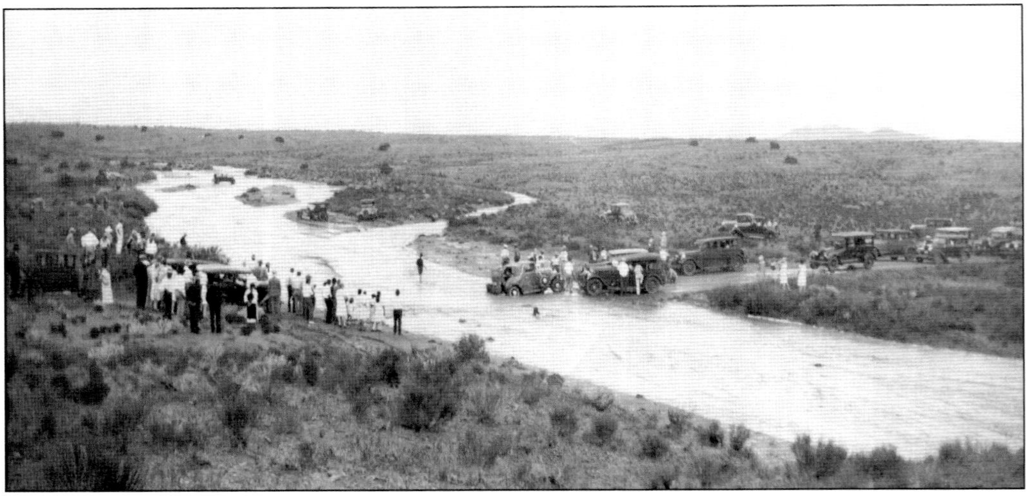

During the rainy season in New Mexico—especially during the months of July and August—dry washes become raging rivers in an instant, as shown in this photograph.

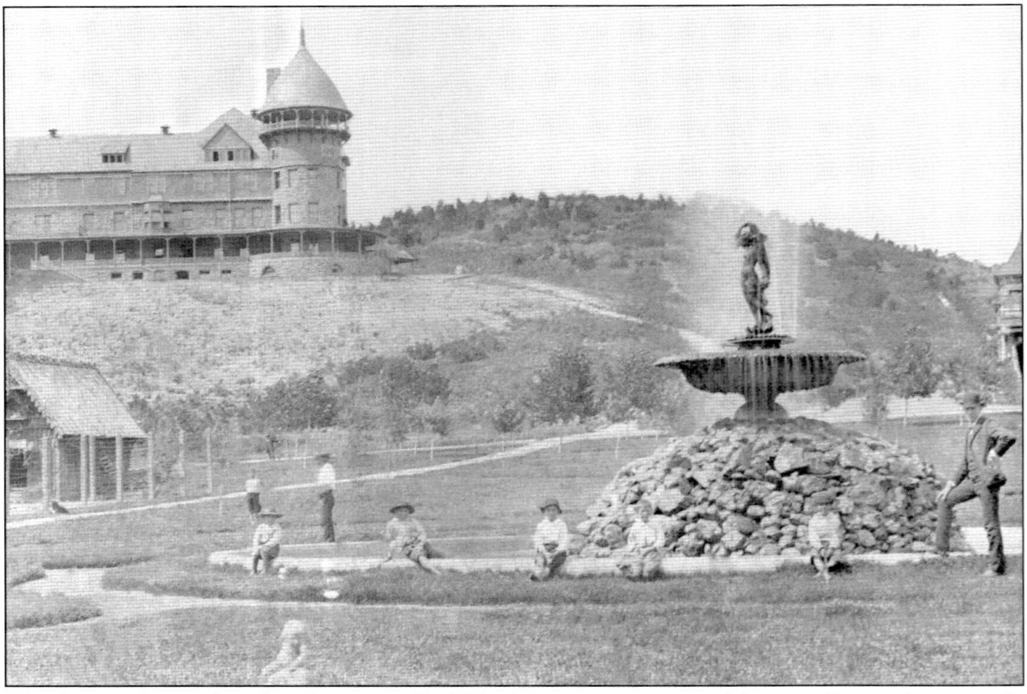

The famous luxury hotel and resort called The Montezuma was a 400-room Queen Anne–style structure located five miles northwest of Las Vegas, New Mexico. The site was formerly known as the Las Vegas Hot Springs. The first hotel, built in 1881, burned down, as did the second one built in 1885. The new hotel erected in 1886 was much grander than the others. It housed a casino, an 11-lane bowling alley, billiard rooms, and a dance floor and stage and featured European stained glass, plus a Steinway piano. Presidents Teddy Roosevelt, Rutherford B. Hayes, and Ulysses S. Grant stayed at the Montezuma, as well as Emperor Hirohito of Japan. John Chisum and other wealthy and influential citizens from Lincoln and other towns stayed at the hotel and bathed in the hot springs, purported to contain healthful mineral waters.

Two

Showdown in Lincoln

A full-fledged battle for control of the town of Lincoln took place between July 15 and July 19, 1878. This famous shootout is known as "The Five-Day Battle" or "The Battle of Lincoln." Friction between the James Dolan faction and the McSween faction had been building up, especially after the death of John H. Tunstall. Constable Atanacio Martinez and the Lincoln County Regulators, a group deputized by Martinez to capture and arrest the killers of Tunstall, set up positions in Lincoln. The Regulators included nearly 60 armed men, the majority of whom were Hispanic cowboys. Dolan's group of around 50 men contained primarily hired white gunmen including the notorious Jesse Evans and John Kinney. The group, led by Sheriff George Peppin, included Bob Olinger, who was known to be unscrupulous in shooting people and getting away with it. Evans was believed to have been the one who killed Tunstall. In a five-day battle, thousands of rounds were fired in a standoff. However, Col. Augustus Nathan Dudley, the commanding officer of Fort Stanton, along with four officers, 35 cavalrymen, a howitzer, and a Gatling gun intervened on Dolan's behalf. Although Dudley was prohibited from participating by the Posse Comitatus Act, which forbade military intervention in civil disturbances, he found an excuse to do so. The end result was the murder of McSween and the defeat of the Regulators. Dudley faced a court of inquiry into his actions and was summarily removed as commander, but he was found not guilty.

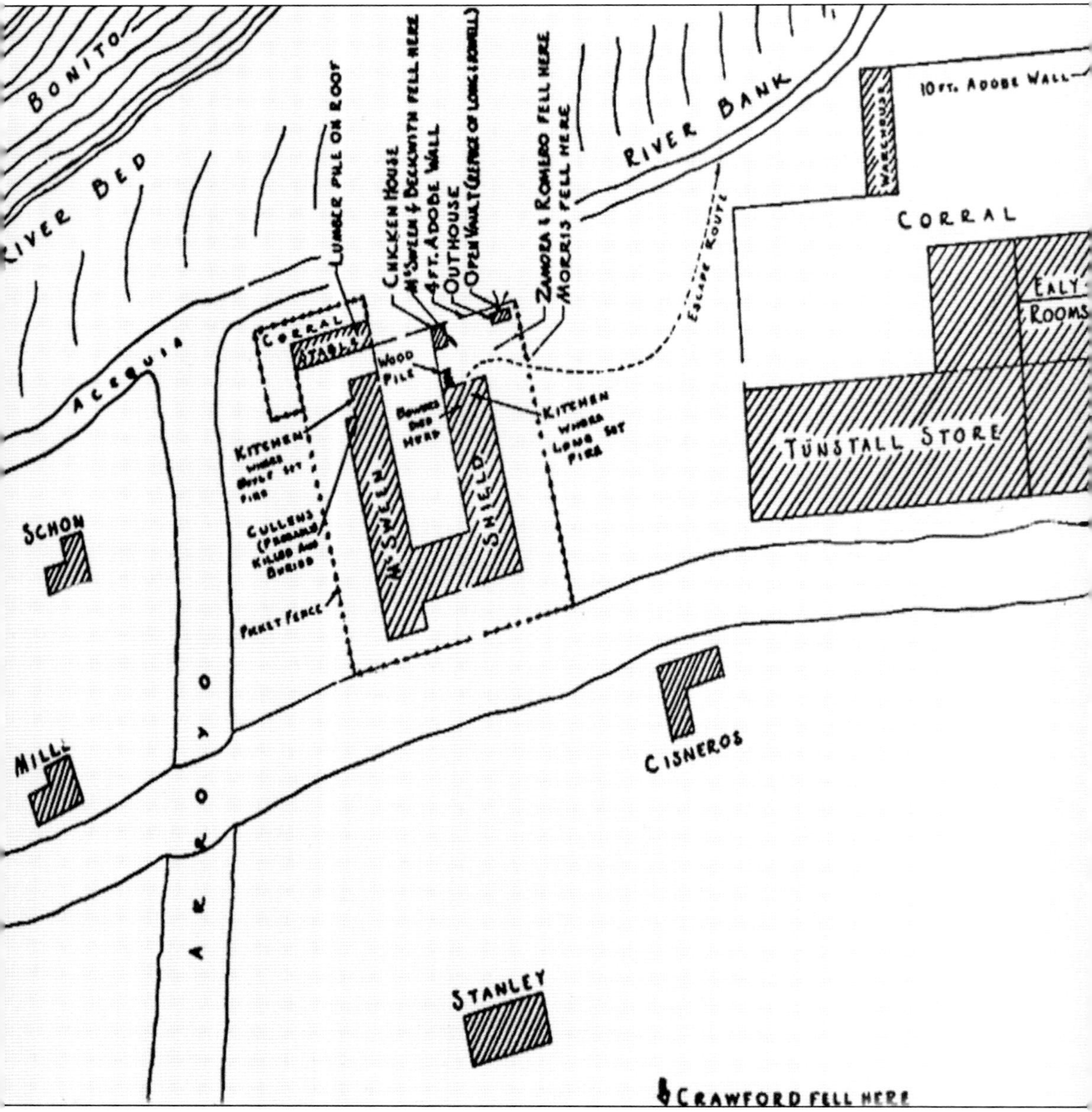

This map of Lincoln's Main Street, produced by historian Robert N. Mullin in 1955, shows the

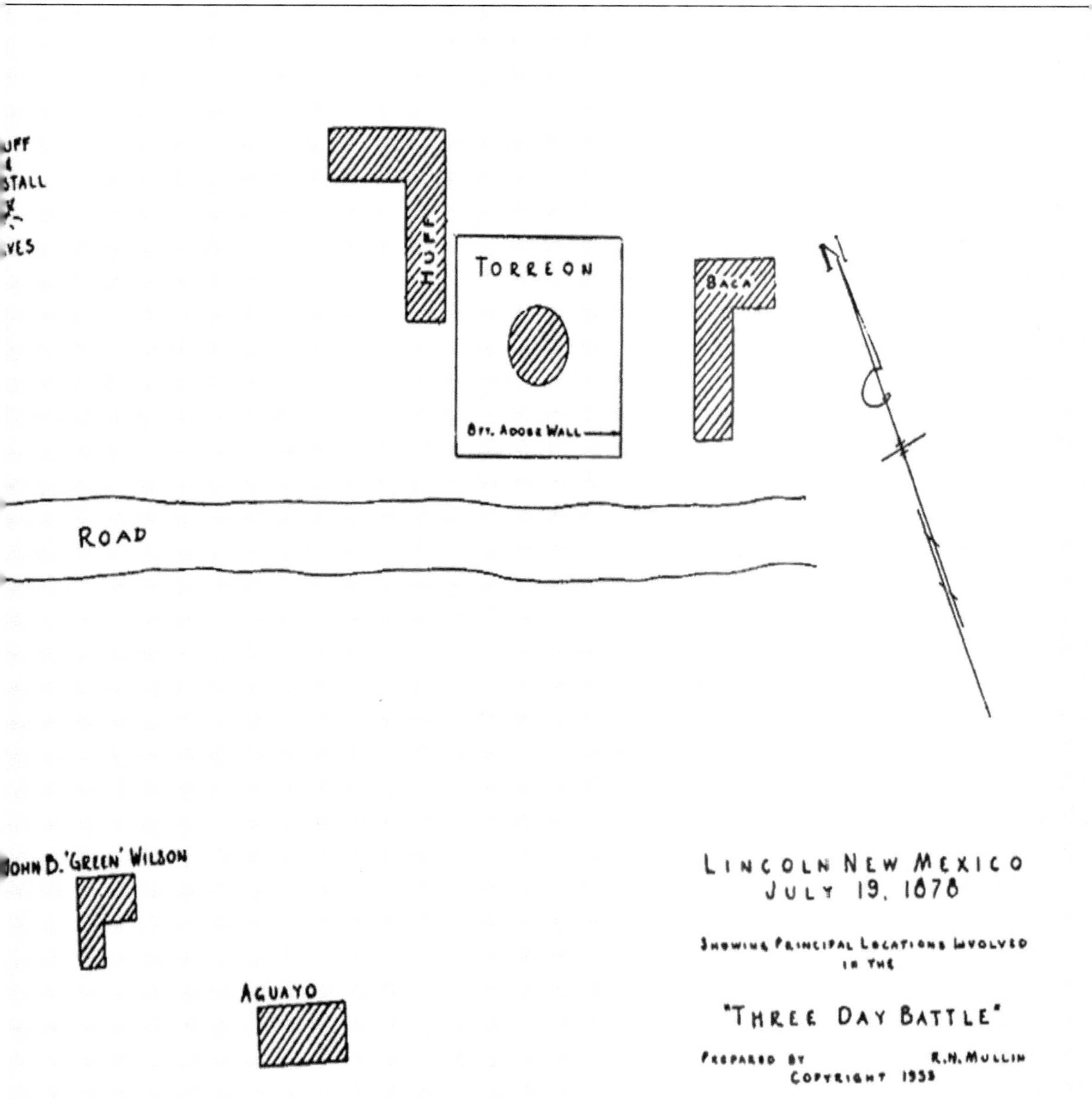

principal locations and places of conflict within the town when major fighting took place.

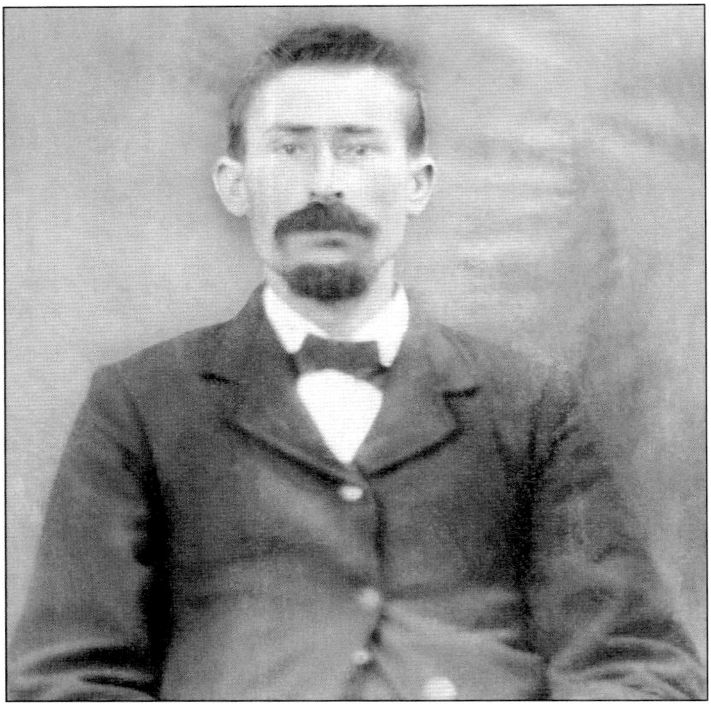

Col. Emil Fritz was a former commanding officer at Fort Stanton. After being mustered out of the Army in 1866, he formed a partnership with Lawrence G. Murphy and both of them became post traders. They both made a fortune with the L.G. Murphy and Company store in Lincoln. Because of failing health, Fritz returned to his hometown of Hamburg, Germany, where he died in 1874. Fritz's life-insurance policy settlement of his estate started a feud with rival Alexander Anderson McSween.

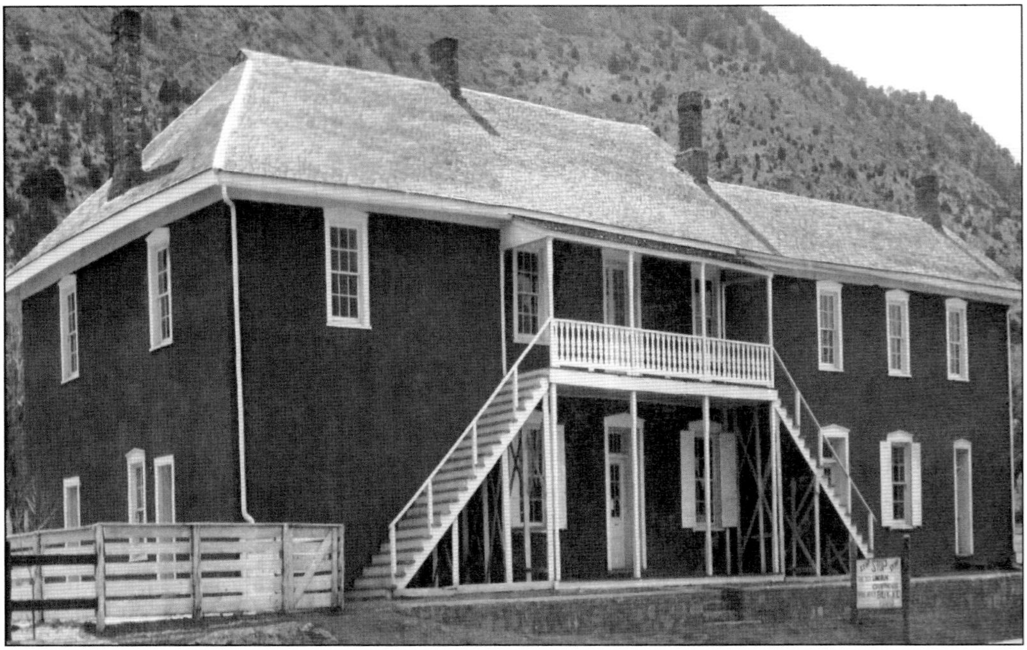

The Lincoln County Courthouse is the most recognizable landmark in the town of Lincoln. The two-story adobe structure originally served as the mercantile of Lawrence G. Murphy and was later known as the Murphy-Dolan Store. During the Lincoln County War, the store was the headquarters of the James J. Dolan faction. After the war, the building served as a courthouse and jail.

In 1872, Charles Fritz moved to Lincoln from Hamburg, Germany, at his brother Emil's request. Charles had a ranch near Lincoln called Spring Ranch where he had several thousand head of cattle. He was married to Catherine Knebling and had eight children, including Carolina "Lina" Fritz. Charles was named to succeed Sheriff William Brady as administrator of his brother's estate when he died.

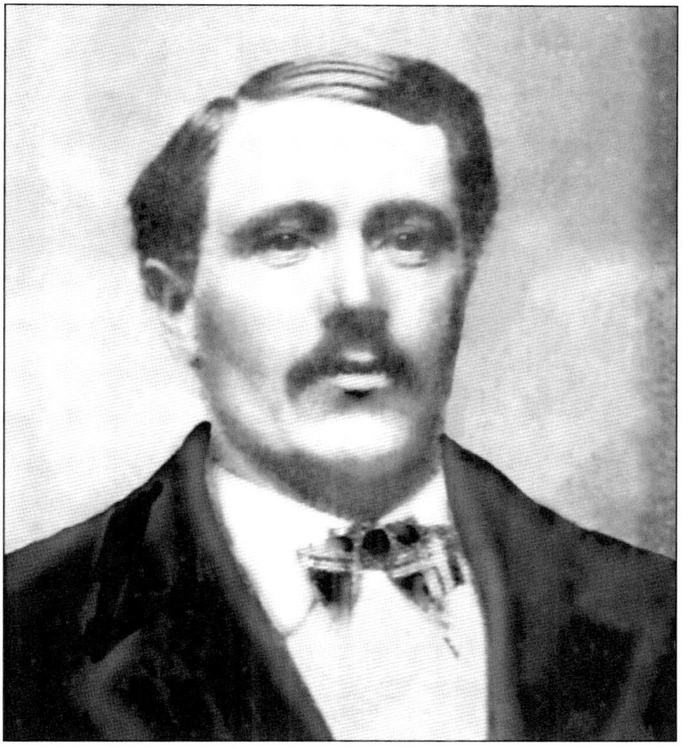

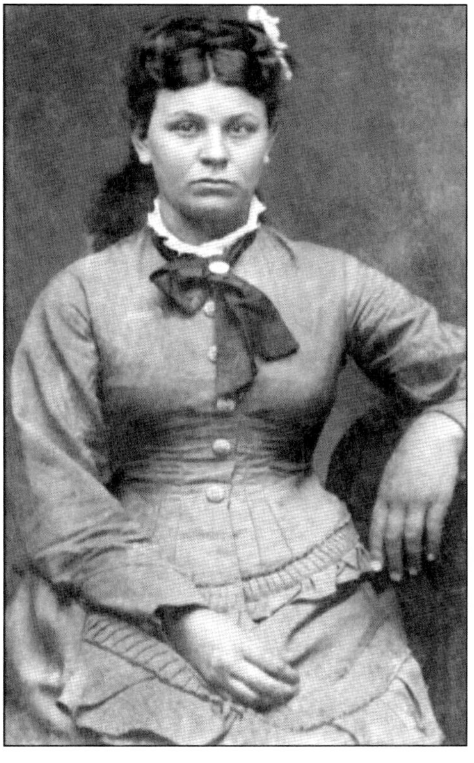

Carolina "Lina" Fritz married James Dolan on July 13, 1879, at the age of 18. Dolan was 31. Her father, Charles, objected to the marriage, but later allowed them to live with him at his ranch until they built their home in Lincoln. They had four children; two died at an early age, and Carolina died in childbirth along with her fourth child.

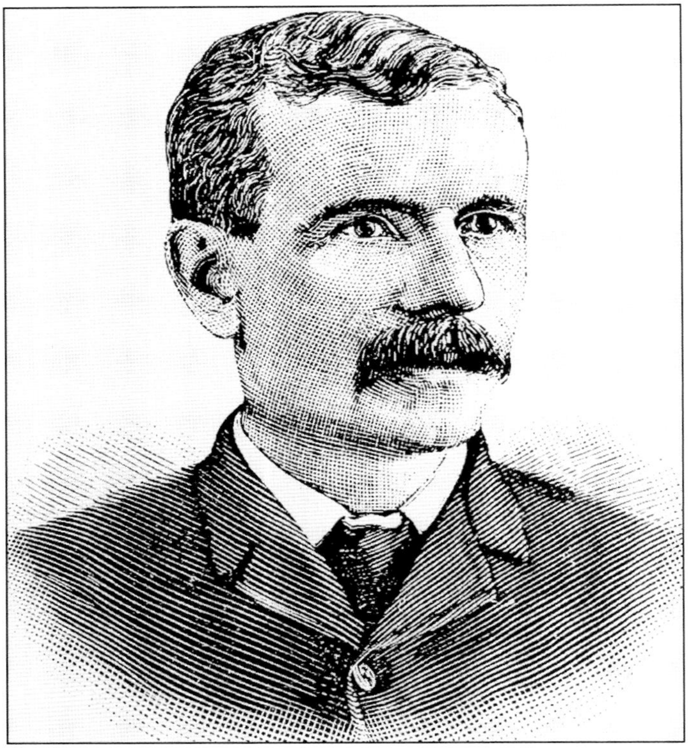

A major part of the lawlessness that resulted in violence in the town of Lincoln can be attributed to James Joseph Dolan, pictured in this engraving. Dolan was reportedly from Ireland and was discharged from the Army at Fort Stanton. His first wife, Carolina, Charles Fritz's daughter, died at the age of 25. He then married Eva Marie Whitlock, from Las Vegas, on February 20, 1888.

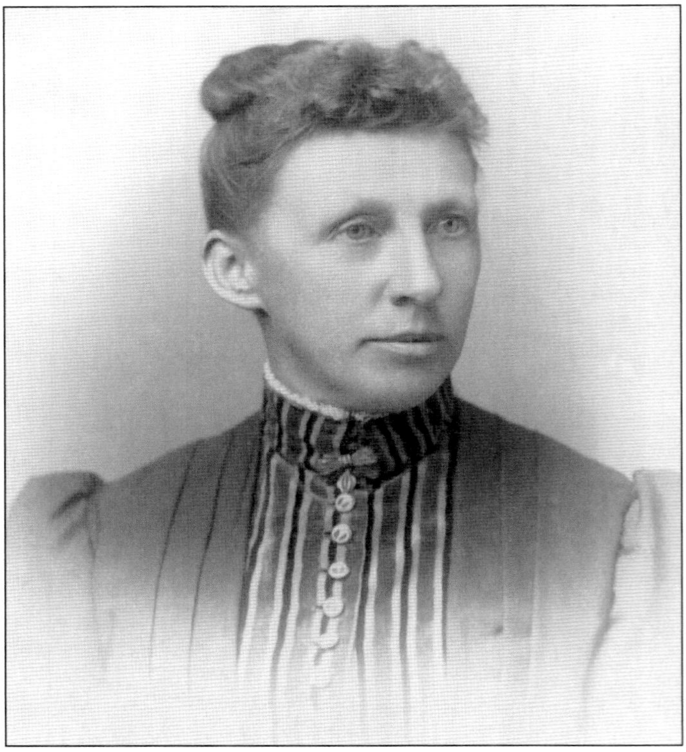

Chief Justice Elisha V. Long, a member of the Santa Fe Ring, wed Eva Marie Whitlock to James Dolan at Lincoln two years after the death of Dolan's first wife. In 1882, Dolan, who maintained herds of cattle along with William Rynerson, moved his cattle to the Tunstall Ranch. Dolan had taken over the Tunstall property at Lincoln and the Tunstall Ranch on the Felíz, which the couple made their home.

James J. Dolan (right) was elected treasurer of Lincoln County in 1884. In 1888, he represented the counties of Lincoln, Doña Anna, Sierra, and Grants as a member of the territorial senate. He formed a partnership with Numa Reymond and William Rynerson and established the Felíz Land and Cattle Company, which was centered on the rangeland of John H. Tunstall. Dolan also helped organize the Lincoln County Stock Association; below is a receipt he issued to James Sutherland, who was a former Army surgeon.

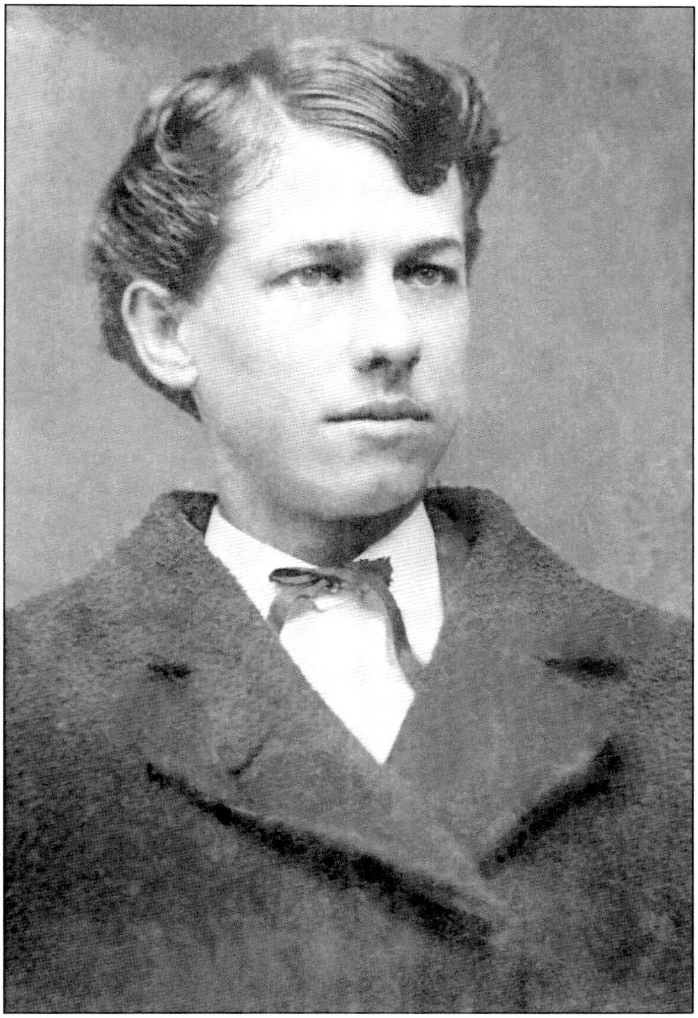

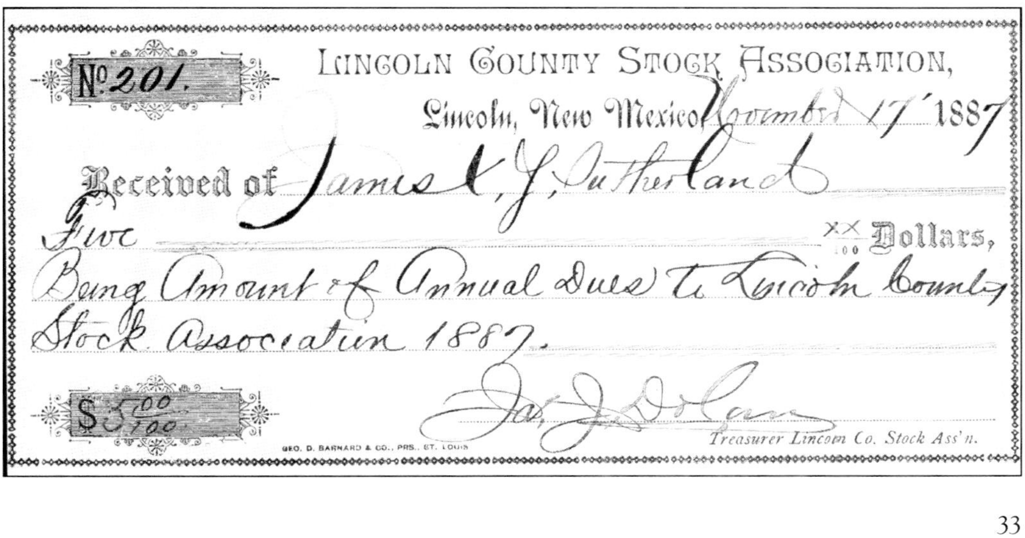

No. 201.

LINCOLN COUNTY STOCK ASSOCIATION,

Lincoln, New Mexico November 17 1887

Received of James C. J. Sutherland

Five xx/100 Dollars,

Being Amount of Annual Dues to Lincoln County Stock Association 1887.

$5 00/100

Jas. J. Dolan

Treasurer Lincoln Co. Stock Ass'n.

GEO. D. BARNARD & CO., PRS., ST. LOUIS

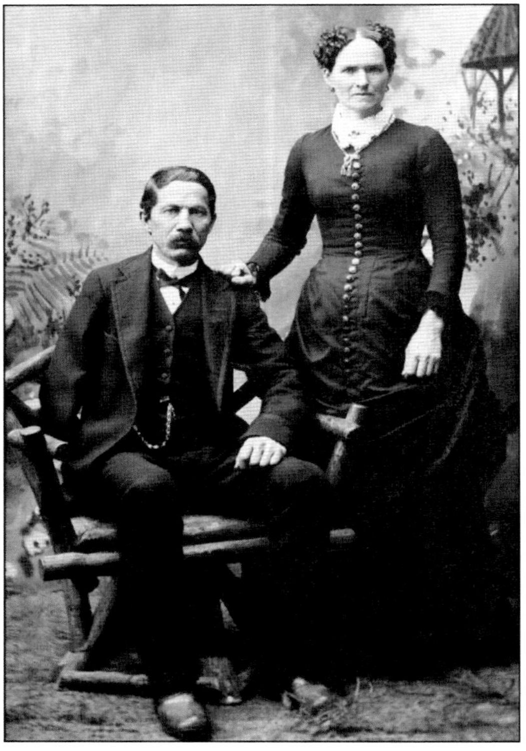

Capt. Saturnino Baca was well known in New Mexico circles. He served in a regiment under the famed Christopher (Kit) Carson during the Civil War and distinguished himself at the Battle of Valverde. Baca was a member of the New Mexico territorial legislature and sponsored a bill in 1869 that led to the creation of Lincoln County, with its seat at Lincoln. He was appointed the county's first probate judge and served as sheriff. In 1889, Baca lost his arm (as shown in this tintype) after he received a bullet wound from an unknown assailant during a dispute over cattle and sheep ranges. Baca married Juana María Chavez (left), and they had nine children, one of whom was María Baca (pictured below).

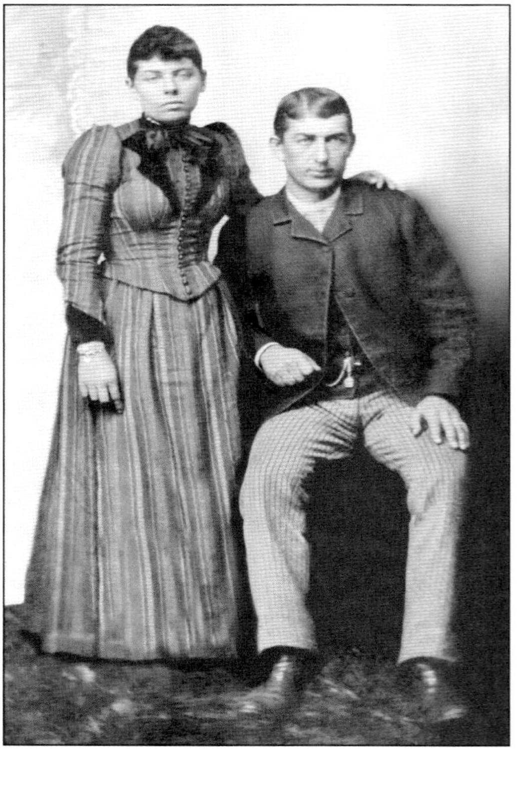

Alexander Anderson McSween and his wife, Susan Ellen McSween, arrived in Lincoln in 1875. McSween set up a law office and began building a sprawling adobe residence. McSween and his wife were equally ambitious; he devised schemes to challenge the control of Murphy and Dolan, which eventually led to his downfall and death.

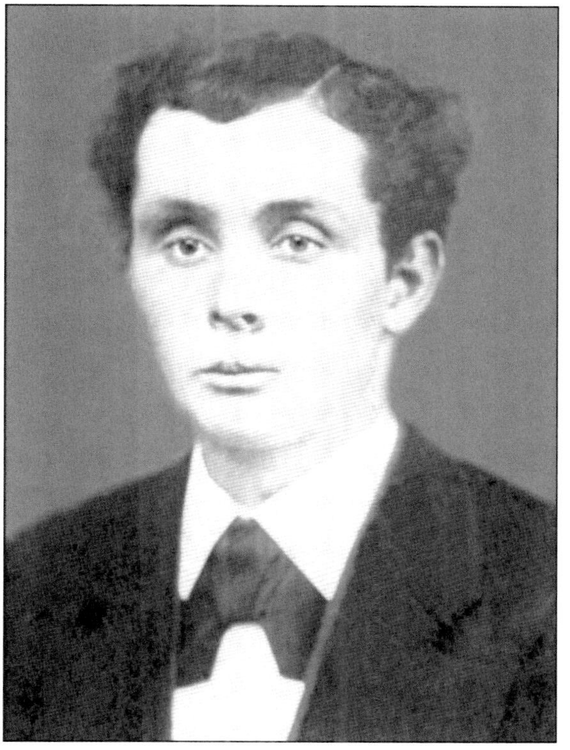

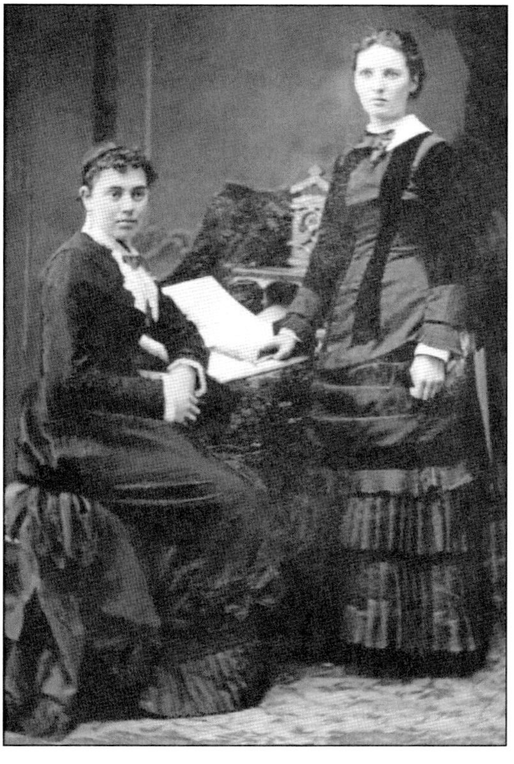

Susan Ellen McSween is pictured here on the left with Mary Ealy. Susan was present during the Five-Day Battle, during which her home was burned down and her husband killed. After his death, she sought justice for his killing but never succeeded. Sometime later, she married another attorney, George Barber. She eventually moved to White Oaks, where she operated a cattle ranch for the rest of her life.

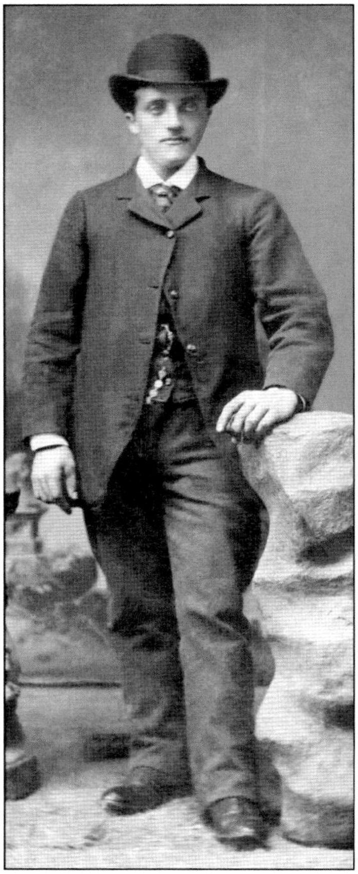

Englishman John Henry Tunstall set up roots in Lincoln after opening up the large mercantile store there in 1877 (below) and purchasing a ranch on the Río Felíz. In partnership with Alex McSween, he challenged the economic monopoly held by J.J. Dolan & Co. As a result, Sheriff William J. Brady murdered Tunstall with a posse controlled by the Dolan faction on February 18, 1878. This precipitated the Lincoln County War.

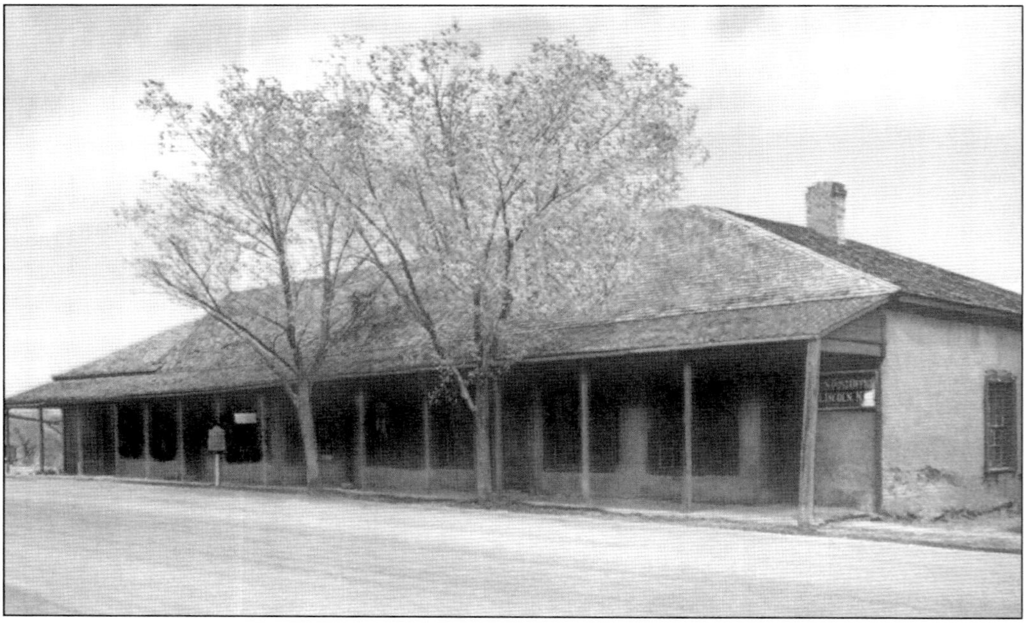

General store owner José Montaño sold groceries, firearms, and ammunition at his place of business in Lincoln. He rented part of his building to Ike Stockton, who operated a popular saloon. Montaño was a Civil War veteran who provided refuge to the McSween faction during the Five-Day Battle.

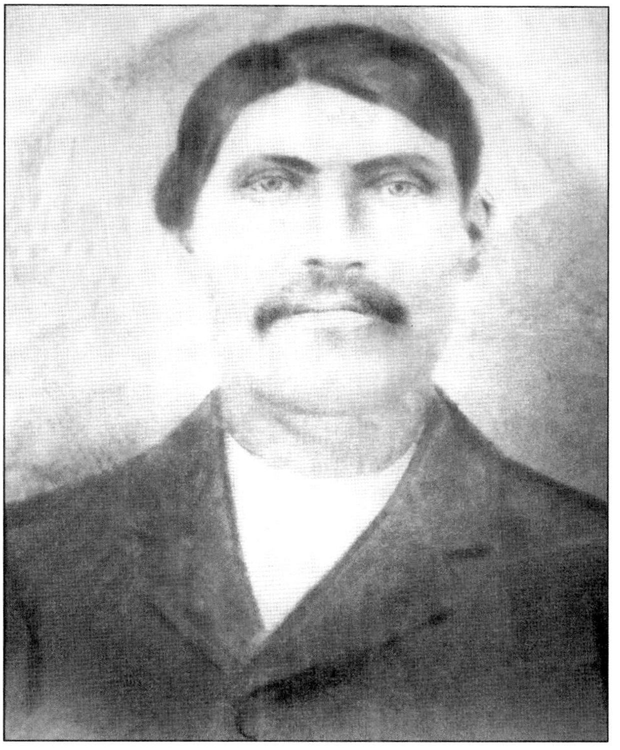

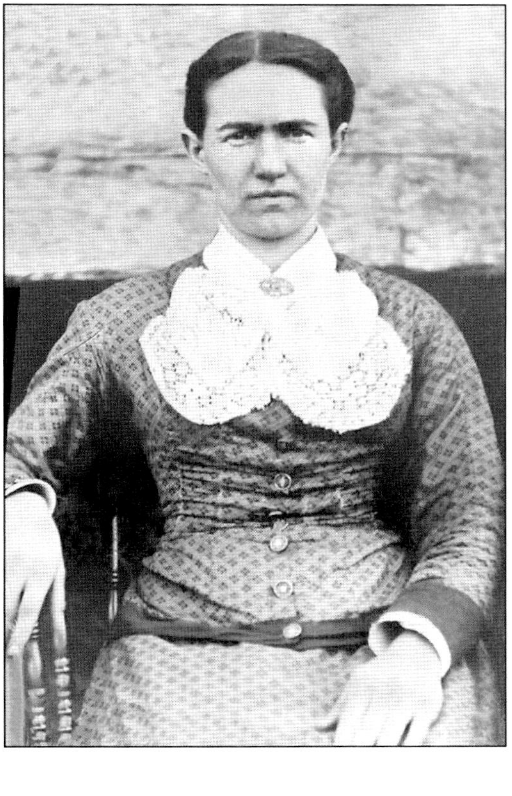

Josefa Lopez married José Montaño, and they had three children—Beatrix, José, and Trinidad. Josefa often cautioned her husband to remain neutral during the Lincoln County War, but he sided with the Regulators and tried to help them.

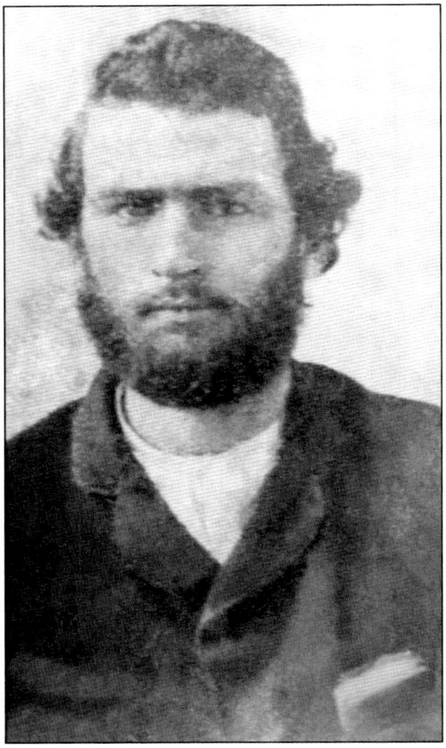

Presbyterian medical missionary Dr. Taylor Filmore Ealy arrived in Lincoln—along with his wife, Mary, and their children, Pearl and Ruth—on February 19, 1878. John Henry Tunstall had been murdered the previous day, so Ealy officiated at his funeral. The unsuspecting Ealy family went on to experience much of the turbulence of the Lincoln County War while trying to set up a school and church in Lincoln.

Presbyterian ministers—possibly including Taylor Ealy—perform a baptism somewhere on the Río Bonito. (Courtesy of Taylor Ealy's great-grandson Lawrence O. Ealy.)

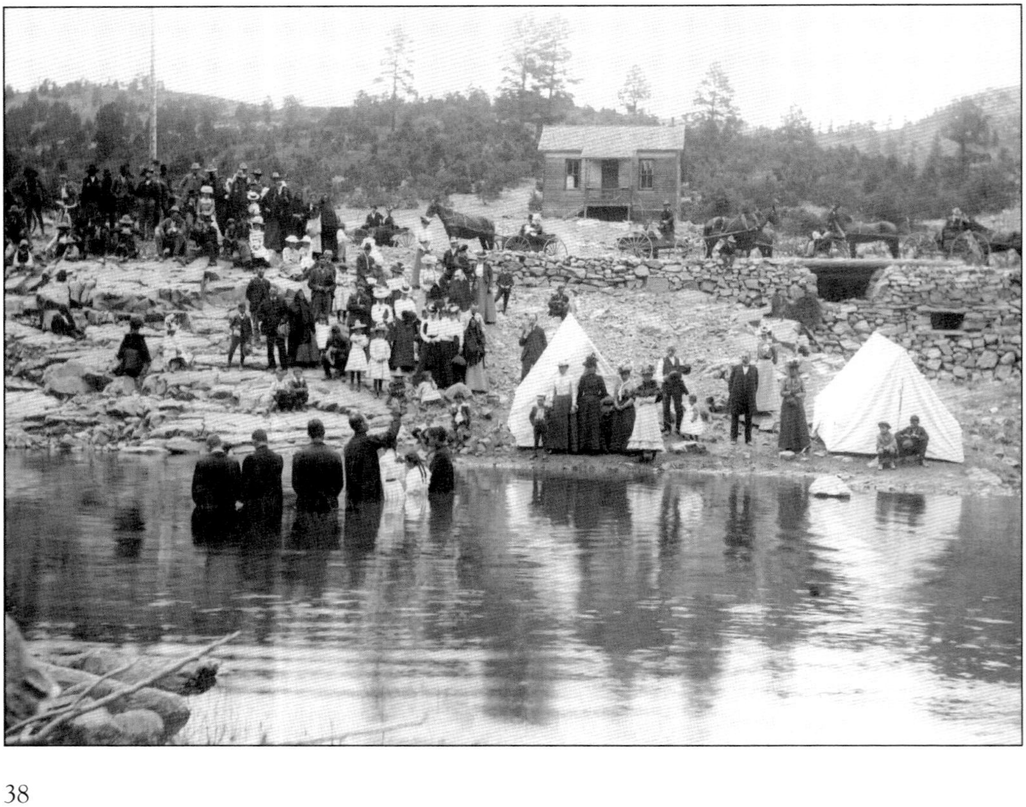

John Simpson Chisum was a cattle baron with 100,000 head of cattle. His South Spring Ranch near Roswell was the headquarters of an empire that stretched for 100 miles. Chisum's "Jingle Bob" brand was one of the most famous brands in the West. Chisum, along with partners Alexander McSween and John Henry Tunstall, set up a bank in Lincoln. Chisum was the president, McSween the vice president, and Tunstall the cashier. Chisum died from a cancerous growth (visible in the tintype at right) in 1884. Some people believe that the gambler's ring on his pinky finger is the one that belonged to Billy the Kid.

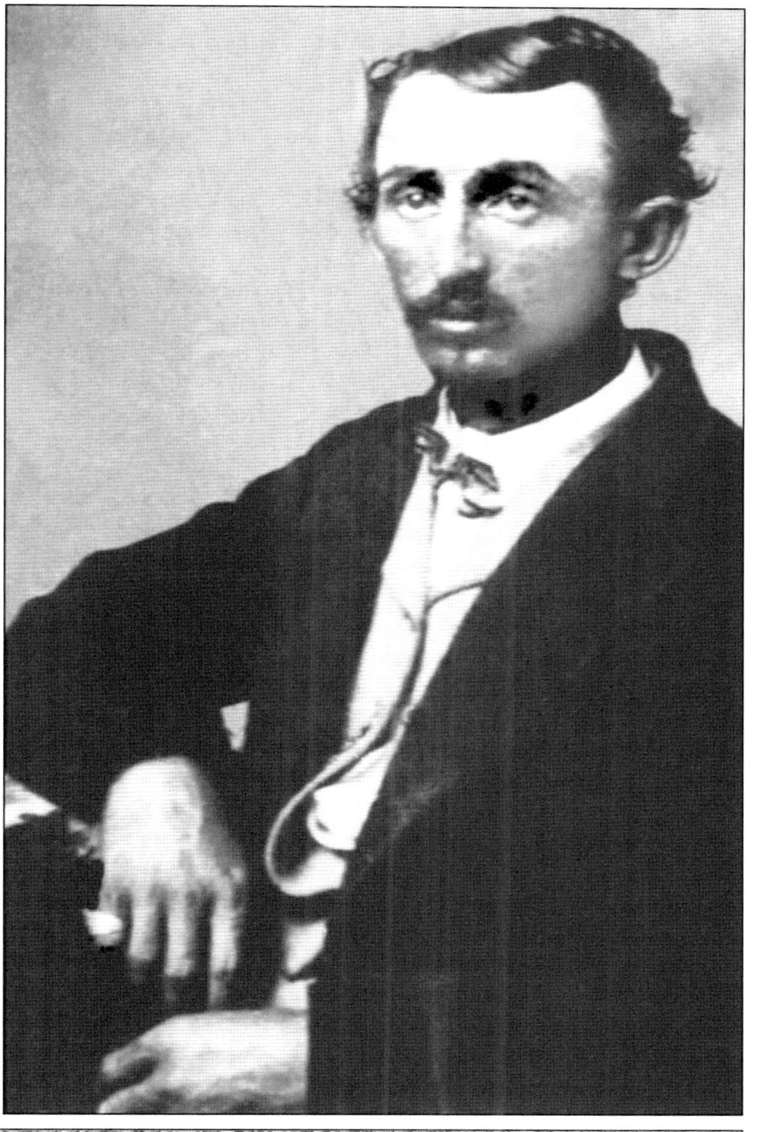

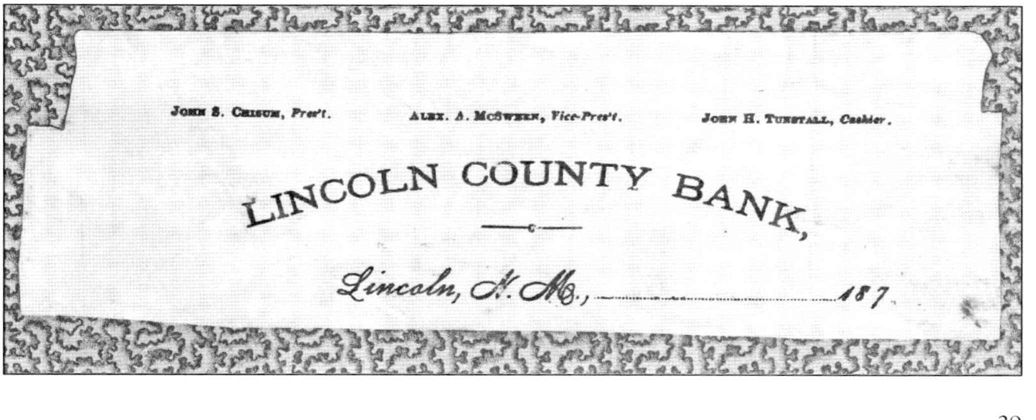

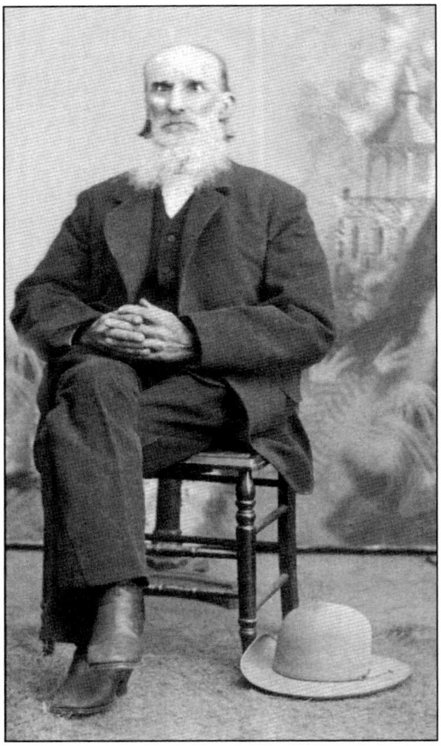

In 1877, Heiskell Jones and his wife, Barbara Culp Jones (popularly called Ma'am Jones), operated a well-known trading post in a place called Seven Rivers, an area located in southeastern Lincoln County and so named because seven springs there formed a stream that flowed into a main channel before the water went into the Pecos River. The post, which had a store, saloon, and post office, was a favorite hangout for cattle rustlers, gamblers, and outlaws. Jones had worked as a post butcher at Fort Stanton. Other families eventually moved into Seven Rivers, including Rebecca Stafford Olinger and her two sons, Wallace and William "Bob" Olinger.

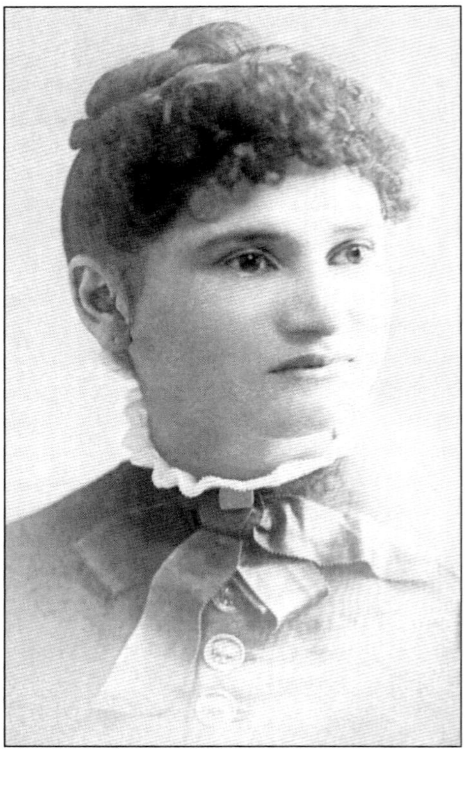

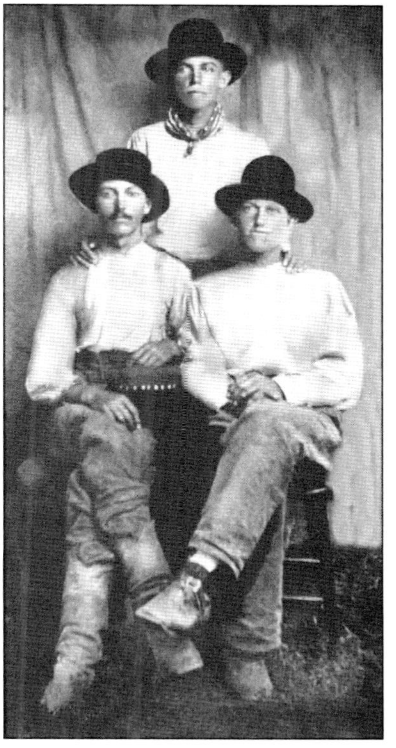

Renegades, outlaws, and cowboy rebels from Seven Rivers added much to the turmoil at Lincoln. Seven Rivers was a wild community, located near Carlsbad on the road to Roswell, founded by cowmen from Texas who rustled cattle from John Chisum's South Spring Ranch. The town became a haven for cowboys (like those pictured at right) who frequented its saloons and bawdy houses. A favorite pastime of the Seven Rivers gang was to ride into Lincoln during cattle drives and shoot up the town. They often fired at windows and scampering residents who ran for their lives. Lincoln lawmen put their lives on the line while standing up to these roustabouts. Little is left today of the violent community of Seven Rivers.

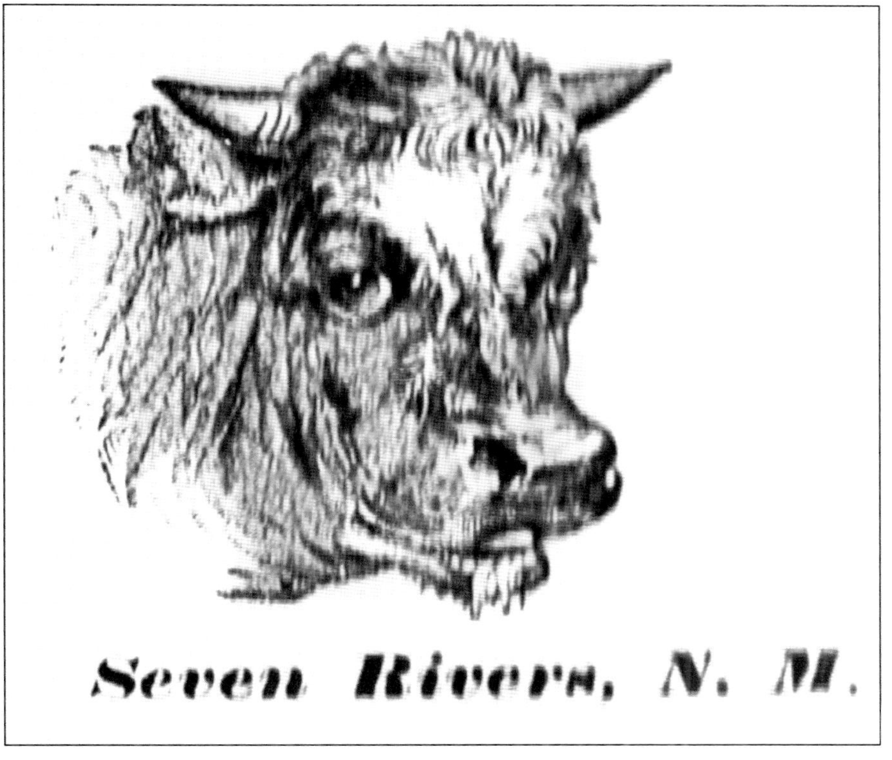

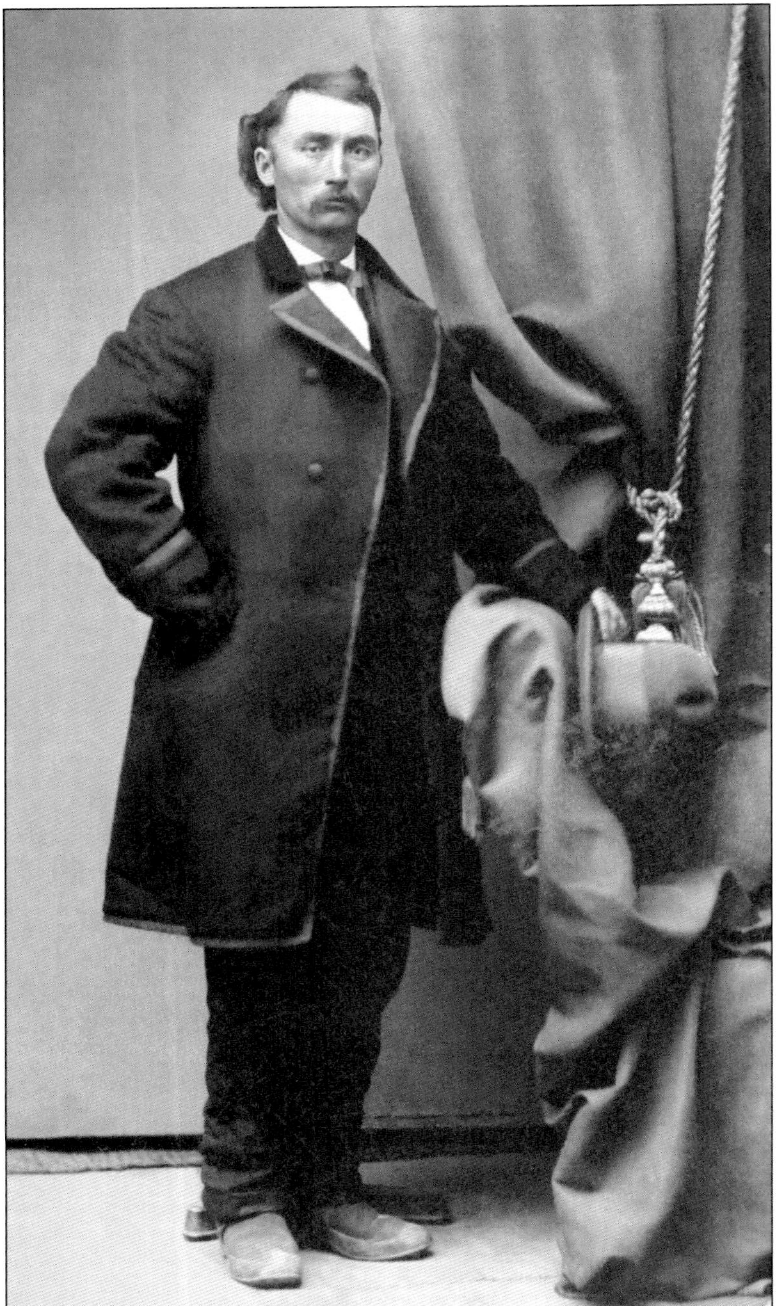

Pres. Ulysses S. Grant appointed Samuel Beach Axtell as governor of Utah in 1874, and Axtell became involved in a bitter feud between the anti-Mormon and Mormon citizens of the area. Axtell was next appointed as governor of the territory of New Mexico and allied himself with the Santa Fe Ring and James Dolan. During his tenure as governor, lawlessness was rampant in New Mexico, so he was dismissed from his position. However, Pres. James Garfield, a friend of Axtell's, appointed him chief justice for the territory—a post he held from 1882 to 1885.

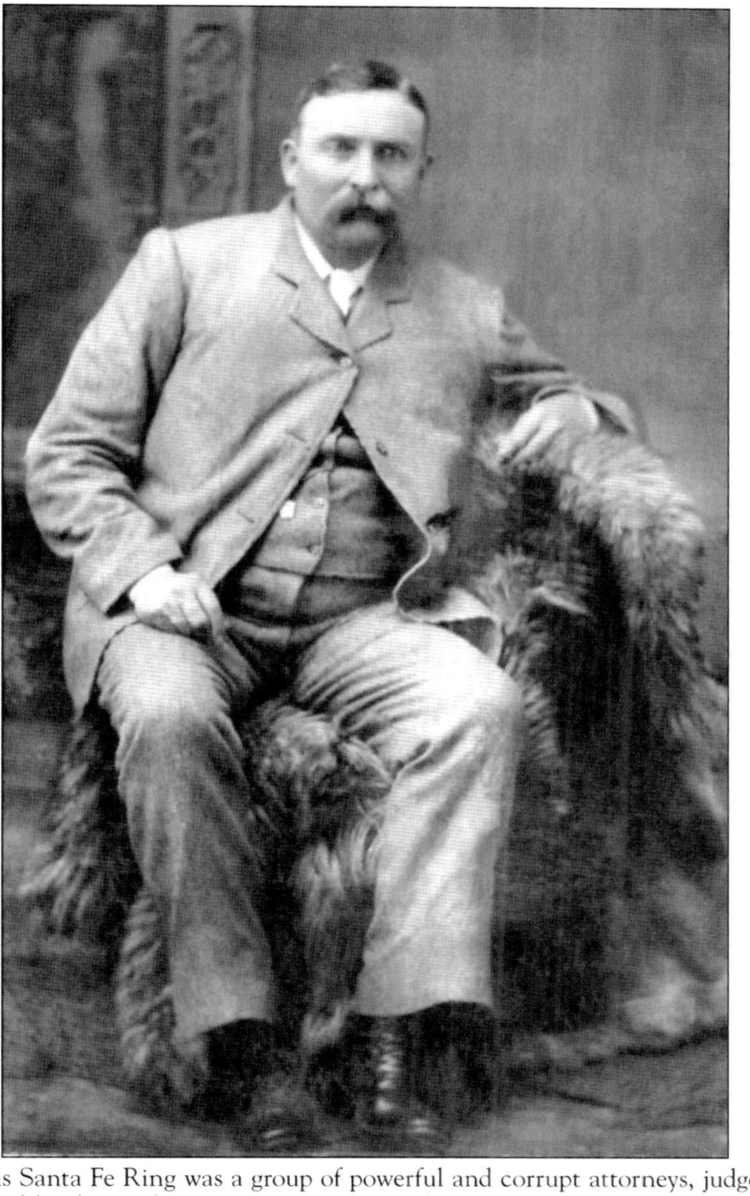

The notorious Santa Fe Ring was a group of powerful and corrupt attorneys, judges, lawmen, politicians, and land speculators in New Mexico. The group was presumably led by Thomas Benton Catron (pictured sitting on a buffalo hide). Some territorial governors, congressmen, and US senators who were ring members used the law to suit themselves. These men amassed considerable wealth through fraudulent land deals, mining, cattle, and railroad ventures. Santa Fe Ring men were known to be involved in stealing elections and influencing the press. Some members in this organized group actively took part in cattle rustling and horse stealing and committed many serious crimes with impunity. Catron served as district attorney for the Third Judicial District Court, which included Lincoln. He was later appointed attorney general for New Mexico. Pres. Ulysses S. Grant appointed him to a term as a federal attorney. Catron became the single largest landowner in New Mexico and one of the largest landowners in the United States by controlling three million acres.

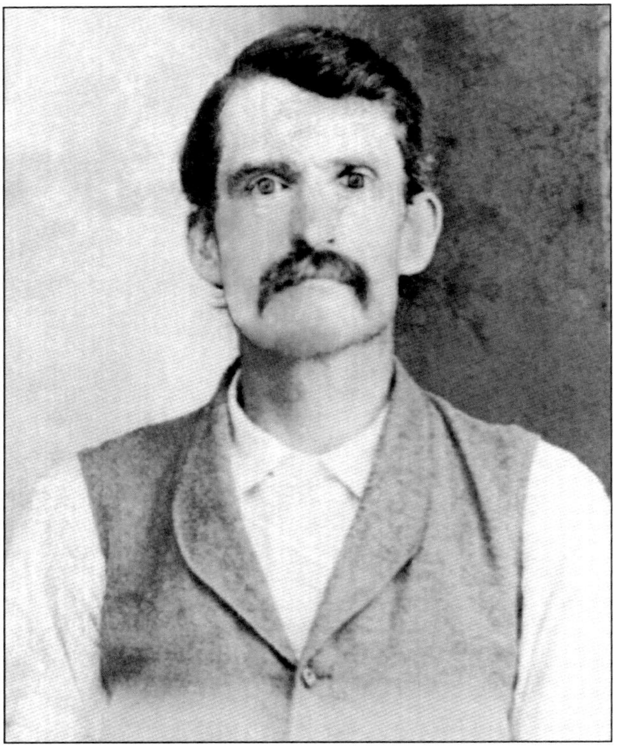

Former soldier Jacob Basil Mathews was Sheriff William Brady's chief deputy. He arrived in Lincoln and worked as a clerk for L.G. Murphy and Company. He squatted on land near Seven Rivers and went into the local cattle business. By 1877, Mathews illegally sold water rights and improvements to John Henry Tunstall on land he did not own. This was the general custom of Lawrence Murphy and James Dolan. Sheriff Brady was in debt to the Murphy store, so, under pressure, he issued warrants for the arrest of Alexander McSween for cattle rustling. Mathews formed a posse, which included notorious killers like George W. Hindman. Dolan went along with the posse to the Tunstall ranch and, not finding McSween, the posse killed Tunstall on February 18, 1878. Sheriff Brady seized Tunstall's property after his death.

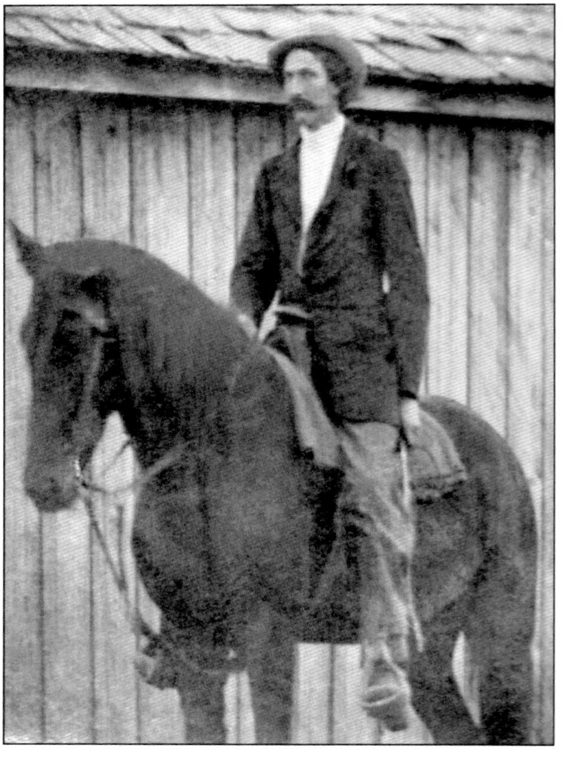

The Seven Rivers rustlers like those pictured at right and below constantly stole cattle from John Chisum's herd. They sold the stolen cattle to Lawrence Murphy and James Dolan, who would resell the cattle at low prices to fill government contracts that Chisum himself competed for. Chisum sought help from Sheriff William Brady to apprehend the thieves, but Brady refused, citing Seven Rivers as out of his jurisdiction. Finding himself with no support from the law, Chisum took matters into his own hands. Interestingly, Brady was deeply in debt at the Murphy-Dolan store, and his chief deputy, Jacob Mathews, became a partner of the J.J. Dolan Company. Brady aligned himself with the Dolan faction, along with Milo Pierce. Since Chisum was a business partner of McSween and Tunstall, this made them targets of the Seven Rivers outlaws and Dolan.

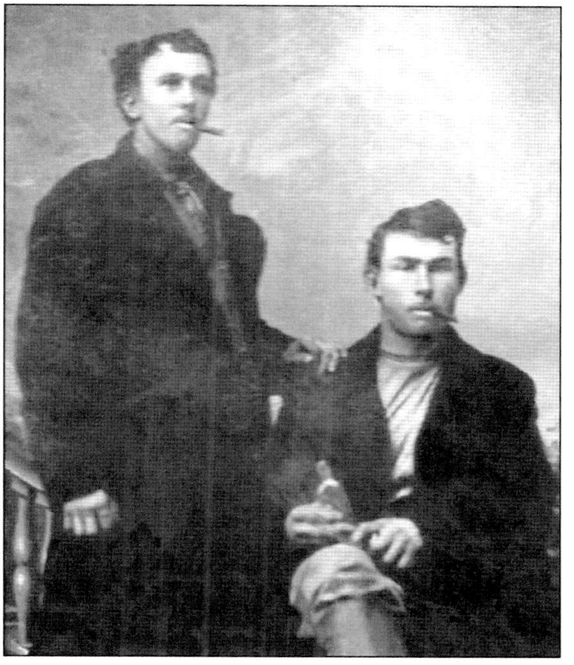

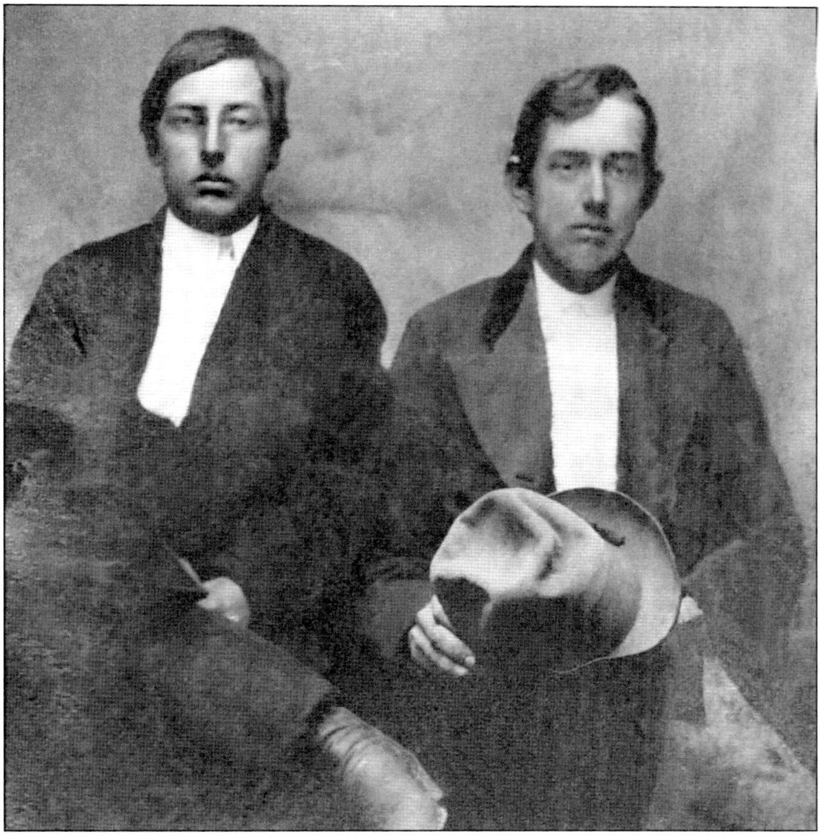

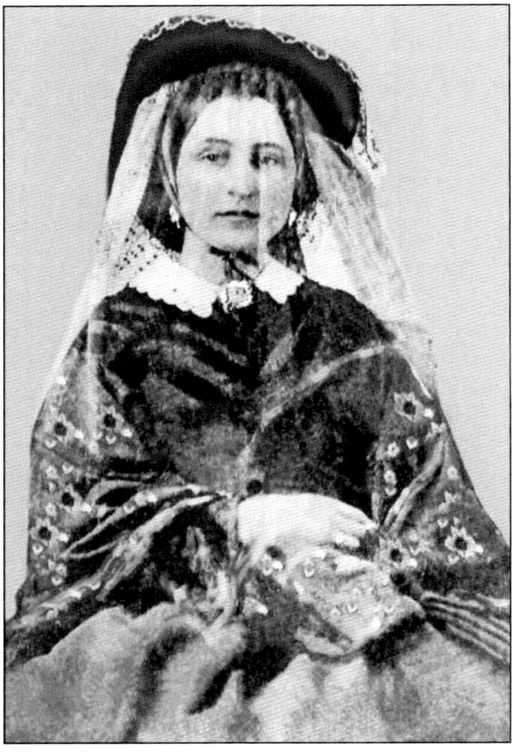

John Tunstall was well liked in Lincoln. Barbara Jones (left) and other residents attended his funeral. The women and children in the town of Lincoln and the surrounding area were victims of the turbulence and violence that the men were going through.

Frank Coe is pictured here (standing) with his dog "Ole Sheep" and three companions. During the Lincoln County War, Coe joined the Alexander McSween faction. He fought along with Billy the Kid and fellow Regulators, including his cousin George Coe, in the Gunfight of Blazer Mills. He was later involved in the Five-Day Battle in Lincoln.

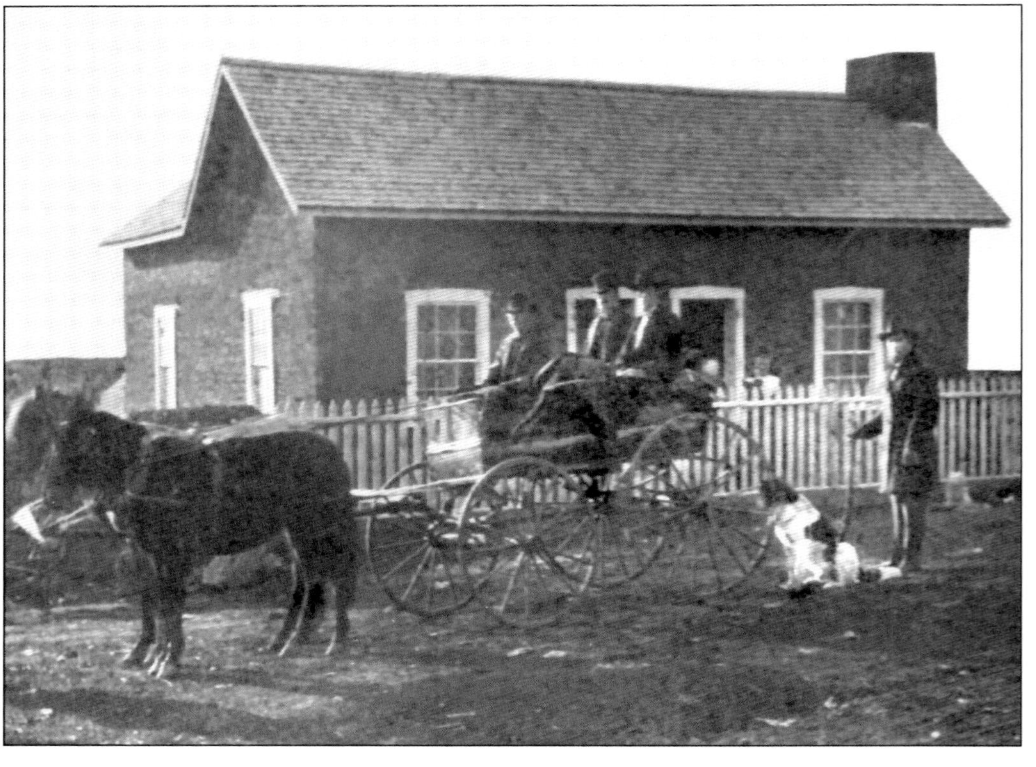

Sheriff William Brady reportedly knew Lawrence G. Murphy when he was discharged from the Army. "Squire" John Wilson, justice of the peace, saw that things were getting out of control in Lincoln, so he deputized Richard M. Brewer as a special constable to form a posse, the Lincoln County Regulators, to apprehend Tunstall's killers and bring them to justice. Billy the Kid was included among Brewer's special deputies. The Regulators wound up being involved in several shootouts, since the Brady group would not surrender or acknowledge the new lawmen. Sheriff William Brady and his deputy George Hindman were killed when shots were fired from a wall with portholes. Brady deputies Jacob Mathews, George Peppin, and Jack Long survived.

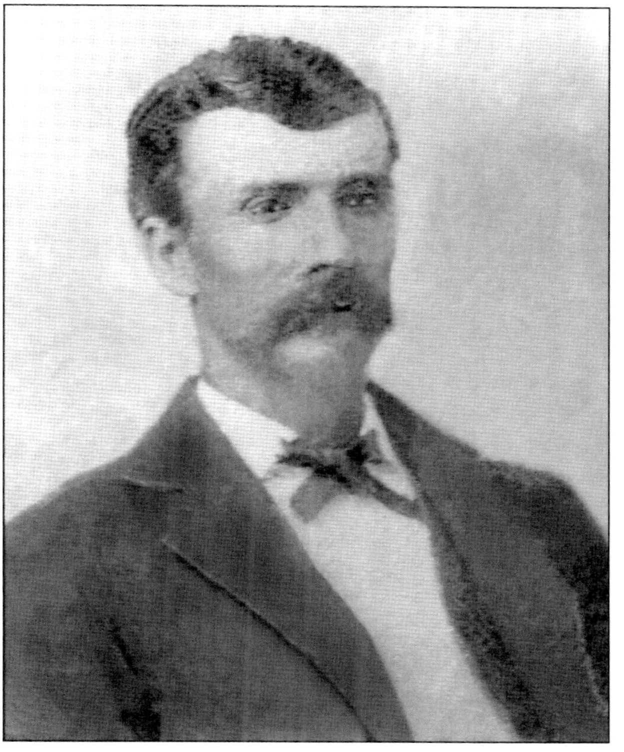

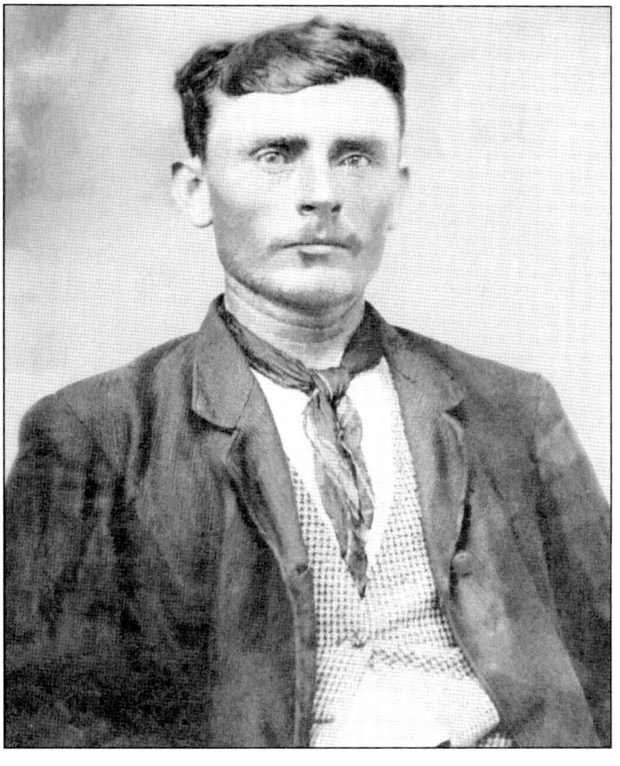

John Hurley ran a saloon near Fort Stanton. Hurley, one of Sheriff Brady's deputies, was in the party that killed Tunstall. He fought along with James Dolan's Seven Rivers outfit during the Five-Day Battle. In January 1886, Nicolás Aragón killed Hurley in a shootout.

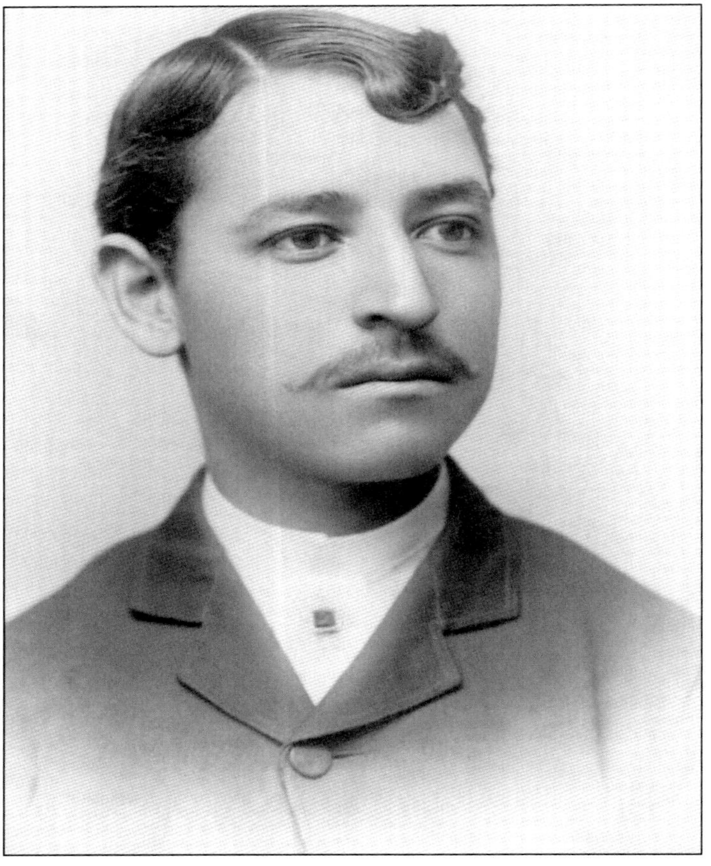

Bonifacio "Bonnie" Baca witnessed the shooting of Sheriff William Brady and deputy George Hindman on the main street of Lincoln on April 1, 1878. Baca had rushed along with his class of students to the nearby torreon, the defensive tower near the street, for protection. From the top of the tower, he saw Billy the Kid and four other men lying in wait behind an adobe wall before the ambush of Brady and four of his deputies. Bonifacio Baca served as a witness against Billy the Kid at his trial in Mesilla in April 1881.

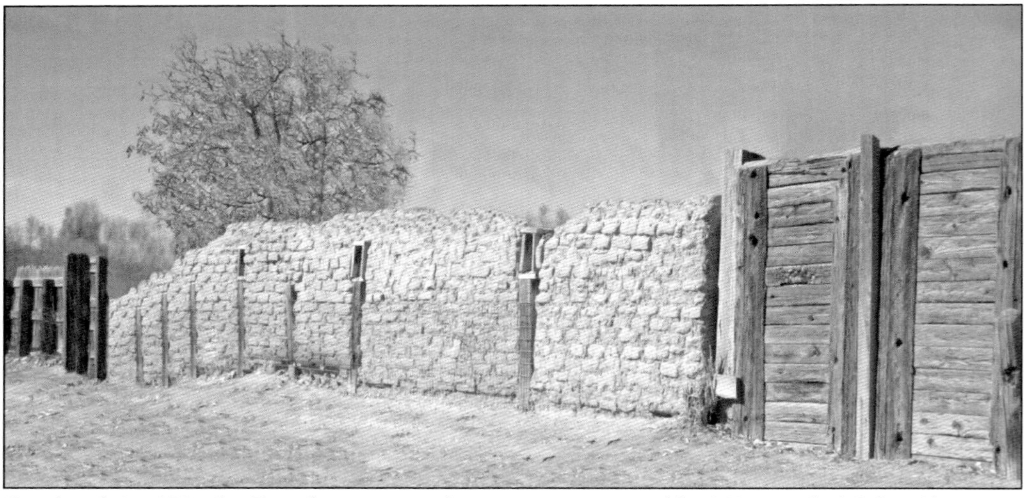

On April 1, 1878, the Regulators, a civilian posse organized by US Marshal John Sherman, ambushed Sheriff William Brady and three deputies. While seeking to serve warrants for Tunstall's murder and firing from portholes in a wall similar to this one, Brady and Hindman fell. US Deputy Marshal Robert Widenmann and William H. Bonney were involved in the shooting. (Photograph by Santiago de Aragón.)

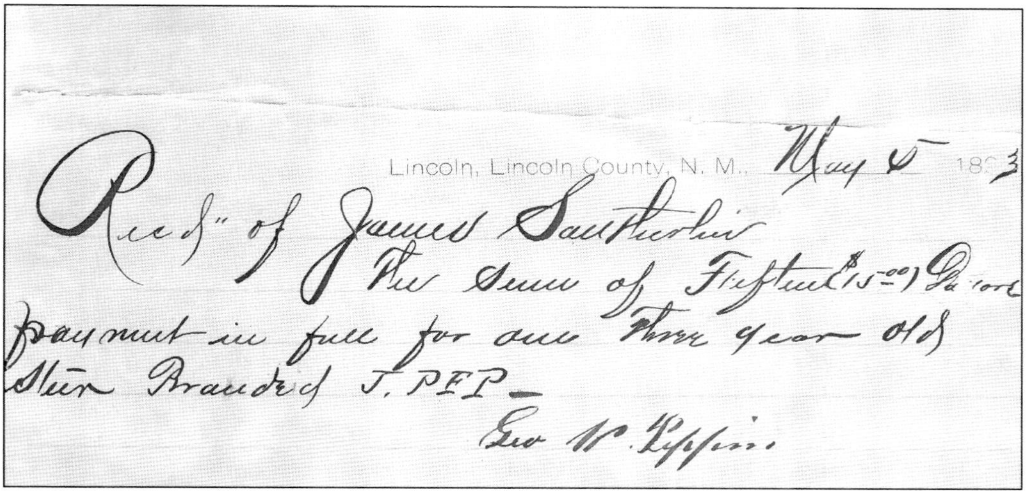

Lincoln, Lincoln County, N. M., May 5 1893

Rec'd of James Southerlin The sum of Fifteen ($15.00) Dollars payment in full for one three year old Steer Branded J. PEP—

Geo W. Peppin.

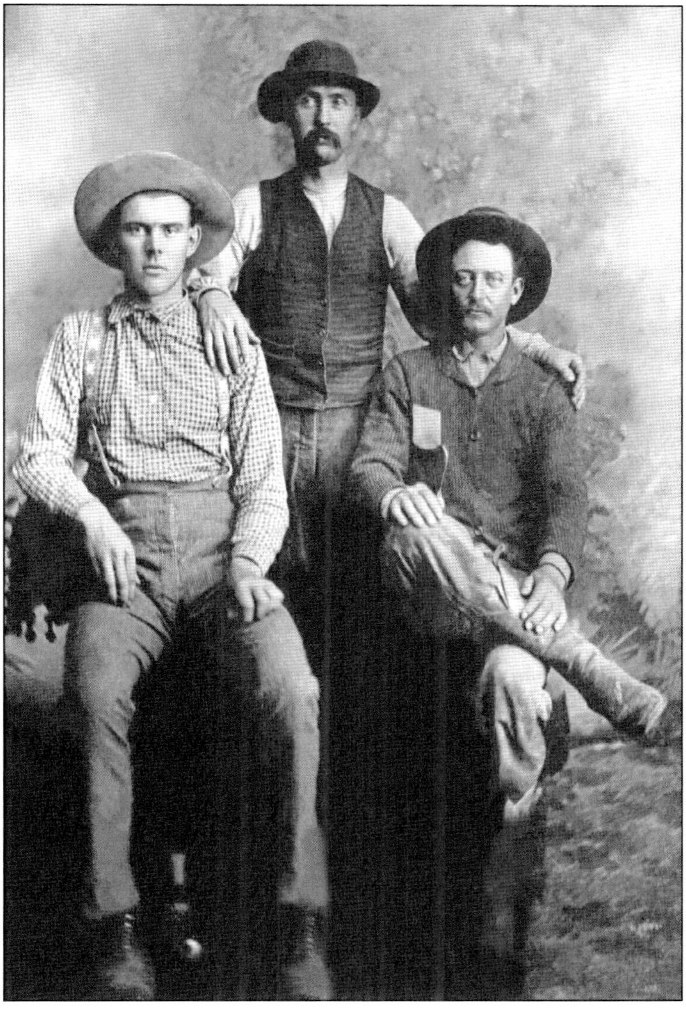

Sheriff George Warden Peppin (center), pictured with two deputies, was a former Army soldier who had worked as a civilian mason at Fort Stanton. Pictured above is a receipt for the sale of a steer issued by George Peppin, bearing the brand of his son, Juan Peppin. Sheriff Peppin helped construct a new jail and houses, including the McSween home, in Lincoln. James Dolan persuaded Gov. Samuel Beach Axtell to side with him to appoint Peppin as Lincoln County sheriff in place of Sheriff John N. Copeland, who was neutral. Peppin's first order of business was to go after the McSween faction.

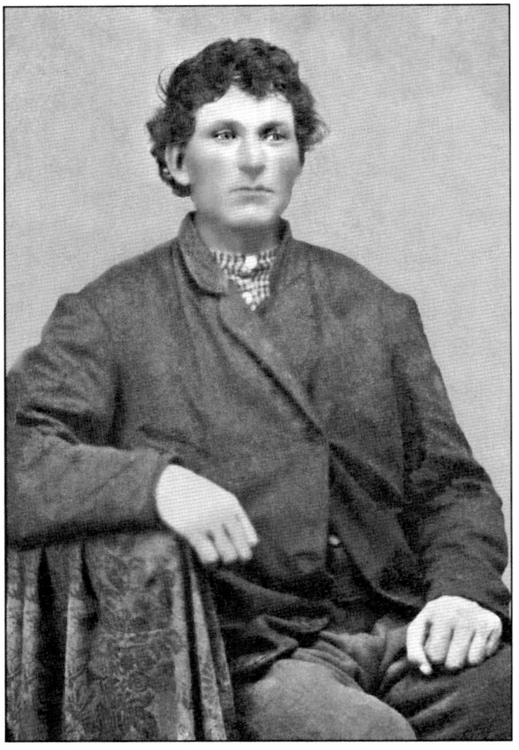

Richard M. Brewer arrived in Lincoln from Missouri sometime around 1870. He worked for L.G. Murphy and Company and was recognized for being aboveboard and honest. He was on friendly terms with John Tunstall. At one point, Seven Rivers cowboys stole horses and mules owned by Brewer, Tunstall, and Alexander McSween. Brewer served as a deputy under Sheriff William Brady.

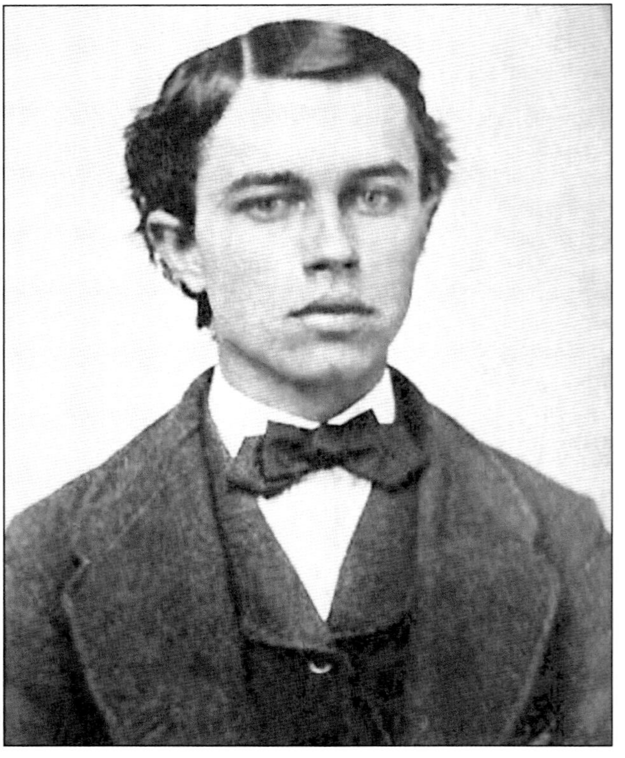

James Albert Saunders arrived in Lincoln in 1875. Saunders and Frank Coe served as deputies in the Regulators. Seven Rivers men ambushed them, and Regulator Frank MacNab was killed. Saunders was wounded and captured. Coe was captured. Deputy US Marshal Robert Widenmann and his posse trapped the Seven Rivers men, who surrendered to Sheriff John N. Copeland. A troop of soldiers under the command of Lt. George Smith incarcerated them at Fort Stanton. Lawrence Murphy and James Dolan succeeded in getting Col. Nathan Dudley to set the Seven Rivers men free. Immediately after their release by Sheriff Copeland, they went on a horse-stealing spree.

In 1873, Capt. Chambers McKibbin from Fort Stanton prohibited James Dolan from entering the fort, but Emil Fritz intervened on his behalf. McKibbin, along with troops under his command, patrolled Lincoln County in order to control hostilities with the Indians and between rival cattlemen.

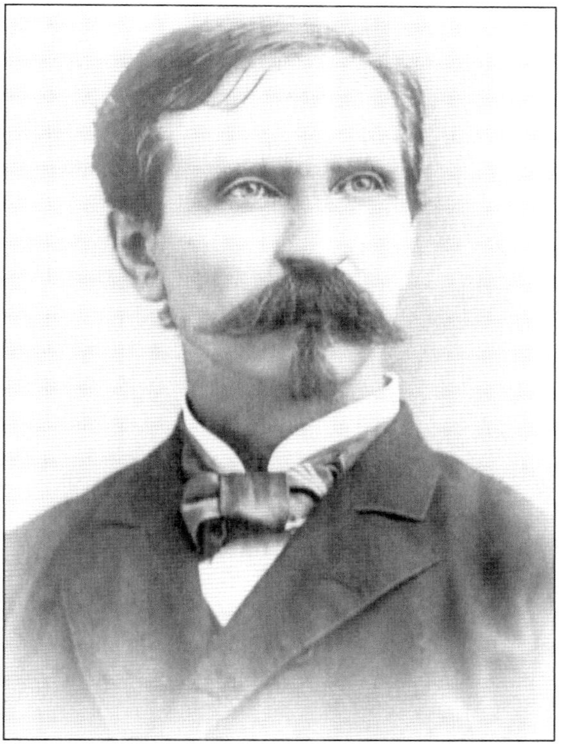

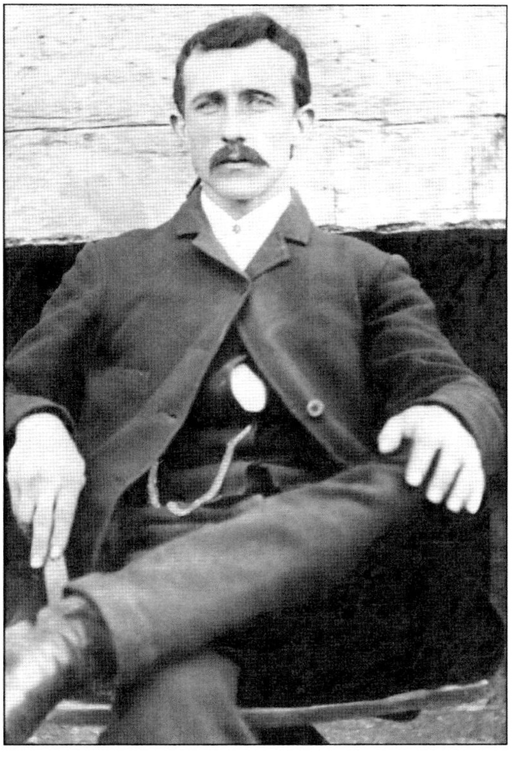

Seven Rivers rancher Milo Lucius Pierce was a willing James Dolan partisan. Pierce—along with George Peppin, John Hurley, Bob and John Beckwith, and Bob Olinger and his brother Wallace Olinger—fought against the Alexander McSween faction in Lincoln, which included Billy the Kid, José Chavez y Chavez, and numerous Hispanic sheep and cattle ranchers and farmers. It appears that the majority of the Hispanic citizenry in and around Lincoln sided with John Tunstall and McSween against the Murphy-Dolan monopoly.

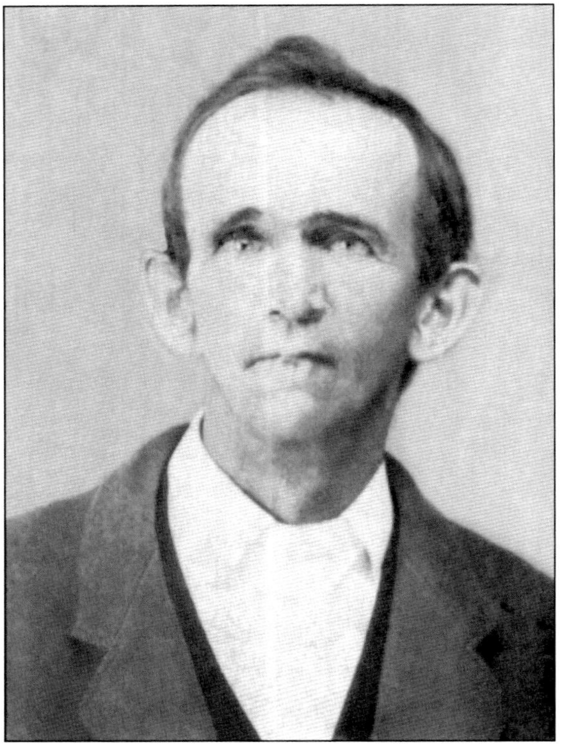

Gov. Lew Wallace gave Capt. Henry Carroll, interim commander at Fort Stanton, authority to apprehend and incarcerate James J. Dolan, Jacob Mathews, Jesse Evans, John Beckwith, Eugenio Salazar, Heiskell Jones, and 30 others with outstanding warrants for murder and cattle rustling. Dolan was wanted for the murder of attorney Huston Ingraham Chapman as well as another murder, but Tom Catron succeeded in getting the charges dropped, as well as a charge of murder against George Peppin. Robert Beckwith (left), a Seven Rivers member of the Dolan faction, was shot and killed at Lincoln. His brother John M. Beckwith (below) was killed in 1879. The Beckwith clan was led by Henry M. "Hugh" Beckwith, who was wanted for treason during the Civil War. Hugh Beckwith shot and killed his son-in-law William H. Johnson. John Chisum and 30 of his men surrounded the Beckwith ranch for three days (for rustling Chisum's cattle) to no avail.

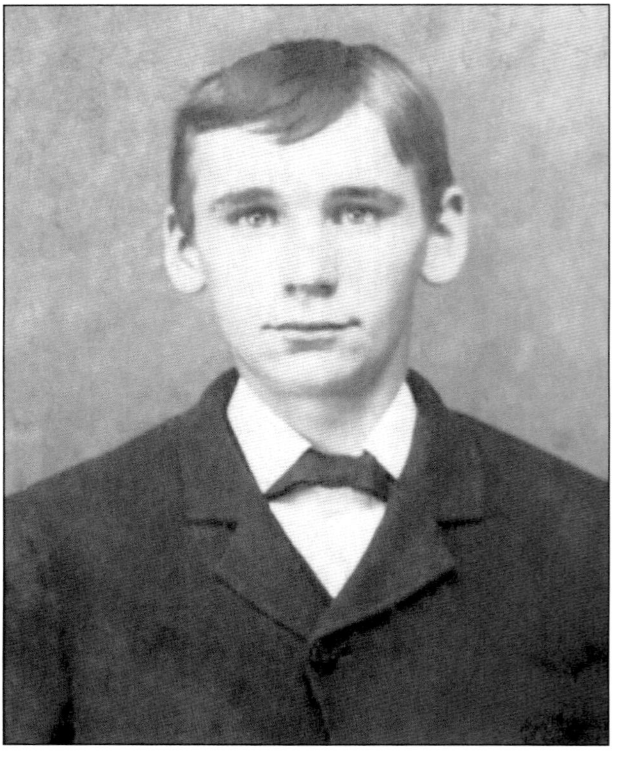

Eugenio Salazar was born on February 14, 1863. At 15, he was one of the youngest members of the Regulators. Salazar miraculously survived the fire at the Alexander McSween house after being shot by James Dolan's men. Salazar crept to the home of José Otero, where his sister-in-law, Nicolosita Pacheco, was staying. Dr. Richard Wells, post surgeon at Fort Stanton, treated his wounds.

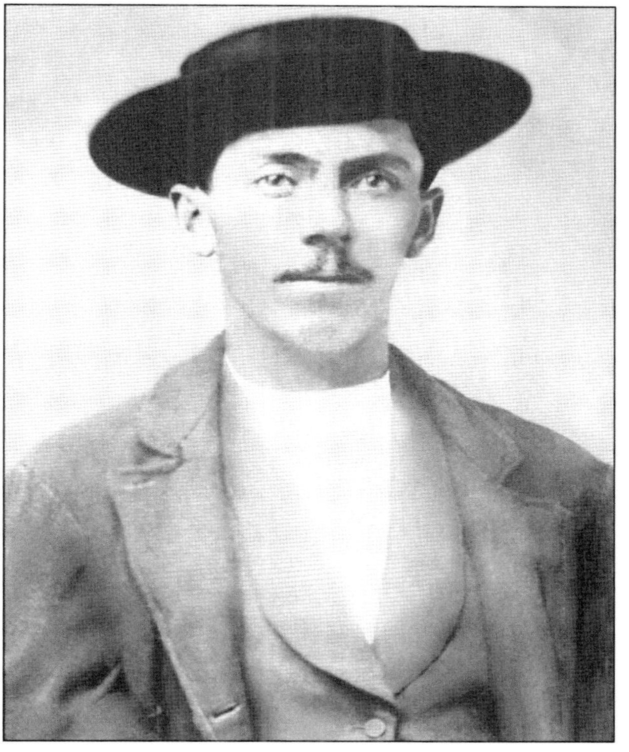

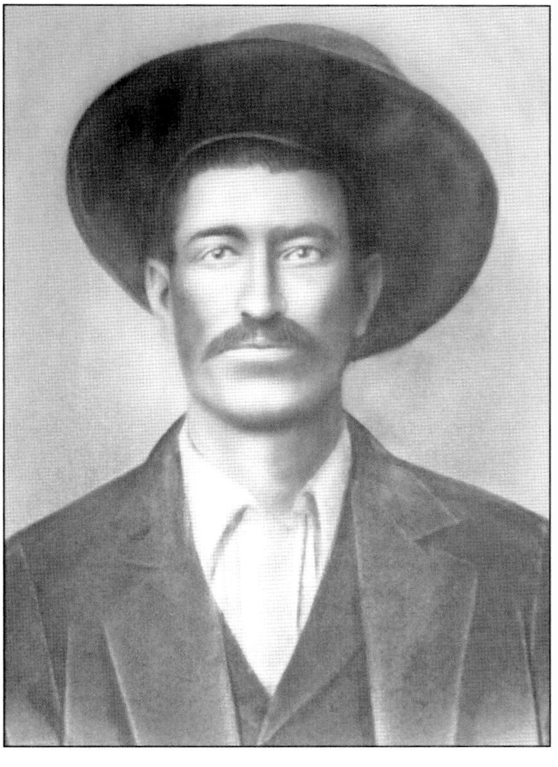

José Chavez y Chavez was Billy the Kid's sidekick. He went back and forth from lawman to outlaw. Chavez joined the Alexander McSween faction. He was sentenced to death for murder, but Gov. Miguel Antonio Otero commuted the sentence. Later, Gov. George Curry pardoned Chavez. He spent the rest of his life thrilling youngsters with stories of Billy the Kid as he sat on a park bench on the Old Town Plaza in Las Vegas, New Mexico.

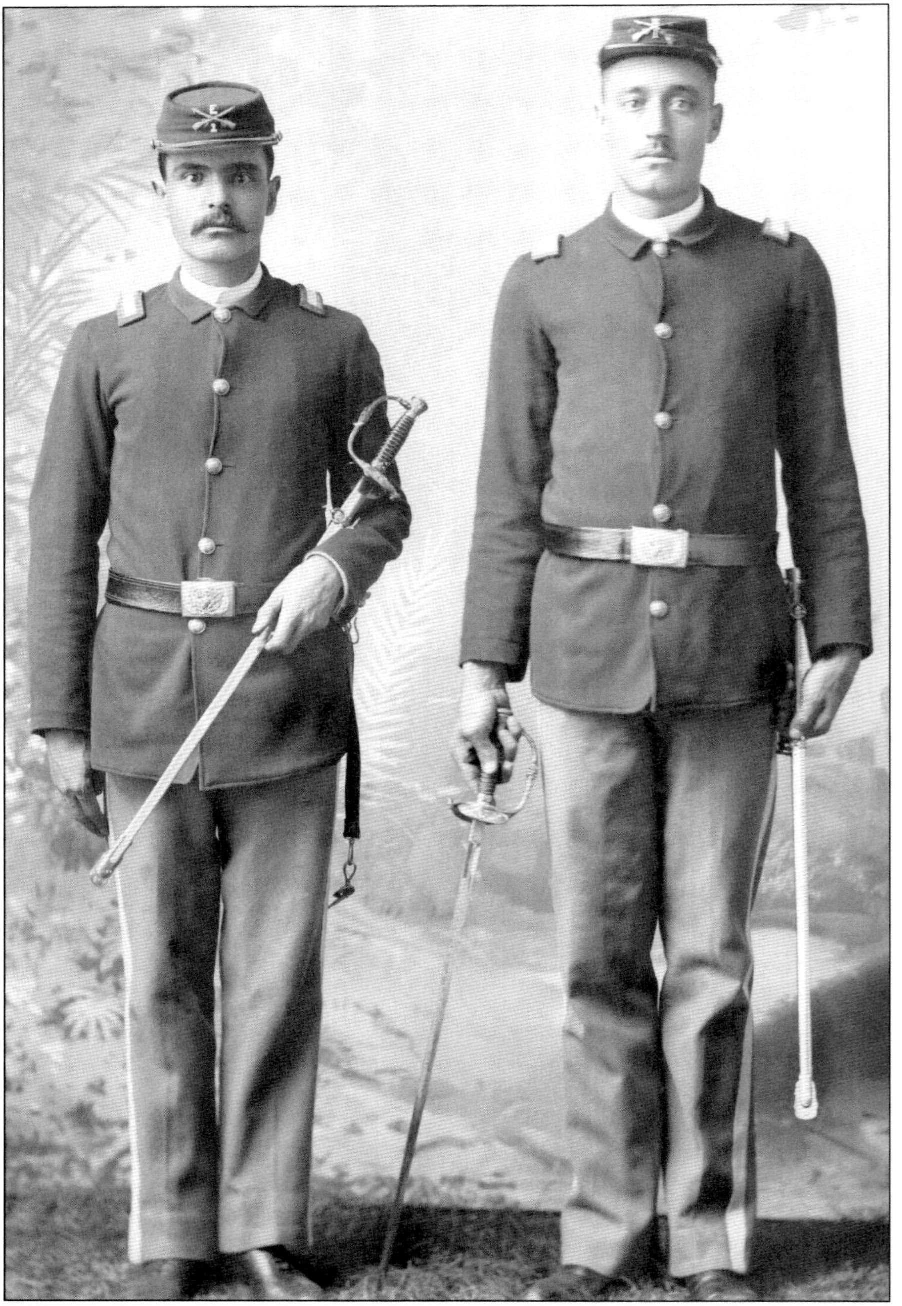

The photographs on this page and the following page were taken by James Furlong in Las Vegas, New Mexico, and represent Fort Stanton soldiers who fought to a draw during the Five-Day Battle between the Regulators and James Dolan's faction. Dolan was frustrated, so he rode to Fort Stanton to try to convince Col. Nathan Dudley, the fort commander, that the lives of civilians in Lincoln were in danger. Colonel Dudley showed up in Lincoln on July 19, 1878, with one company of infantry, one of cavalry, four officers, a Gatling gun with 2,000 rounds of ammunition, and a 12-pound brass howitzer. Dudley posted his men on the Dolan side.

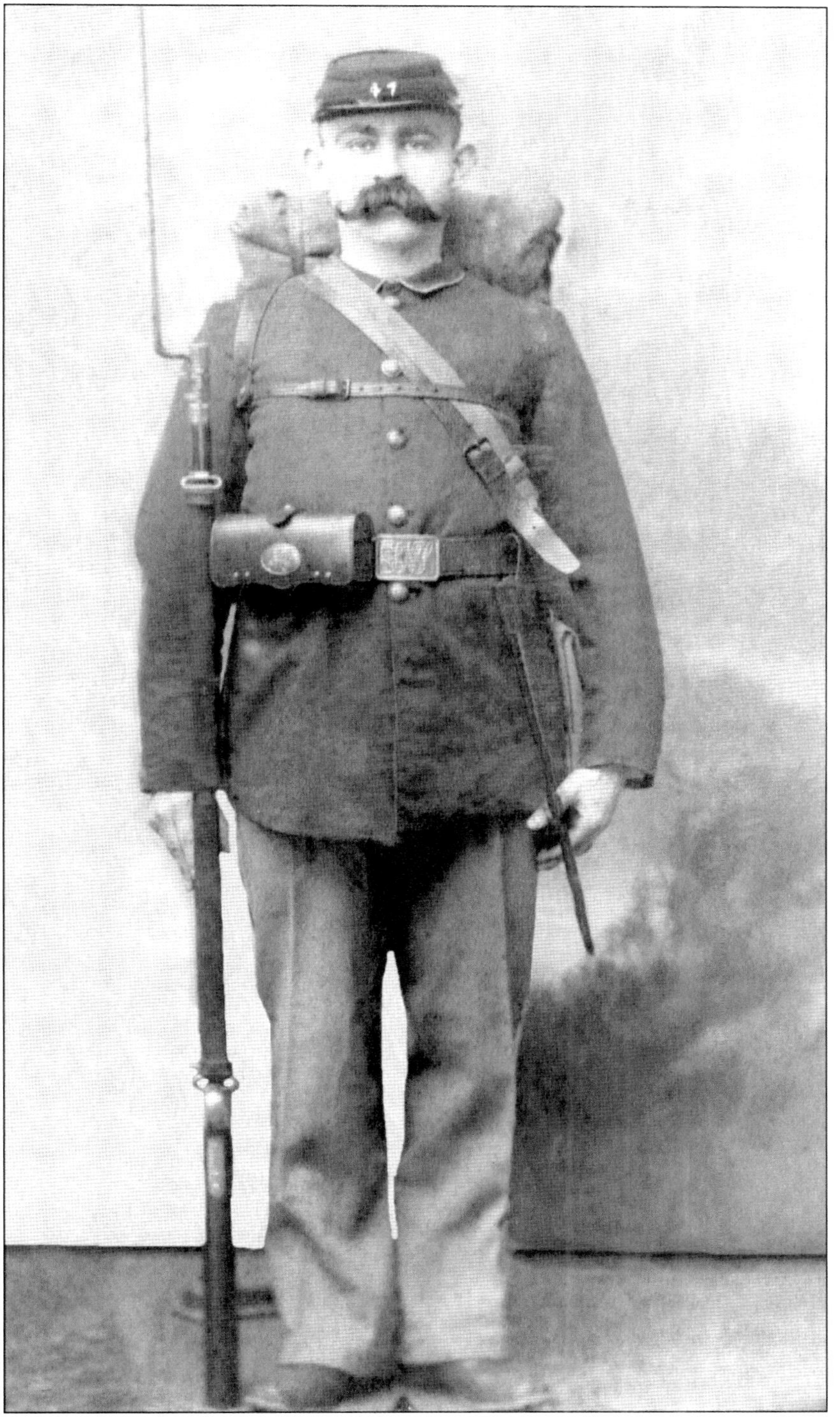

It is not known to what extent the soldiers participated in the fighting, but their presence tipped the scales in James Dolan's favor. Alexander McSween's house was burned to the ground, and only a few Regulators trapped inside managed to escape.

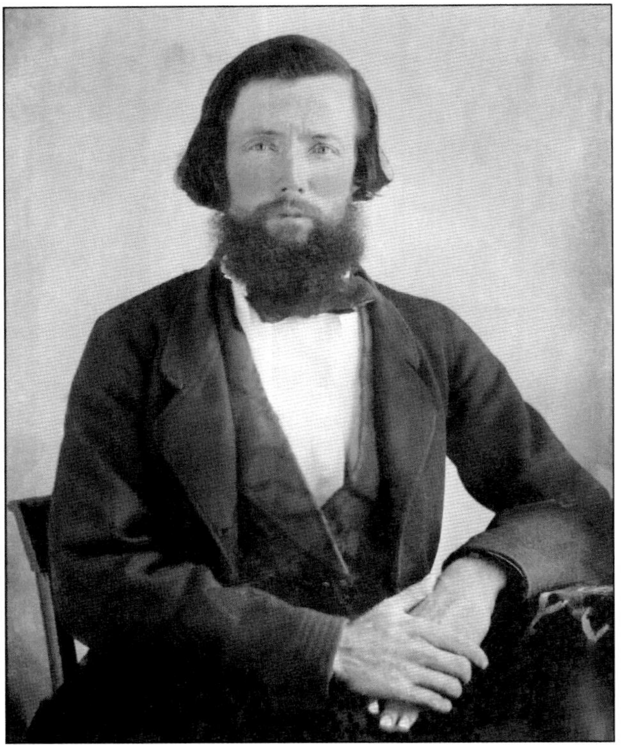

Third judicial district attorney William L. Rynerson was a powerful member of the notorious Santa Fe Ring. He bent the rules of the law to suit himself and only prosecuted those who were not allied with the ring. The town of Lincoln fell in Rynerson's jurisdiction, so he manipulated trials and juries to go his way.

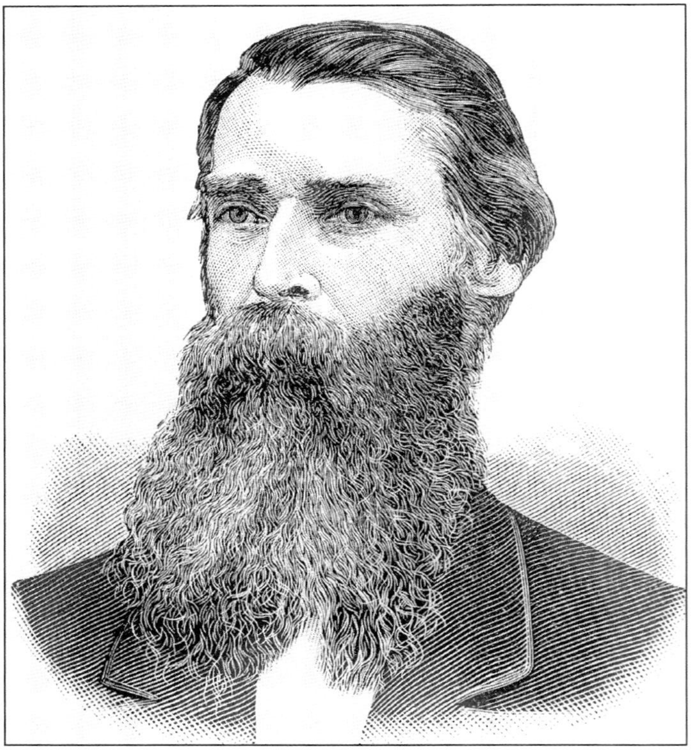

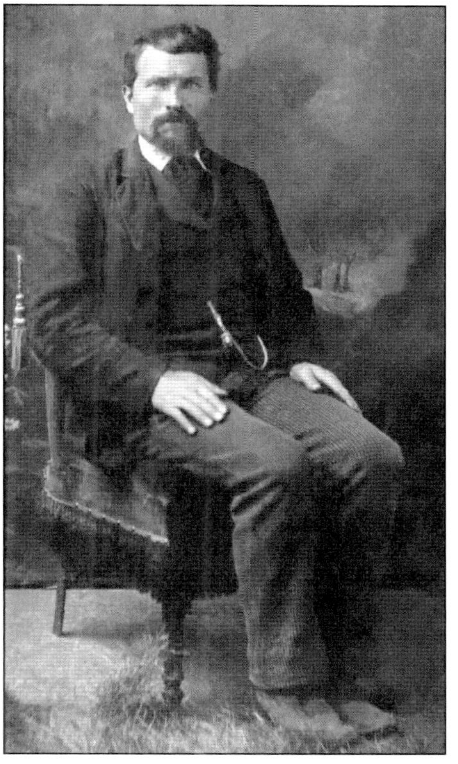

Robert Adam Casey and his wife, Ellen Eveline Casey, owned a mill and ranch about 25 miles from Fort Stanton. "Casey's Mill" was the only gristmill in the area. Ash Upson served as a clerk at a store Casey owned. Robert Casey was highly critical of Lawrence Murphy and James Dolan. On August 1, 1875, Casey went to eat lunch at the Wortley hotel in Lincoln, which was a popular hangout for the Murphy-Dolan faction. After eating, Casey was killed by William Wilson. It was thought that Murphy paid Wilson to kill Casey, promising Wilson he would have protection from the law. Juan Bautista Patrón, who was a probate judge in Lincoln in 1876, was also outspoken in the community against Murphy and Dolan; he was killed under suspicious circumstances in 1884. It is not surprising that Ellen Casey (pictured below) had serious financial problems after her husband's death. The tintype photograph of John Chisum in this volume was given to Ellen Casey by the famous cowman. On the back of it, Chisum wrote, "Ellen remember your promise."

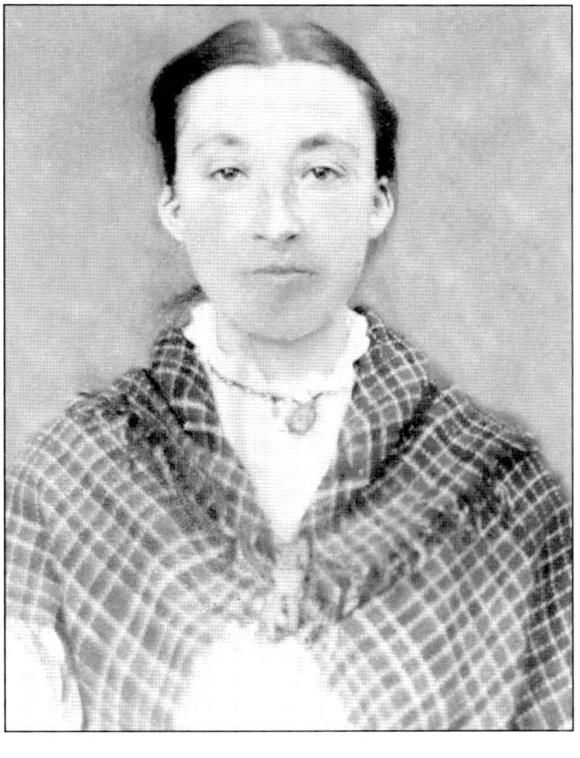

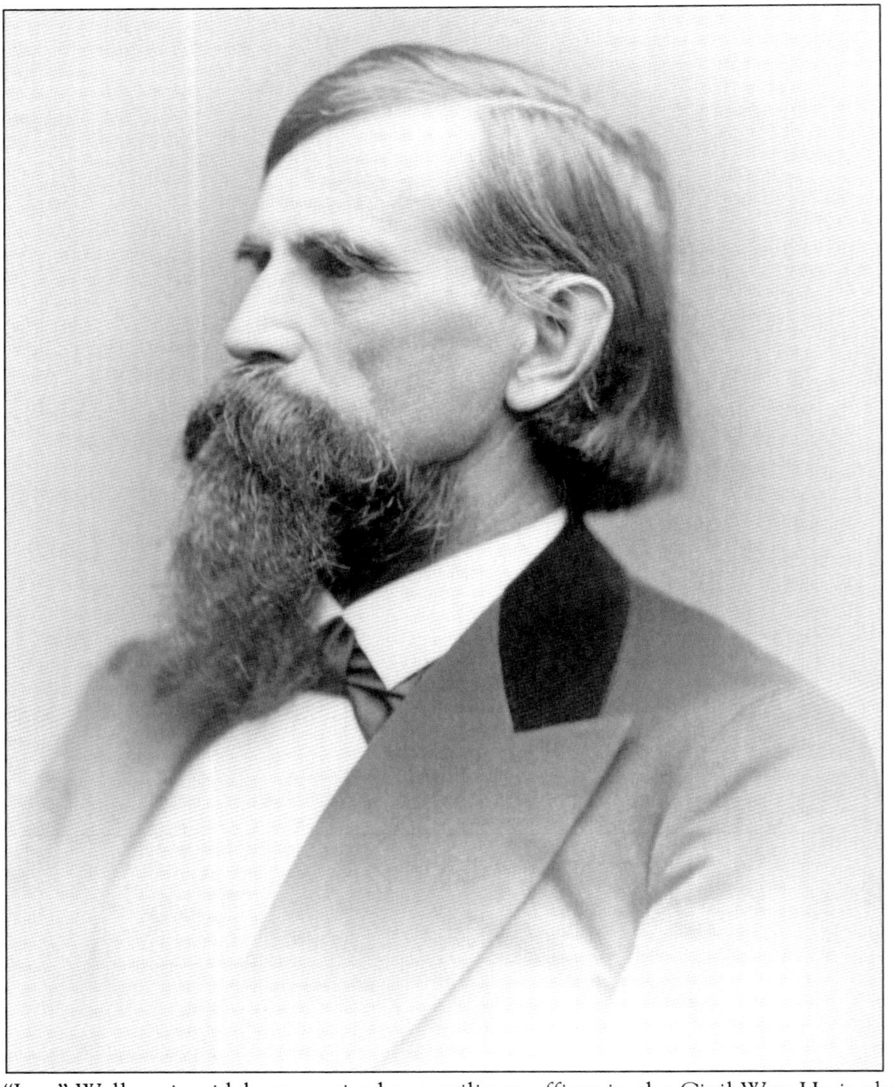

Lewis "Lew" Wallace is widely recognized as a military officer in the Civil War. He is also well known for writing *Ben Hur: A Tale of the Christ*, the best-selling novel of the 19th century. Wallace also served as governor of New Mexico Territory. Pres. Rutherford B. Hayes appointed Wallace governor in 1878 to clean up lawlessness and corruption, which was running rampant. Governor Wallace served from September 1878 to May 30, 1881. Murders of prominent citizens, rape, and pillaging were common in certain parts of the territory, including Lincoln County, so the governor organized citizen militias, assigned special agents, offered rewards, and signed death warrants. He organized the Lincoln County Rifles, commanded by Juan Patron, a New Mexican who was educated at Notre Dame University in Indiana, to search out bandits for trial. The Rifles consisted of nearly 40 mounted and armed Hispanic riders from Lincoln. Wallace went to Lincoln in March 1879 to personally investigate the situation and to find witnesses in pending criminal prosecutions. His most famous meeting took place on March 17 with local legend Billy the Kid, whom he promised to pardon for his misdeeds. Wallace resigned his post in 1881 after experiencing unending difficulties with the Santa Fe Ring, but he did provide some sense of hope in the territory.

Three

Lincoln Spawns a Legend

Amidst the flames of the burning Alexander McSween house during the five-day siege of 1878, Billy the Kid was looking for a way out. The Kid was one of the Lincoln County Regulators trapped inside by the Dolan gunmen. Billy the Kid finally made a run for it while firing his pistols, and escaped. Others were not as lucky, including McSween himself, who was shot unarmed while holding on to his Bible and reportedly carrying a white flag. The Five-Day Battle brought an end to the Lincoln County War, but not to the lawlessness that plagued the territory. Lew Wallace was appointed governor of New Mexico Territory, replacing Gov. Samuel Beach Axtell, who had connections to the Santa Fe Ring and supported James Dolan. Wallace was sent to clean up the lawlessness, and his methods included attempting to bring criminals to justice and granting amnesty to those who were deemed worthy of it. Sheriff Patrick Floyd Garrett was to help accomplish this formidable feat. Garrett—or Juan Largo, as the Hispanic population called him because of his great height—was thought of as being fearless and unerring. He set his sights on bringing Billy the Kid to justice for the killing of Sheriff William Brady, although several of the Regulators were involved in the incident. The general population felt there was no jail that could hold the Kid, since he had built up a reputation for daring escapes. Garrett captured Billy the Kid and took him to trial in Mesilla, New Mexico, where he was found guilty on April 13, 1881, and sentenced to hang in Lincoln. On April 28, 1881, Billy the Kid made his most famous escape by killing Lincoln deputies Bob Olinger and James Bell and riding out of town. Both Billy the Kid and Lincoln garnered national attention, creating a legend and entering the pages of history.

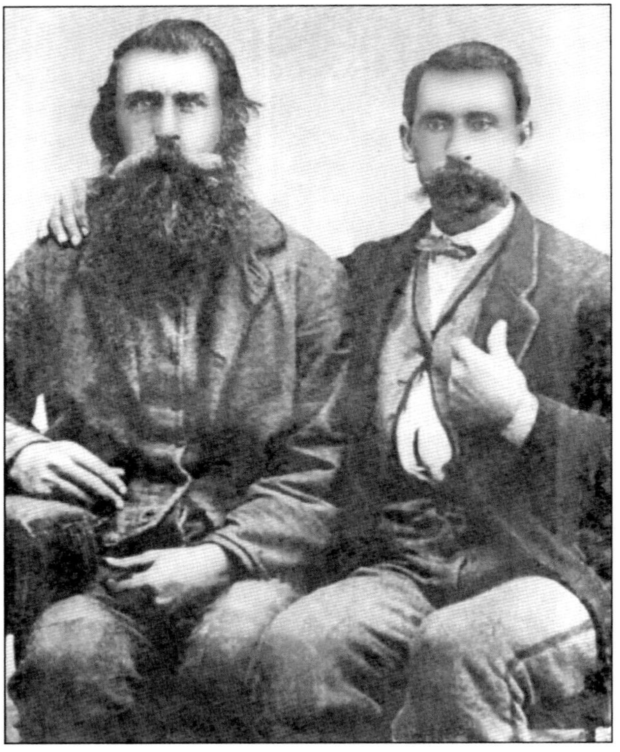

Dr. Joseph H. Blazer (left) was a former dentist from Iowa who operated a sawmill and gristmill on the Mescalero Apache Reservation, where he served as an Indian agent. Blazer's intent was to provide lumber for construction in Lincoln and other areas. Lt. Col. Nathan A. Dudley (right) was a Fort Stanton commander who sided with the James Dolan faction during the Five-Day Battle.

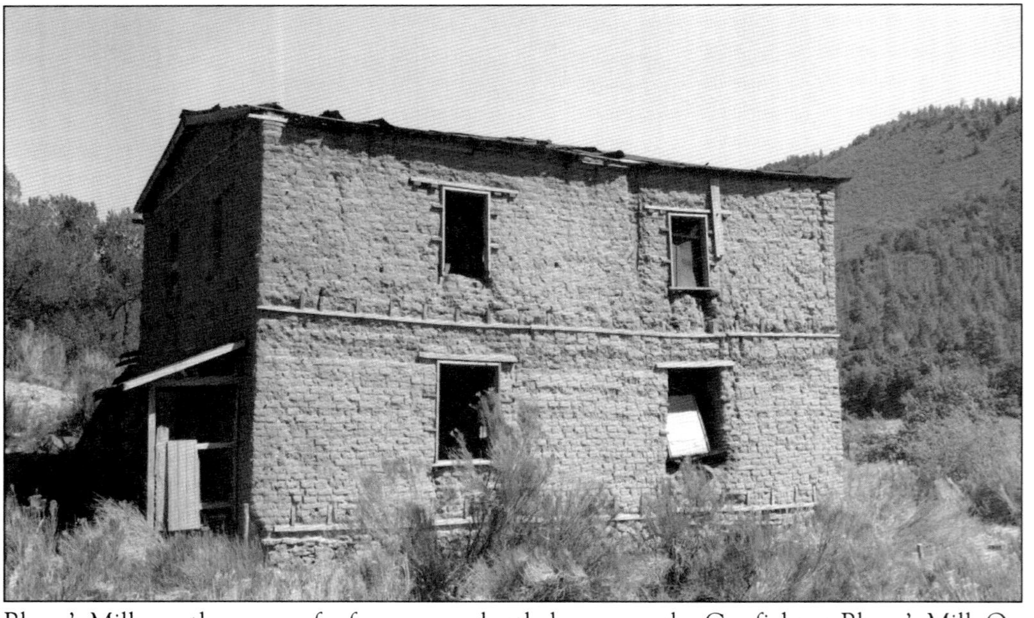

Blazer's Mill was the scene of a famous gun battle known as the Gunfight at Blazer's Mill. On April 4, 1878, William H. Bonney, alias Billy the Kid, and other deputies sought to arrest Buckshot Roberts, a former buffalo hunter who was implicated in John Tunstall's murder and refused to surrender. During the ensuing gunfight, Roberts was shot, but one member of the posse attempting to serve warrants for Tunstall's murder died and four others were wounded.

There were many saloons in Lincoln. The L.G. Murphy and Co. store housed a saloon on the first floor. Isaac "Ike" Stockton had a saloon at the Montaño store. Some saloons were in such close proximity that partygoers could go from one to the next. Entertainment also included performers such as the popular Elle Chapman (pictured), who sang and danced. Chapman traveled a circuit that included saloons in New Mexico and Colorado.

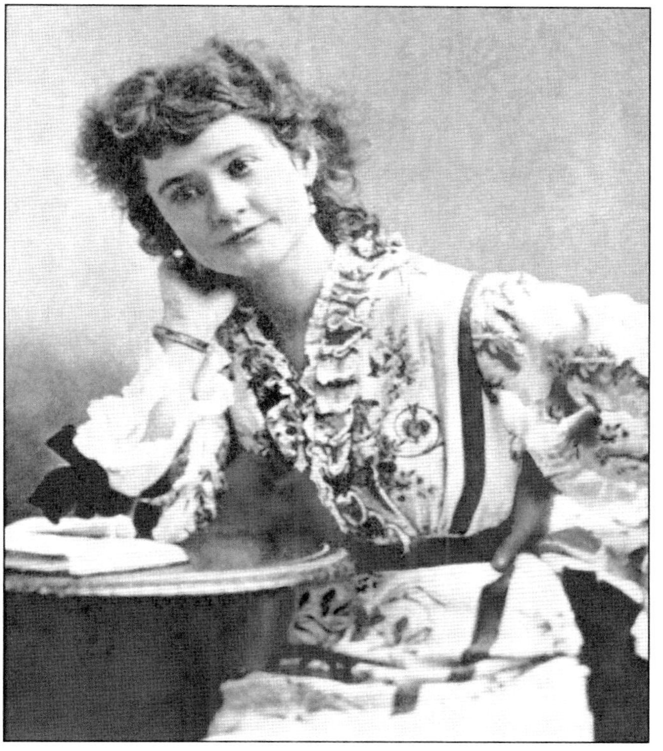

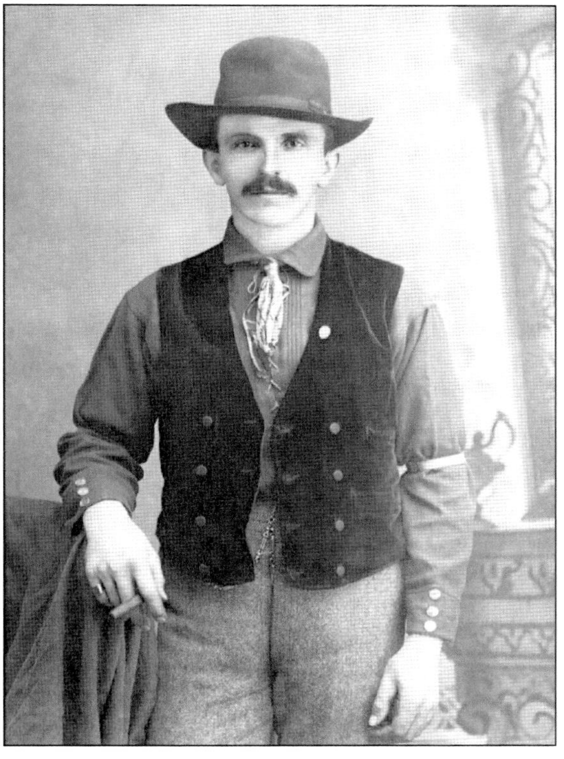

Professional gamblers plied their trade at saloons. Billy the Kid was recognized as a card player in Las Vegas, Fort Sumner, and other towns. Winning at the card table was the Kid's hallmark, which provided him with nice clothes, guns, and ammunition. Here, an unidentified gambler at the Montezuma Saloon flashes a gold gambler's pinky ring like the one worn by the Kid. Gamblers often carried concealed weapons that they could use in a pinch if needed.

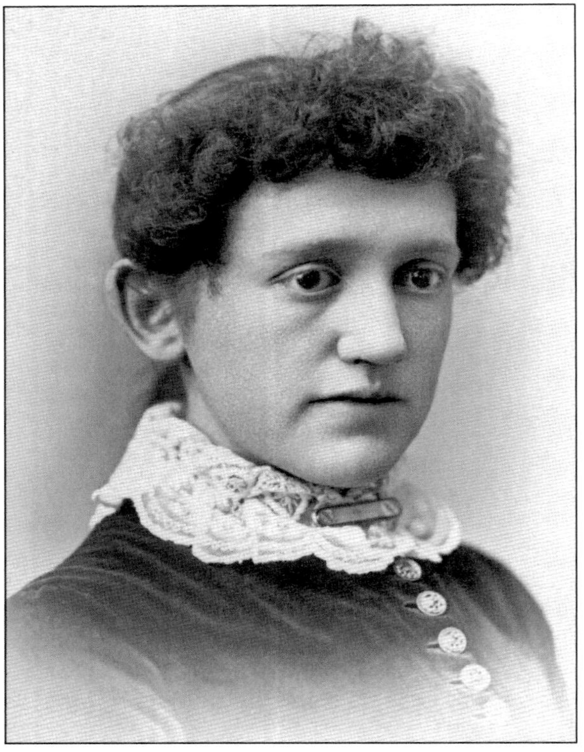

Mary "Minnie" Shield (pictured) was David and Elizabeth Shield's daughter. Minnie was 10 years old and living with her parents in Lincoln when the James Dolan faction killed Alexander McSween.

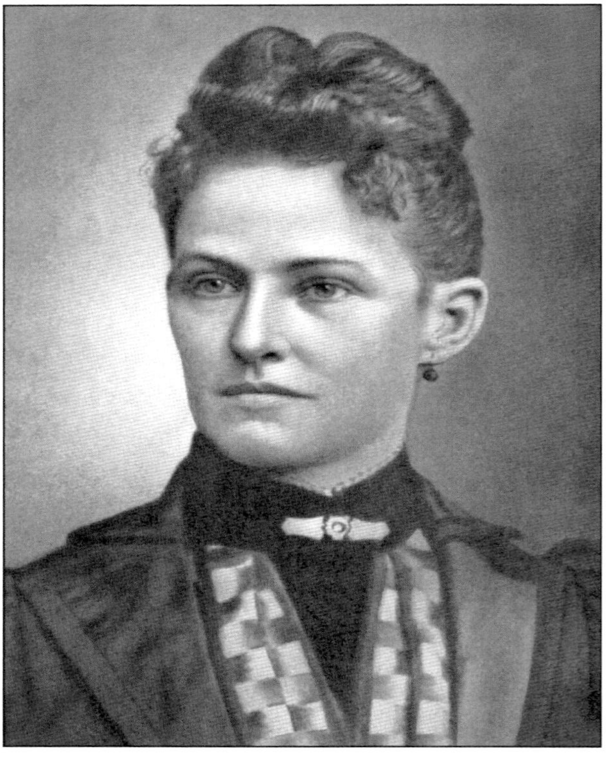

John Chisum's favorite niece was Sallie Lucy Chisum (pictured). Sallie was recognized as the cattle king's niece, and she got to know some of her uncle's ranch hands, including Billy the Kid. She was a beloved figure in Lincoln and thought of the Kid as a gentleman. She recorded in her diary, "As far as dress was concerned he always looked as if he had just stepped out of a bandbox…"

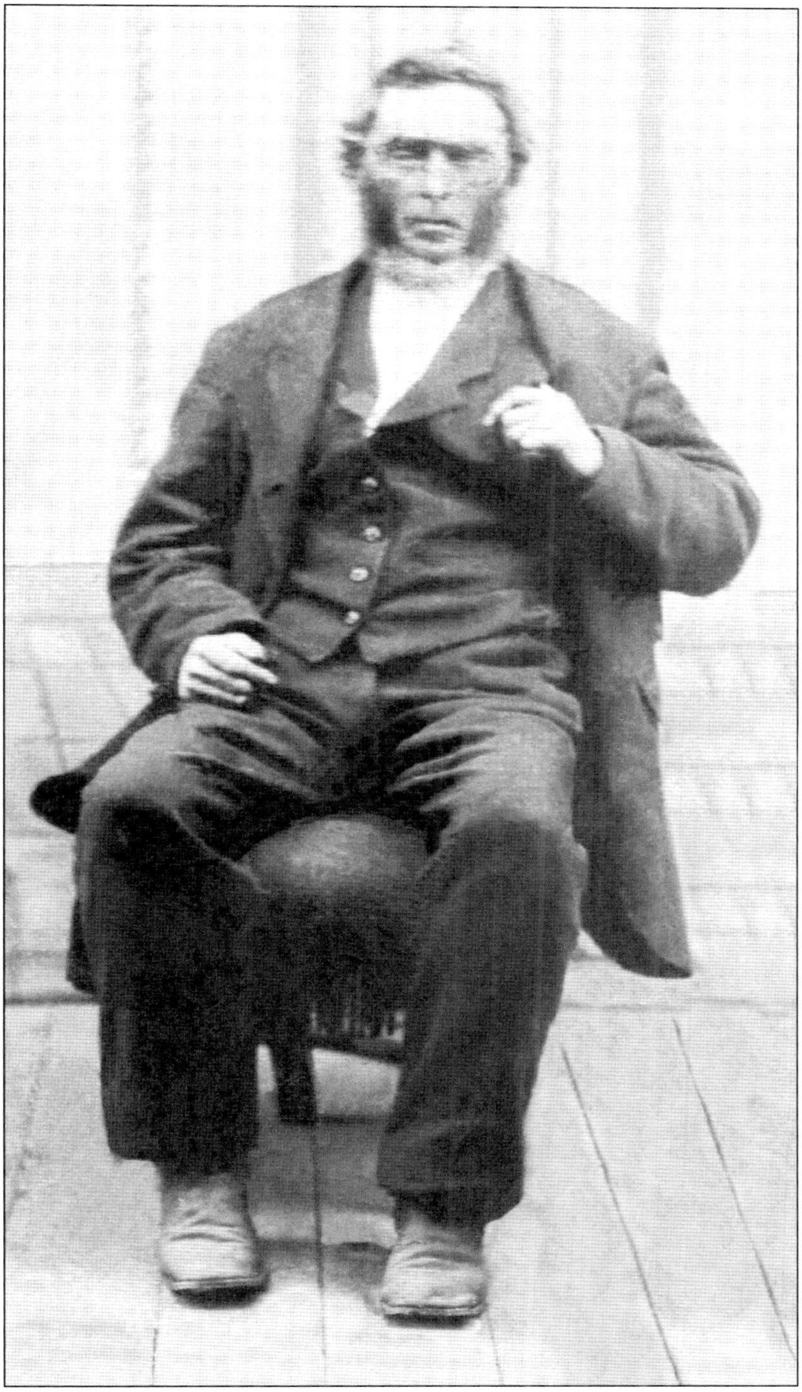

Remembered as cattle king John Chisum's brother, James Chisum was Sallie Chisum's father. His claim to fame in Lincoln was helping nurse his brother day and night when he was dying from a terminal illness. James Chisum was at John Chisum's bedside when he died in Eureka Springs, Arkansas, on December 22, 1884.

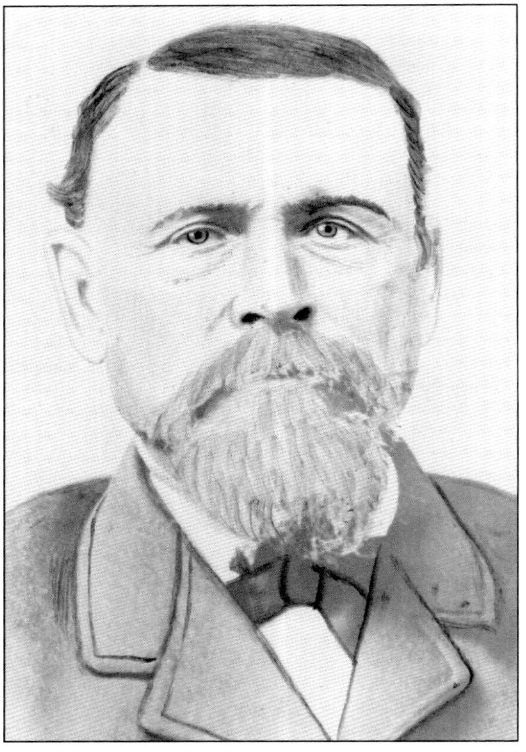

George W. Coe (pictured) was one of the Regulators who fought against the James Dolan faction during the Five-Days Battle at Lincoln. Although Coe was involved in numerous skirmishes, he survived the violence of Lincoln and wrote his autobiography, *Frontier Fighter*, published in 1934.

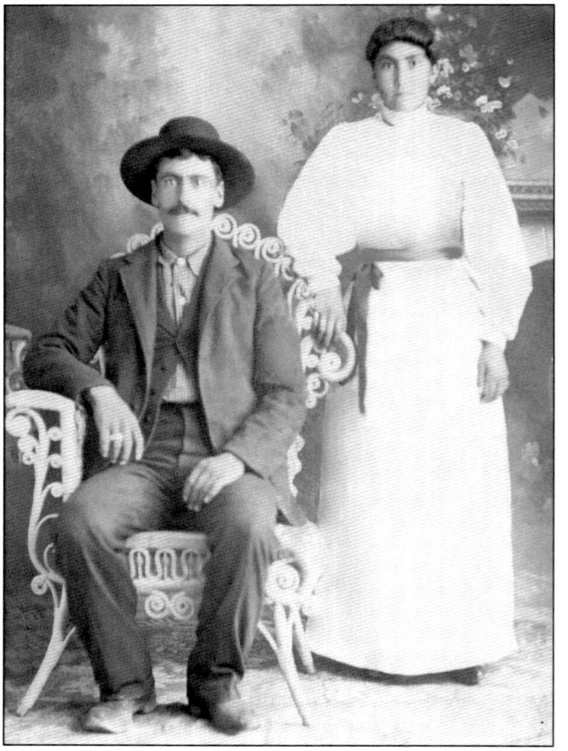

This is a rare photograph of David Rudabaugh. Kansan Wyatt Earp hunted Rudabaugh at one time. Rudabaugh was captured by Bat Masterson and briefly held in jail. By 1879, Rudabaugh wound up in Las Vegas, New Mexico, serving as a policeman and eventually robbing stagecoaches. He joined with Billy the Kid, and when things got too hot for him in New Mexico, he reportedly fled south to Mexico.

Charlie Bowdre's wife, María Manuela Herrera Bowdre, is pictured here. Charlie Bowdre served on several posses that pursued cattle rustlers. He joined the Regulators, who fought against James Dolan. After the Lincoln County War, Bowdre joined Billy the Kid's gang. Manuela was born at Santa Cruz de la Cañada, New Mexico. Her parents were José Herrera and María Martinez.

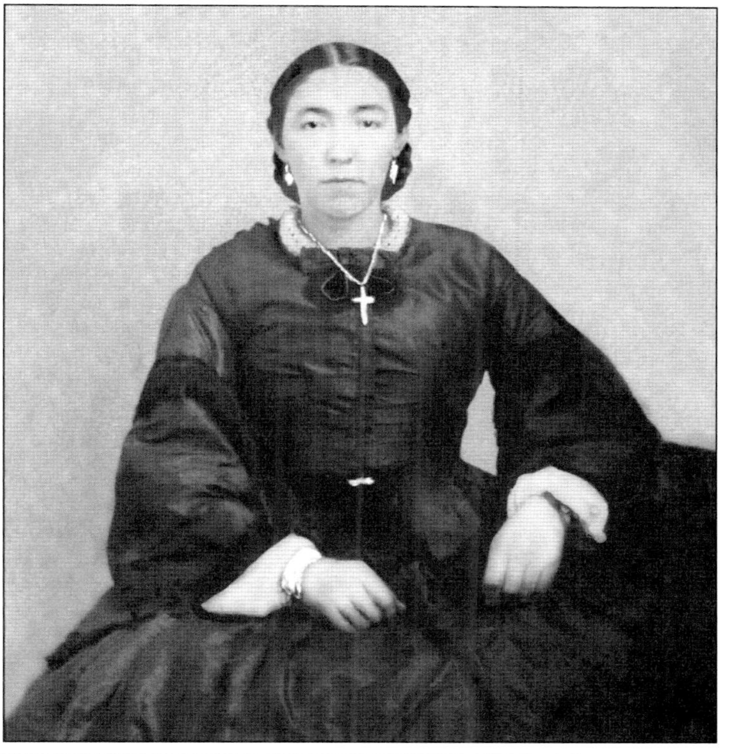

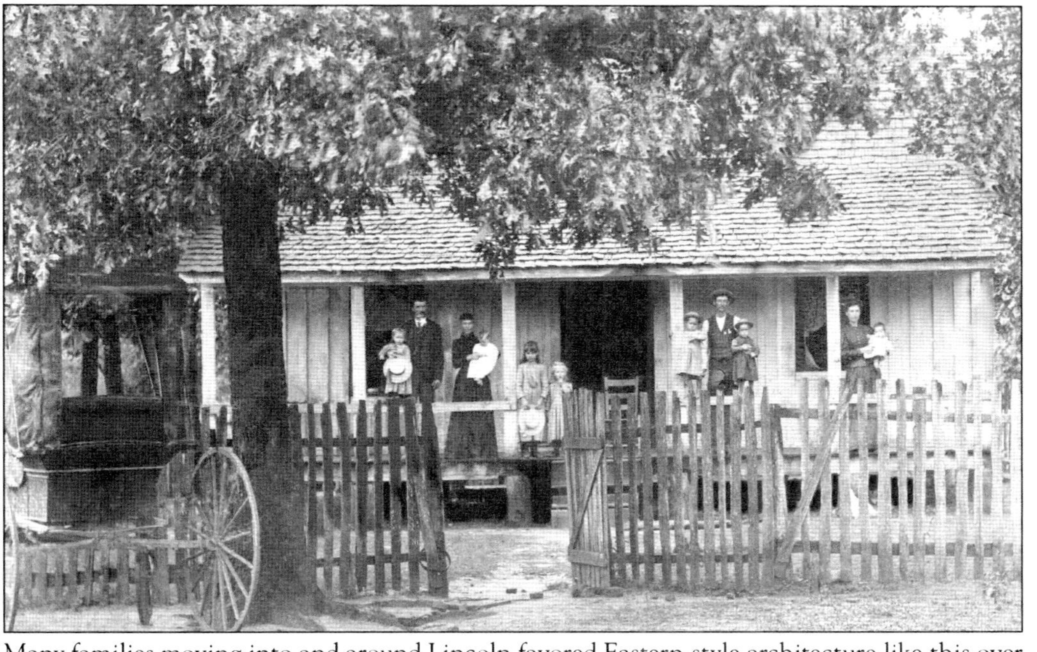

Many families moving into and around Lincoln favored Eastern-style architecture like this over New Mexico's Spanish adobe buildings. New arrivals referred to the adobe homes in Lincoln as mud huts or primitive hovels. Now called Territorial, or Santa Fe–style architecture, these early Lincoln homes are popular again.

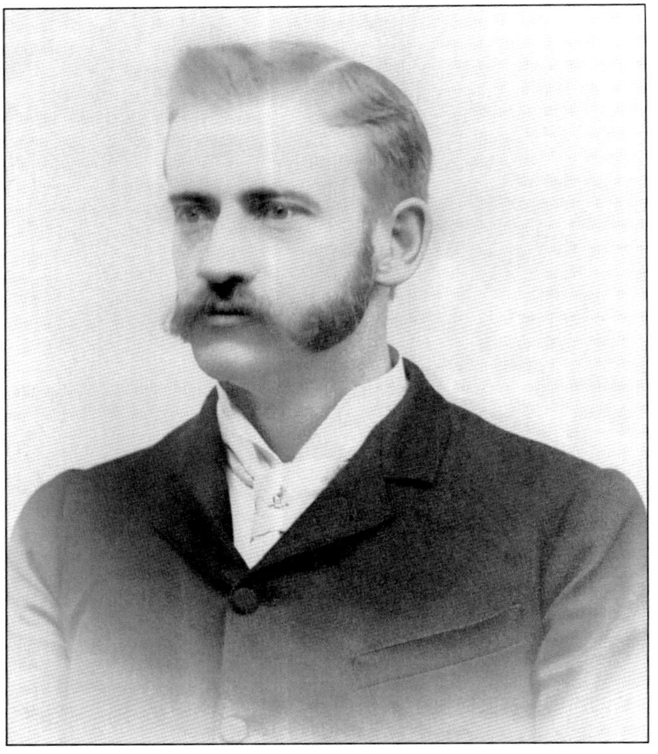

Charles Frederick Rudolph, Milnor Rudolph's son, served on Pat Garrett's posse when Billy the Kid was captured at Stinking Springs near Taiban, New Mexico, on December 24, 1880. Charles Rudolph went on to write a ballad in Spanish about the chase and capture of the famous outlaw.

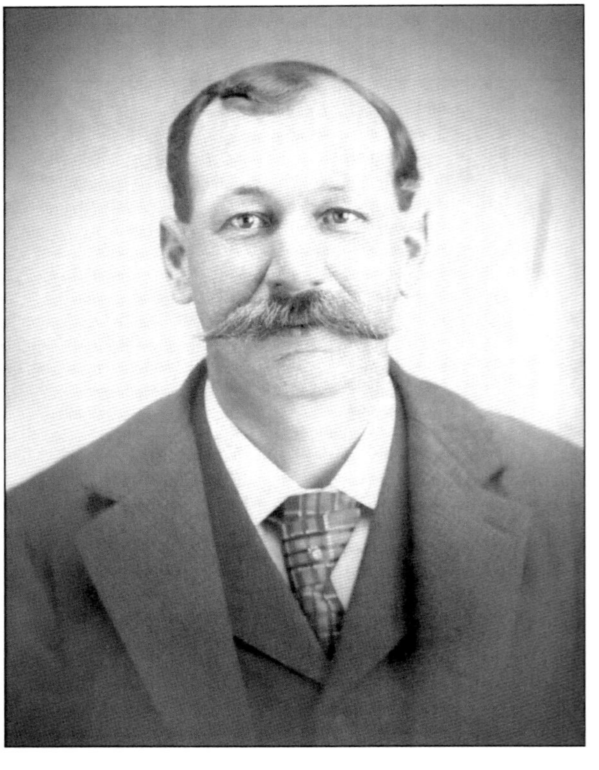

Col. Albert Jennings Fountain was the defense attorney for Billy the Kid. Since District Attorney William Rynerson knew he could not get a conviction against the Kid in Lincoln for the death of Sheriff William Brady, he got a change of venue to Mesilla, New Mexico. The Kid was one of a dozen posse members, including US Deputy Marshal Robert A. Widenmann, who shot at Brady and his men.

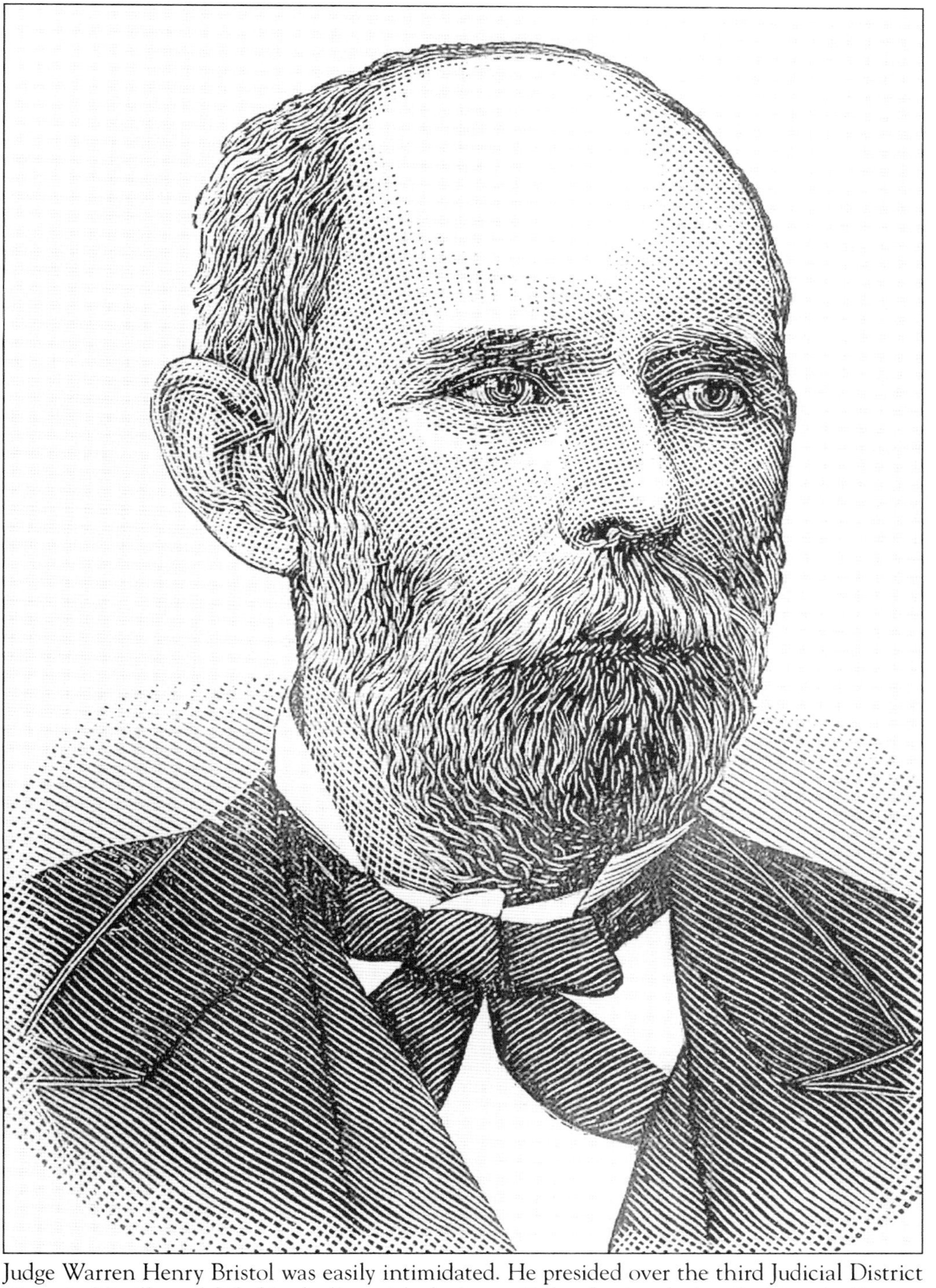

Judge Warren Henry Bristol was easily intimidated. He presided over the third Judicial District Court in Mesilla and failed in dealing with the James Dolan faction during the Lincoln County War. A jury, which leaned toward conviction, tried Billy the Kid in Judge Bristol's court, and Bristol sentenced him to hang; it was feared he would have been acquitted in Lincoln.

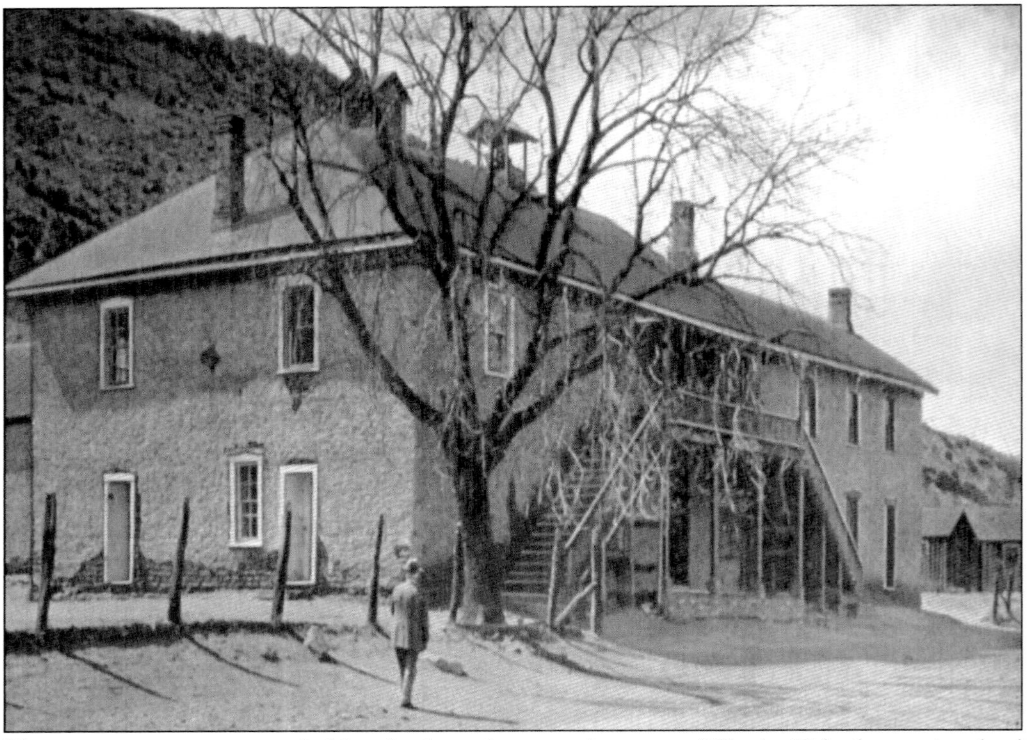

The most notorious prisoner held in this legendary courthouse was Billy the Kid, who was involved in a famous escape on April 28, 1881, in which he killed two deputies. The escape has figured prominently in many motion pictures and documentaries. The courthouse is the main location of an annual Billy the Kid Pageant, which includes a reenactment of the events that led to the famous getaway.

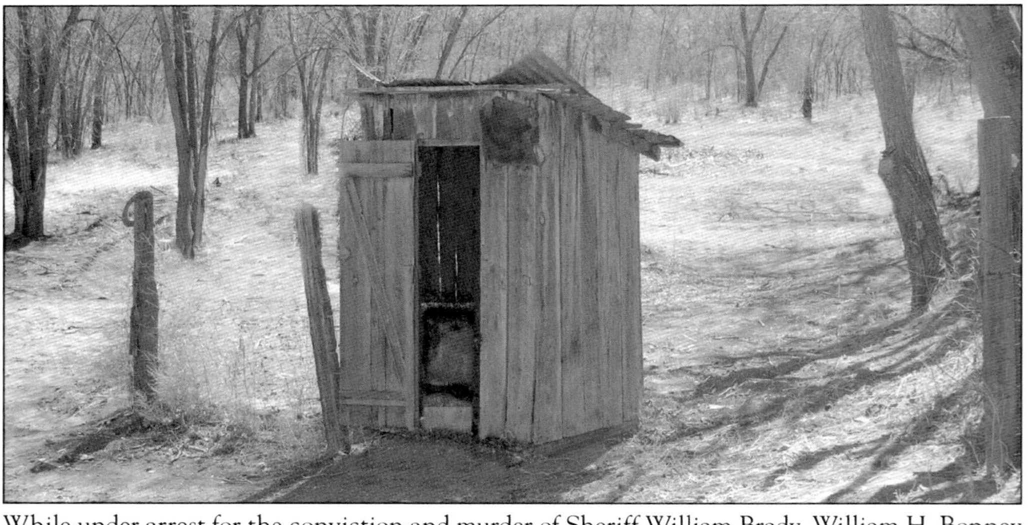

While under arrest for the conviction and murder of Sheriff William Brady, William H. Bonney asked to use the privy. Deputy James W. Bell led Bonney out of the jail to an outhouse like this one. Legend has it that someone planted a gun in the outhouse, and Bonney used it to escape. He killed Bell and Robert Olinger and rode into legend. (Photograph by Santiago de Aragón.)

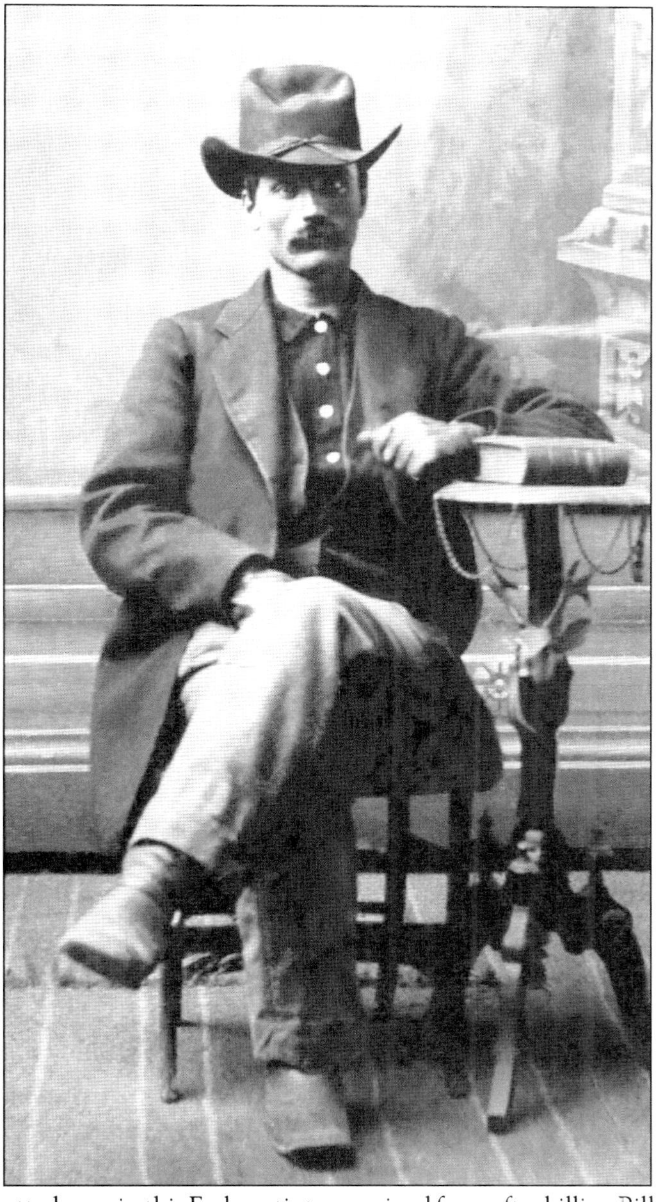

Sheriff Pat F. Garrett, shown in this Furlong tintype, gained fame after killing Billy the Kid. Garrett began his career as a buffalo hunter. He later worked as a bartender at Beaver Smith's Saloon at Fort Sumner. His sister-in-law, Celsa Gutierrez, and her husband, Sabal, lived near the saloon. Garrett steered away from most of the Lincoln troubles, but finally got involved when he was elected sheriff of Lincoln County on November 2, 1880. His first order of business was tracking down Billy. On March 17, 1879, the Kid had met with Gov. Lew Wallace, who promised him amnesty if he testified against James Dolan for a murder. District Attorney William Rynerson, however, had other plans for the Kid. After being sentenced to hang by Dolan and Rynerson partisans, Billy the Kid escaped. It is believed he accidently shot a deputy who struggled for a gun and shot another who had it in for him. After Garrett killed the Kid, many questions arose. Accused of planting evidence and giving a false report, Garrett wrote a book to clear his name.

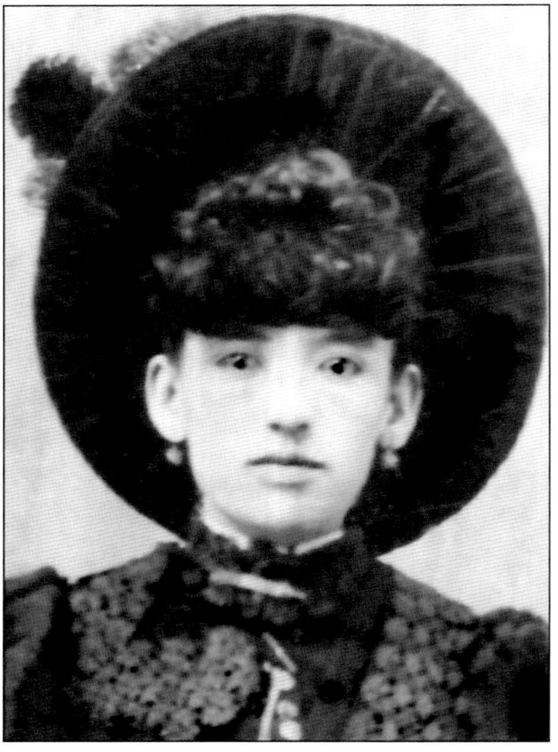

Apolinaria Gutierrez was born in 1861 in Tecolote, a hamlet near Las Vegas, New Mexico. She married Pat Garrett in Anton Chico on January 14, 1880. The two had nine children. Apolinaria raised the children by herself for the most part, since Garrett was gone most of the time. She was grief-stricken when her husband was murdered on February 29, 1908.

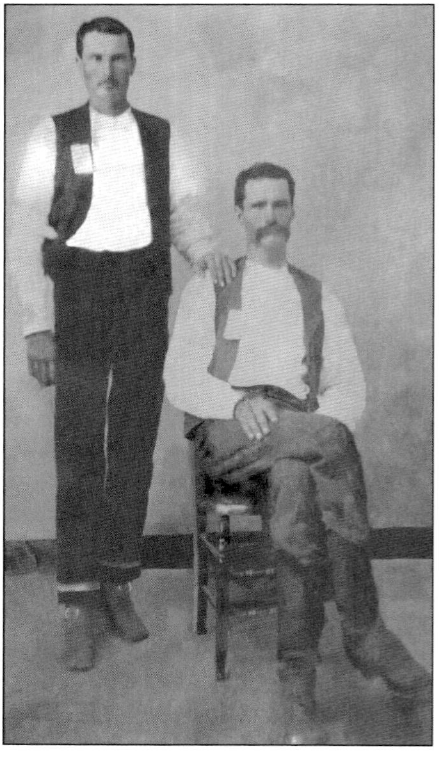

In this photograph, Pat Garrett is sitting while his younger brother Hillary W. Garrett stands. Not much is known about Hillary or what kind of relationship he had with his siblings.

John William Poe (right) worked with a railroad construction crew as a buffalo shooter. It is estimated that in the business of buffalo hunting, John Poe killed 20,000 animals. In 1881, the Canadian River Cattle Association hired him as a detective. Pat Garrett deputized Poe to help him track down Billy the Kid. In 1882, Garrett decided not to run for reelection as Lincoln County sheriff. Instead of supporting his deputy, Garrett threw his support to James J. Dolan, who was running for sheriff. John Poe beat Dolan. Poe then ran against Garrett for the Chavez County sheriff's office, defeating him once again. Poe wrote a book called *The Death of Billy the Kid*. He is pictured below with his wife, Sophie Alberding Poe.

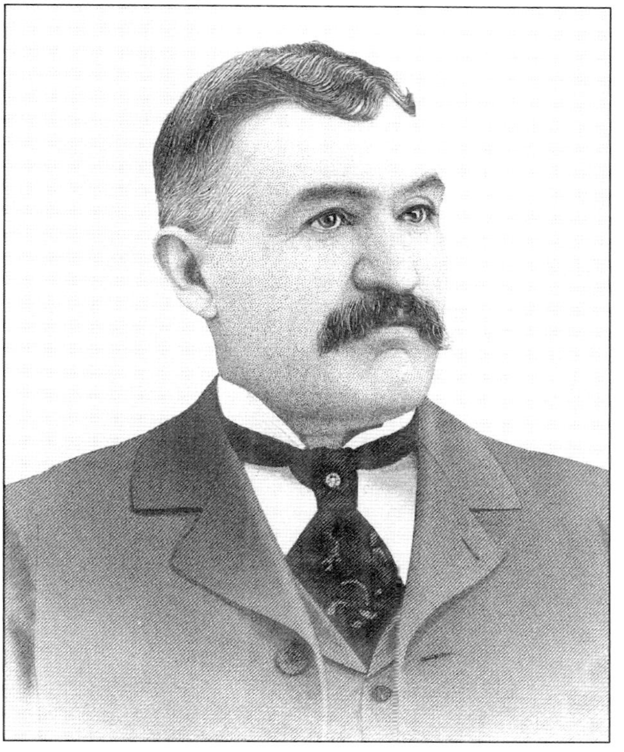

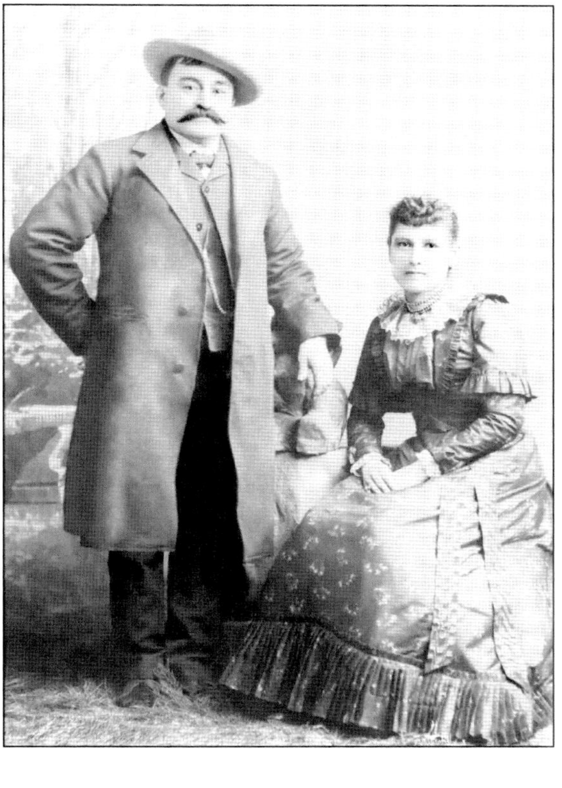

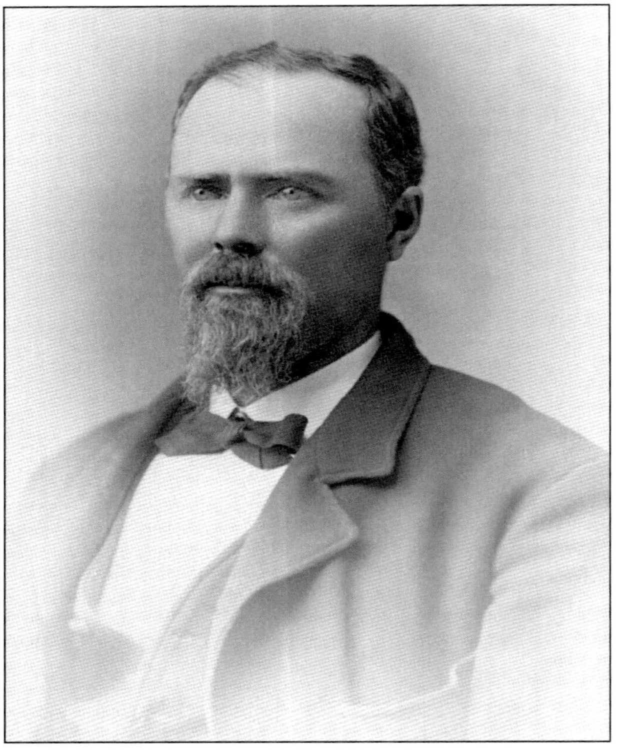

Buffalo hunter James R. Brent was Saturnino Baca's son-in-law. He was married to Carlota Baca. When John Tunstall first traveled from Santa Fe to Lincoln, Baca, Brent, and Juan Patron rode along with Tunstall. Carlota said of Billy the Kid, "I knew this young man to be kind and gentlemanly with me and all the inhabitants of Lincoln." Brent assisted Garrett in trailing the Kid.

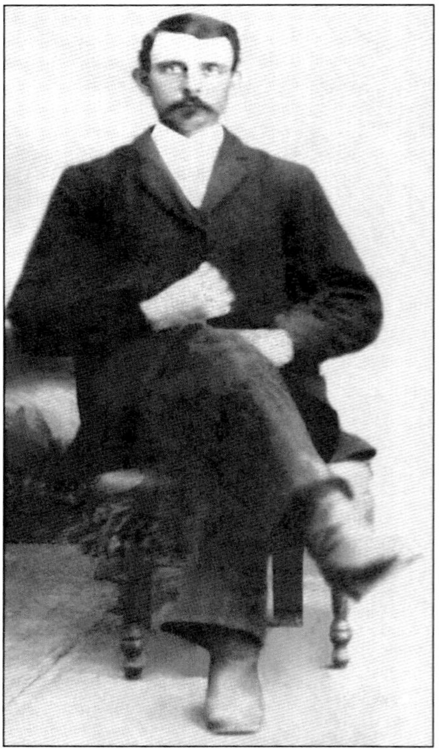

Lincoln attorney George Barber served on the coroner's jury assembled by justice of the peace John B. Wilson to provide an inquest into the death of John H. Tunstall. The jury concluded that Tunstall was shot in the back in a murder committed by James Dolan, George Hindman, and others. Barber married Sue McSween, Alexander McSween's widow, on June 20, 1880. He went on to become a respected lawyer in Lincoln.

Peter Menard Maxwell lived in the shadows of his well-known father Lucien Bonaparte Maxwell. Lucien purchased the former military post of Fort Sumner and turned it into the headquarters of a vast ranch. Peter inherited the ranch holdings after his father's death in 1875. Present-day historians contend that Maxwell conspired with Garrett to kill Billy the Kid because his sister Paulita was planning to elope with him.

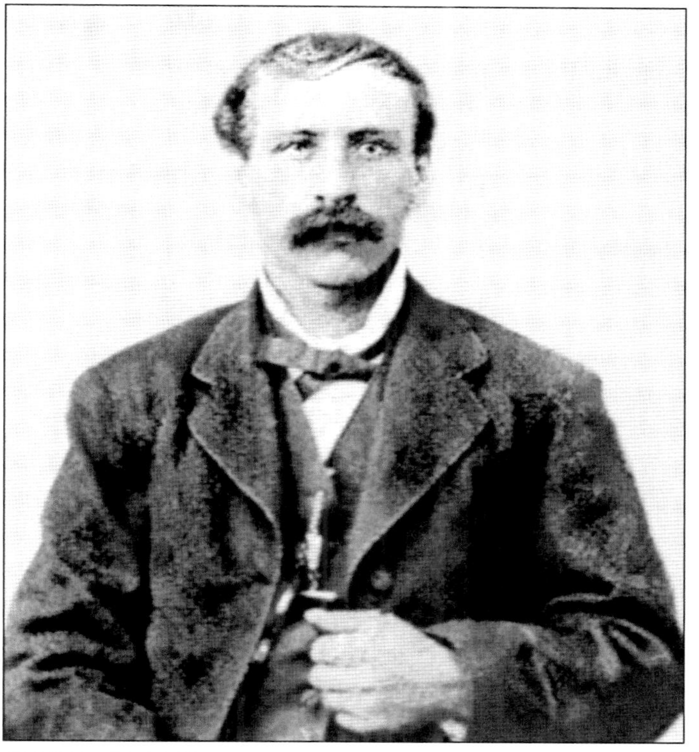

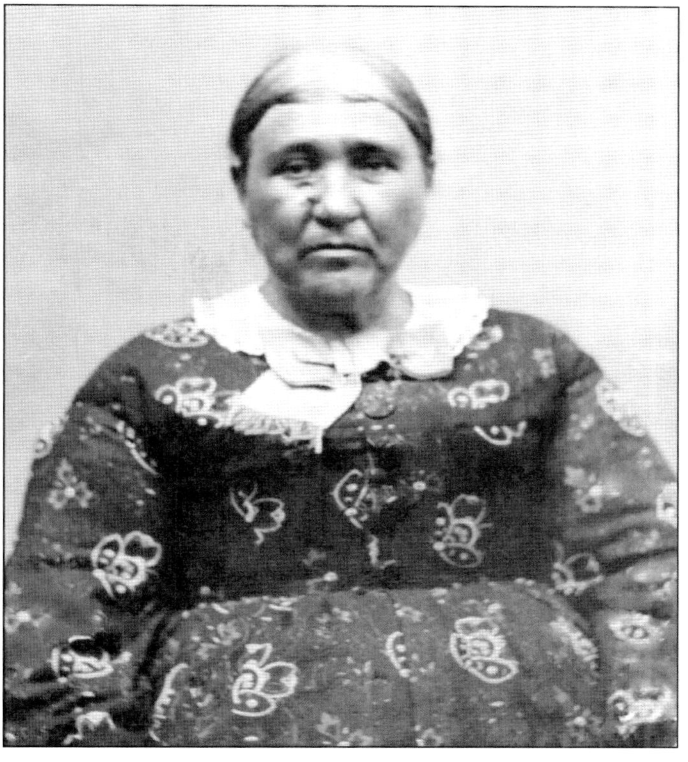

Deluvina Maxwell was a Navajo slave owned by land baron Lucien Bonaparte Maxwell. She was entrusted with the care of Lucien's daughter, Paulita Maxwell. It is written that Deluvina arranged secret meetings between Paulita and Billy the Kid. She was present in the Maxwell residence when Pat Garrett shot the Kid in Paulita's bedroom. Deluvina Maxwell's hatred for Garrett was well known in Lincoln and Fort Sumner.

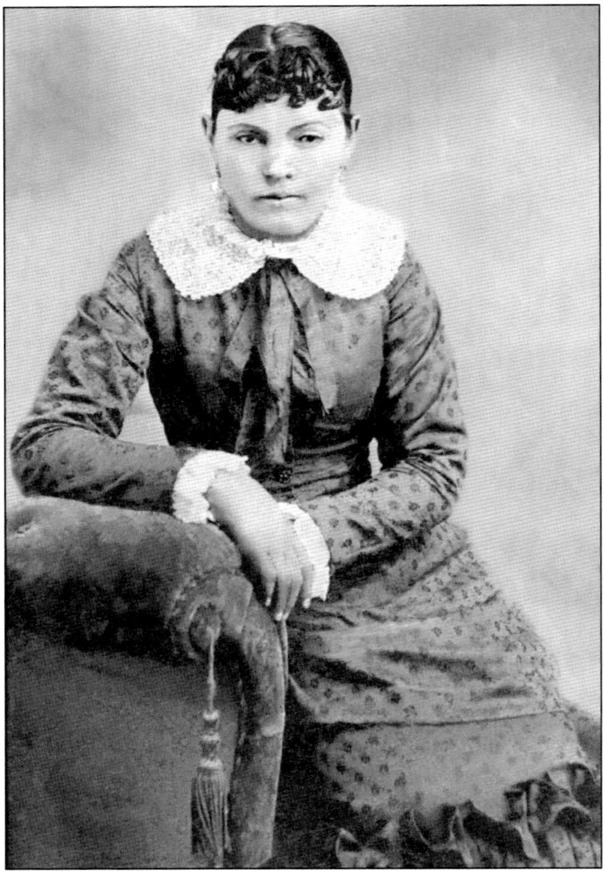

Paulita Maxwell (pictured) was the "Belle of Fort Sumner." Paulita was pampered and protected by her older brother Peter Maxwell. Weekly dances held at Fort Sumner were attended by Paulita and those who traveled from other towns, including Lincoln. Although Paulita had four other sisters—Emilia, Odile, Sofia, and Virginia—she was the one who attracted attention. Some say a fatal attraction existed between Paulita and Billy the Kid, who met his death in her bedroom at the hands of Sheriff Pat Garrett. Paulita reportedly wrote the note pictured below to give to Billy the Kid.

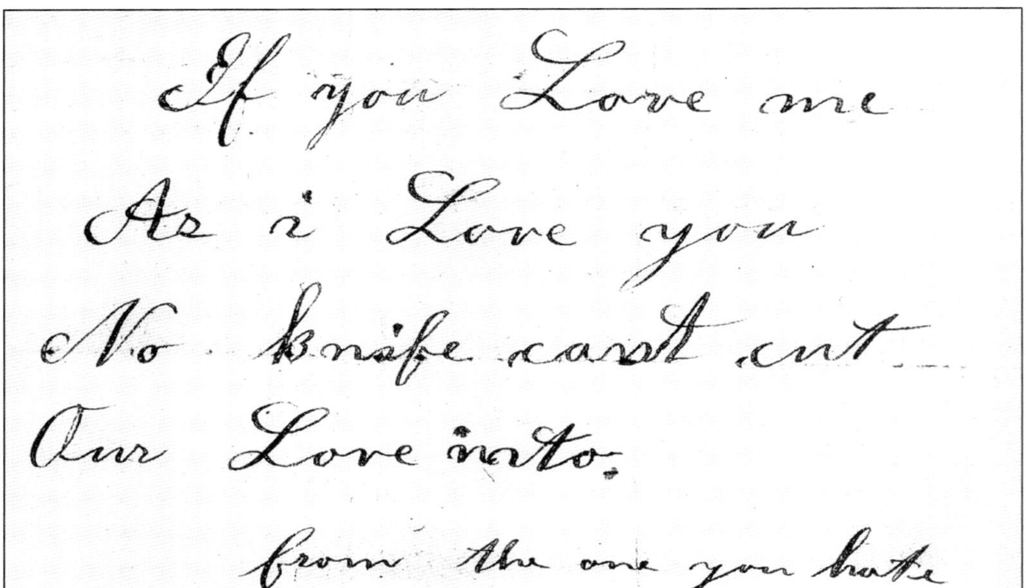

If you Love me
As i Love you
No knife cant cut
Our Love inato.
from the one you hate

Joseph C. Lea was a high-ranking officer in William Clarke Quantrill's Guerilla Raiders during the Civil War. This ruthless group of Confederates was hunted for stealing horses, cattle, and slaves. The Raiders sacked the towns of Olathe and Lawrence, Kansas, where buildings were burned and residents were massacred. What Lea's role was is not known. What is known is that the Hispanic town of El Berrendo, located near where he established a ranch in New Mexico, eventually disappeared.

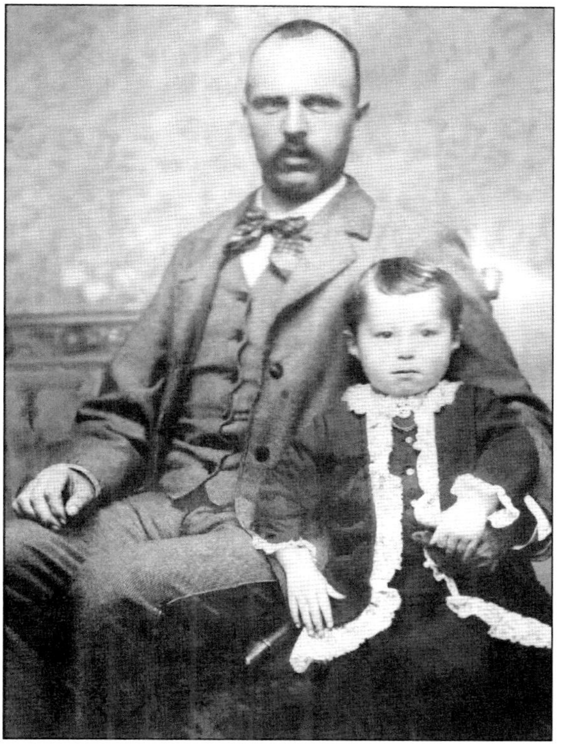

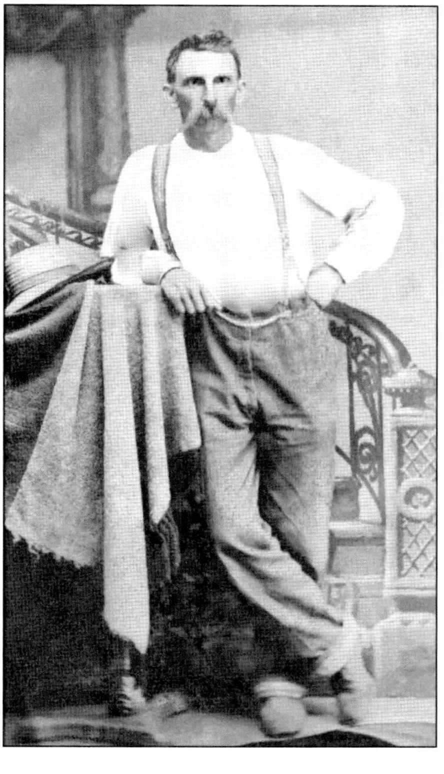

Colonel Albert J. Fountain got 32 indictments at Lincoln against ranchers for cattle rustling, horse theft, and altering brands. Oliver Milton Lee (pictured) was one of the ranchers. Lee and Albert Fall were closely allied. Lee and his cowhand James Gilliland went to trial for Fountain's mysterious disappearance. Fall was the defense attorney, and both Lee and Gilliland were acquitted.

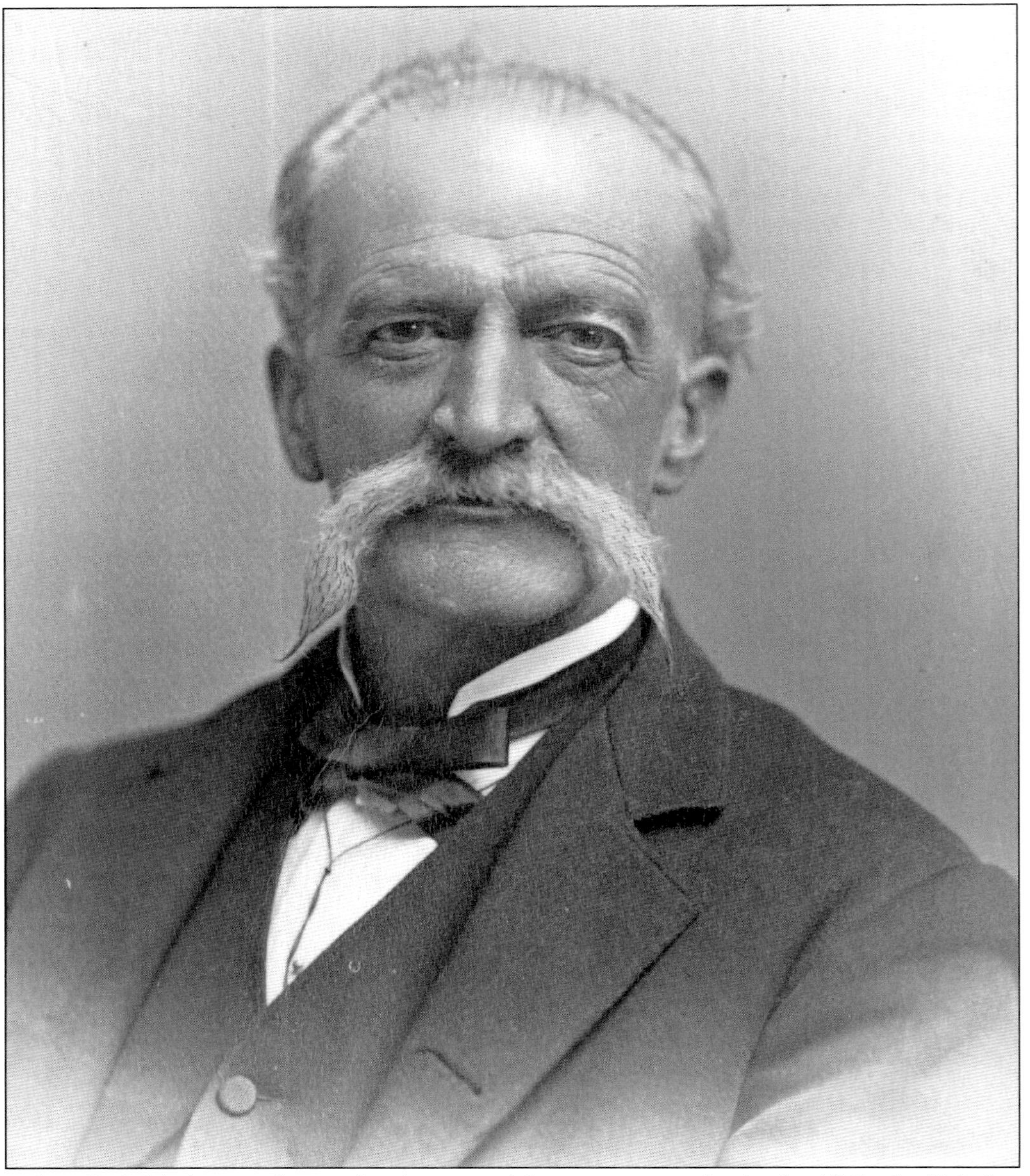

Milnor Rudolph (pictured) served as foreman of the inquest into the death of Billy the Kid after Sheriff Pat Garrett shot him on July 15, 1881. Rudolph was related to Pres. James A. Garfield's wife, Lucretia Rudolph Garfield. He served as speaker of the house for the New Mexico territorial legislature in 1870 and befriended both Garrett and Billy the Kid.

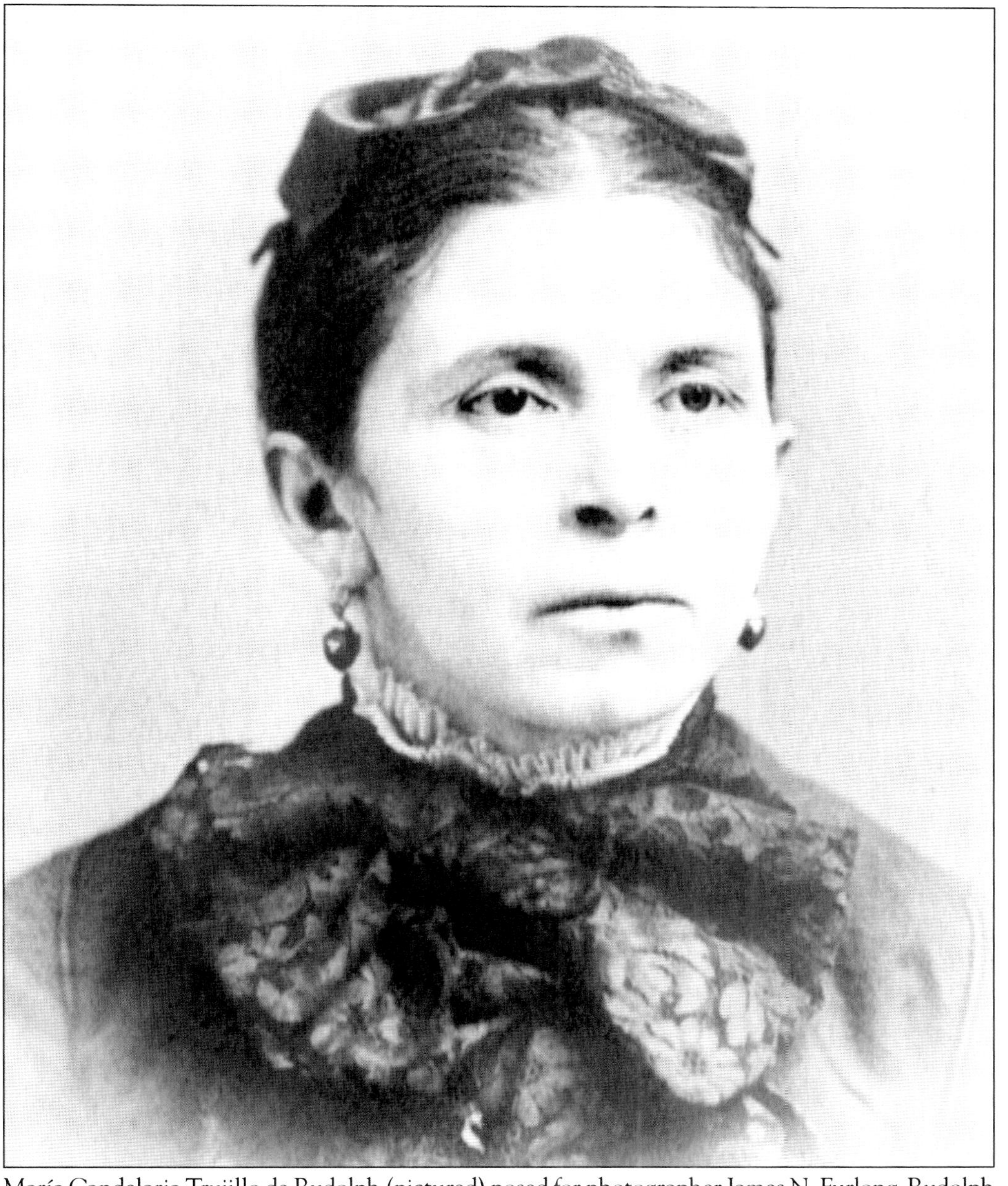

María Candelaria Trujillo de Rudolph (pictured) posed for photographer James N. Furlong. Rudolph and her husband, Milnor, often hosted Billy the Kid at their Sunnyside Ranch. She enjoyed reminiscing about cooking for the Kid and called him "a courteous gentleman." The Rudolphs were frequently in Lincoln visiting friends and buying supplies and provisions for their ranch.

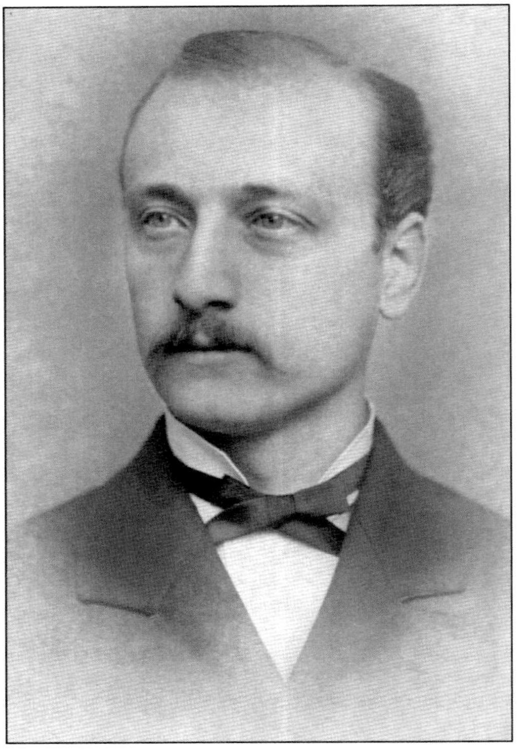

On March 1, 1873, William Henry Harrison Antrim (pictured) married Catherine McCarty at the First Presbyterian Church in Santa Fe. Witnesses included her two sons, Joseph "Josie" McCarty and Henry McCarty, later known as Henry Antrim, William H. Bonney, and Billy the Kid. The family moved to Silver City, New Mexico, where William worked as a carpenter and butcher. He was also a traveling prospector, which kept him away from home most of the time. Antrim spent little time with his young stepsons.

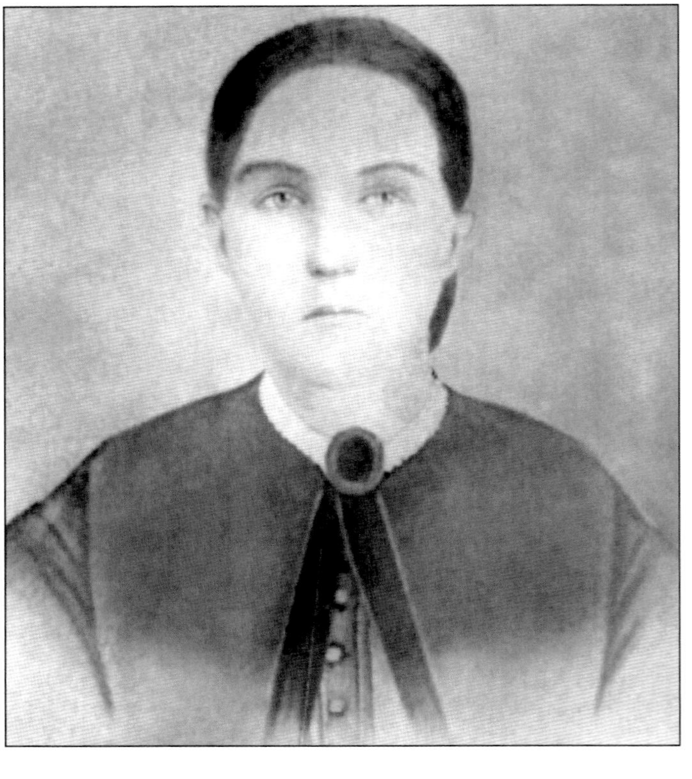

It is known that Catherine McCarty and her sons Joseph and Henry were in Indiana in 1868. By 1870 they had moved to Kansas, where the family lived on a homestead. Catherine McCarty later sold her land to move, because she suffered from tuberculosis. A Bonney family in northern New Mexico claims Catherine's maiden name was Bonney and that she and her boys stayed with the Bonneys before going to Santa Fe.

It is not known when Joseph McCarty was born. What is known is that he and his brother, Henry, attended school in Silver City. They were both typical boys. Their father had died, and they did not seem to have much of a relationship with their stepfather, William Antrim. Joseph did odd jobs at some area businesses and more than likely helped his mother at her boarding house.

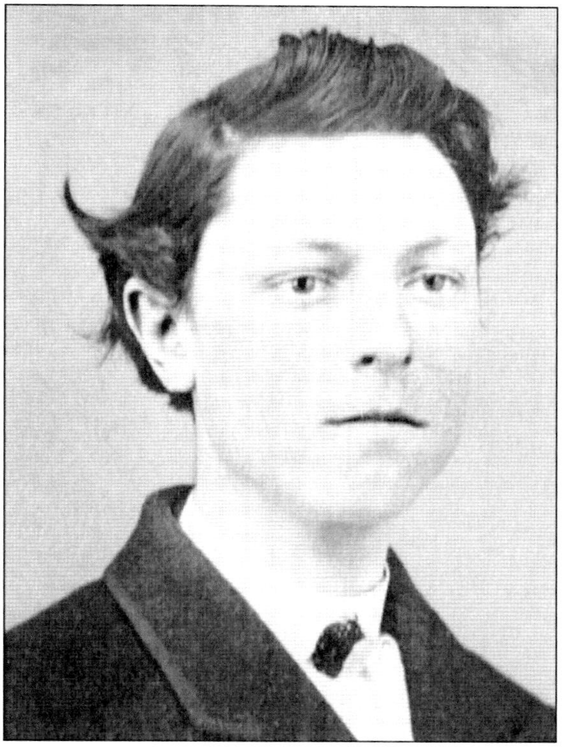

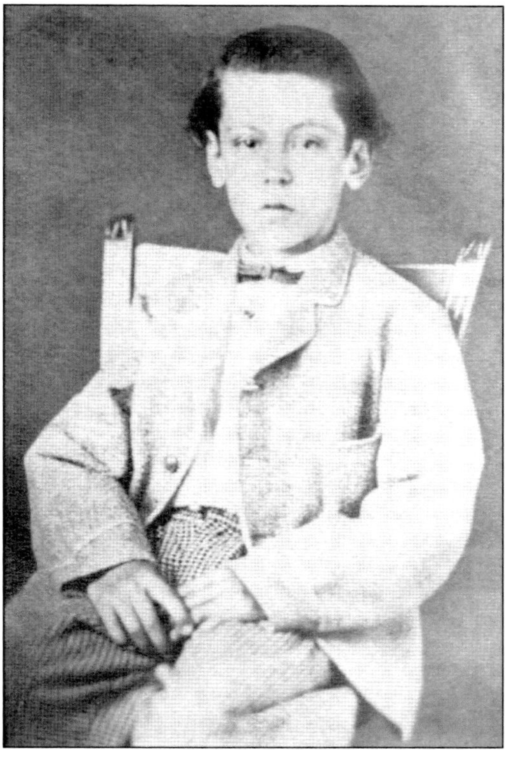

Henry McCarty—shown in this photograph by James Adams in Elmore, Ohio—was strongly attached to his mother, Catherine McCarty. Henry supposedly excelled in school and participated in plays. He learned how to read and write well and also how to fluently speak Spanish. His mother took on boarders and baked to make ends meet. Henry was grief-stricken when his mother died on September 16, 1874.

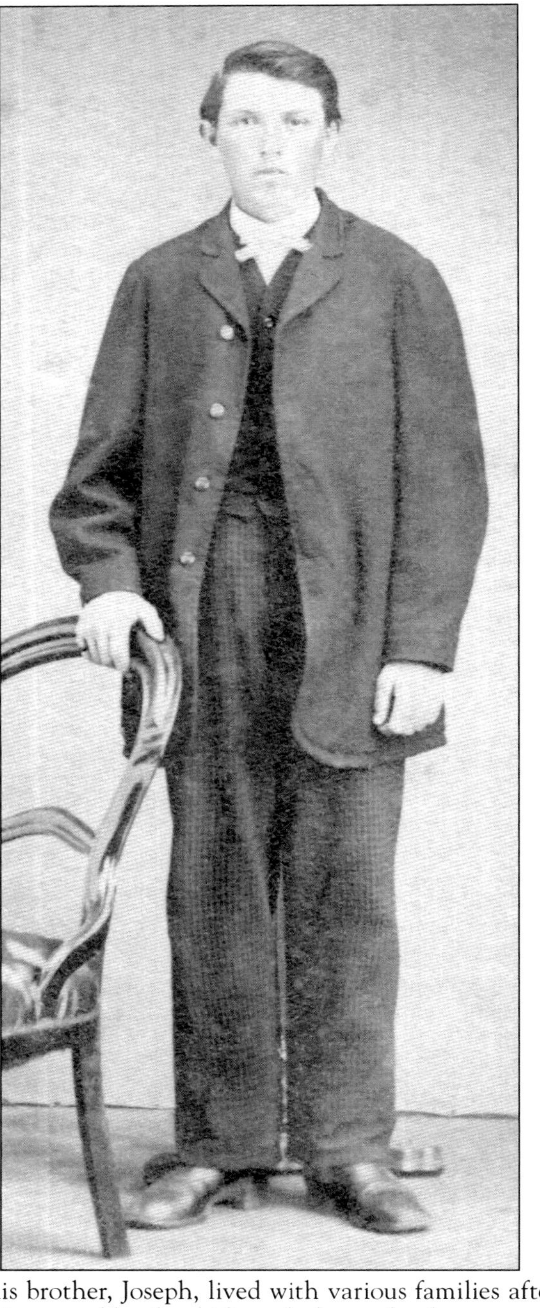

Henry McCarty and his brother, Joseph, lived with various families after their mother died. Henry managed to get into trouble after hiding clothes stolen by a companion, so he traveled to Arizona in 1875 after escaping from custody. This image of Henry McCarty may have been taken in Arizona territory by itinerant photographer Harry Lucas and mounted at his studio in Silver City. In Arizona, Henry went by the name Henry Antrim. It is said he worked as a cook at a hotel and also as a ranch hand. By 1877, Henry was in trouble once again. This time he was accused of stealing a horse. He escaped and rode to Lincoln County, where he started calling himself Kid Antrim and William H. Bonney.

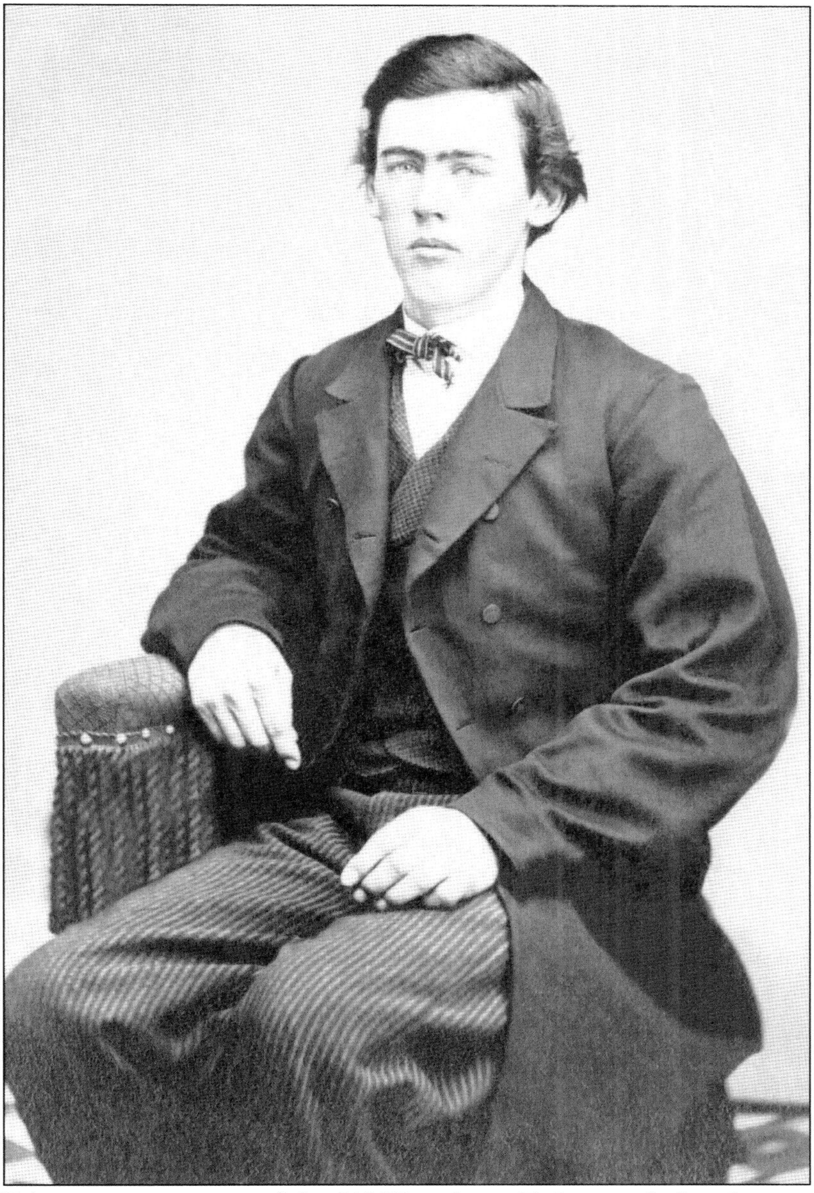

Billy the Kid remains an enigma of the Old West. James Furlong took this photograph in Las Vegas, New Mexico, in 1880. Very little about Billy the Kid's early life has been confirmed, and even the date of his birth, given as 1859, is questioned. Historians have problems separating myth from fact when researching his career. Billy the Kid was employed in New Mexico as a cowboy. He wound up working at the Tunstall Río Felíz Ranch where Richard Brewer worked as foreman. After John Tunstall's death, justice of the peace John B. Wilson appointed Brewer, who had served as a deputy sheriff, as special constable to apprehend Tunstall's killers. The Kid was a deputy constable. He was also a deputy under US deputy marshal Robert A. Widenmann, who was serving under John Sherman, US marshal for New Mexico appointed by the US Senate. The Kid and other members of the posse were, under Widenmann's orders, serving arrest warrants when Brady was killed. Billy the Kid himself was wounded in the line of duty.

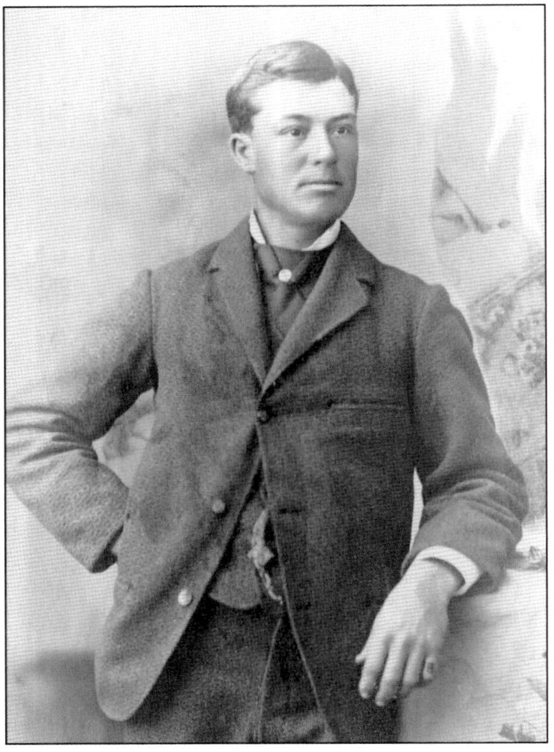

James N. Furlong, who had a photography studio at Bridge Street in Las Vegas, is noted for having photographed many participants of the Lincoln County War. His famous Lincoln and New Mexico subjects included Sheriff Pat Garrett; Billy the Kid's father-in-law William Henry Harrison; Charles Bowdre and his wife, Manuela Herrera Bowdre; Samuel R. Corbet; John William Poe; and many others. Furlong often traveled long distances to take pictures.

This building served as the headquarters of the Optic Publishing Company in Las Vegas, New Mexico. For a short time, Russell Kistler claimed he had Billy the Kid's trigger finger pickled in a jar on display at the Optic offices. He said that he had so many curiosity seekers going in to see it that he decided to sell the trophy for $150.

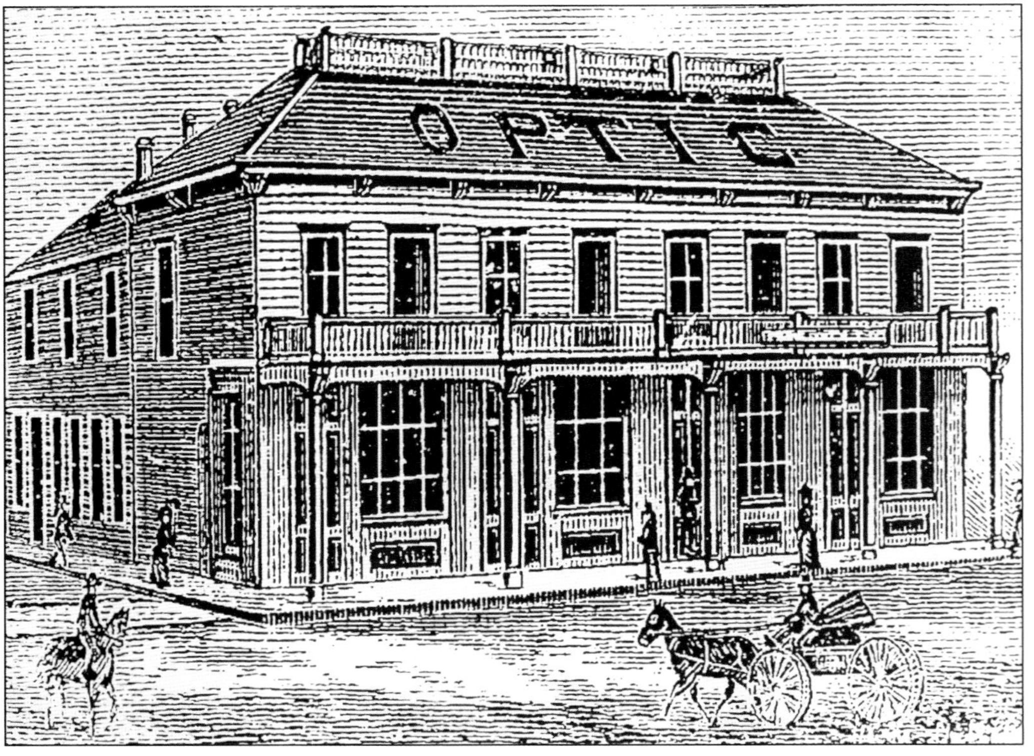

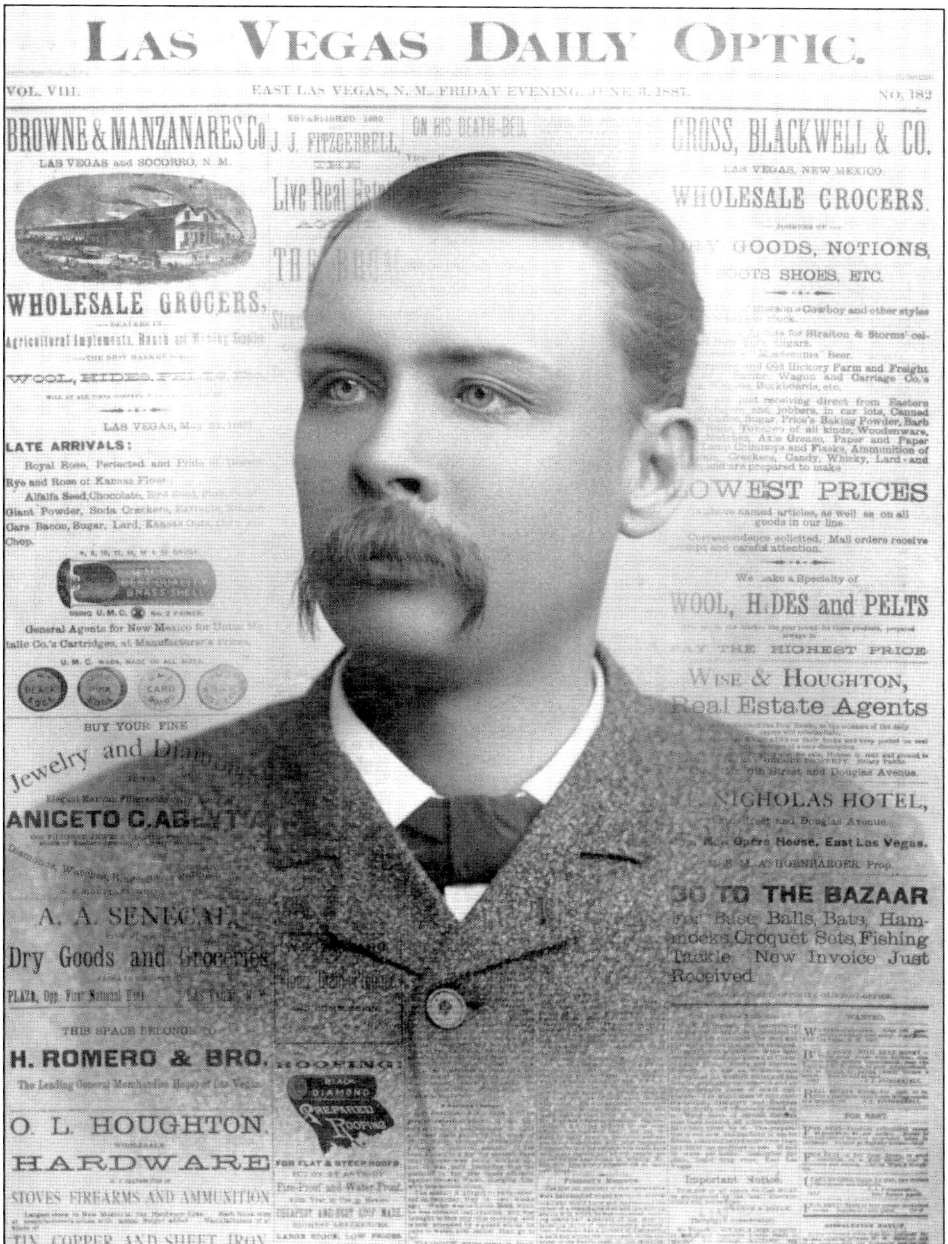

Newspaper publisher Russell A. Kistler started the *Otero Optic* in Otero, New Mexico, in 1879. Within a short time, he moved and founded the *Las Vegas Daily Optic*, which operated from 1879 through the 1890s. As editor and writer for his newspaper, Kistler published many accounts about well-known Lincoln residents. He did much to spread word of the Lincoln County War and the exploits of Billy the Kid as a famous New Mexico desperado. Newspapers across the United States carried his stories, thereby helping to create the legend of Billy the Kid. Not to be outdone, J.H. Koogler, editor of the *Las Vegas Gazette*, a rival newspaper, featured a romanticized serial of the Kid called the "Forty Thieves." Koogler also had his reporters interview the famous outlaw.

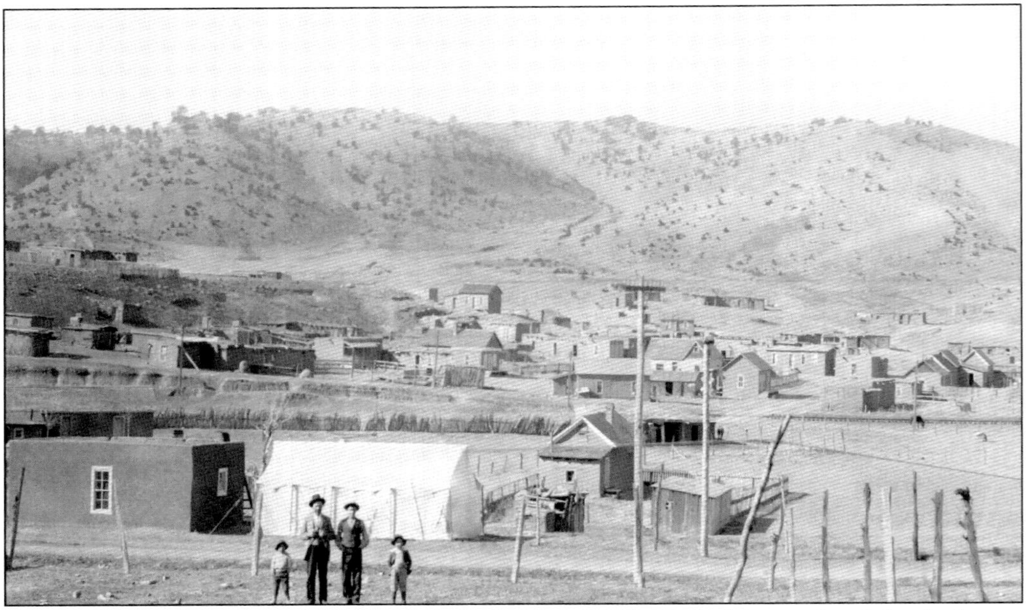

This is Otero, a town in Colfax County, New Mexico, at the end of the tracks of the Atchison, Topeka & Santa Fe Railroad. The town was named after New Mexico territorial governor Miguel Antonio Otero. When the railroad reached Otero in 1879, a celebration was held in his honor. When the division point of the railroad was moved five miles north to Raton, New Mexico, the town died. Otero residents then moved to other areas, including Lincoln. In the 1879 picture above, photographer John Martinez captured an image of his mobile photography tent. Martinez traveled as an itinerant photographer, as did other early territorial photographers, setting up shop and peddling his wares in many fledgling towns like Lincoln. Sometimes Martinez placed his rubber-stamped imprint (which included the name of the town Wagon Mound) on the backs of photographs; he thought of setting up a permanent studio in Wagon Mound.

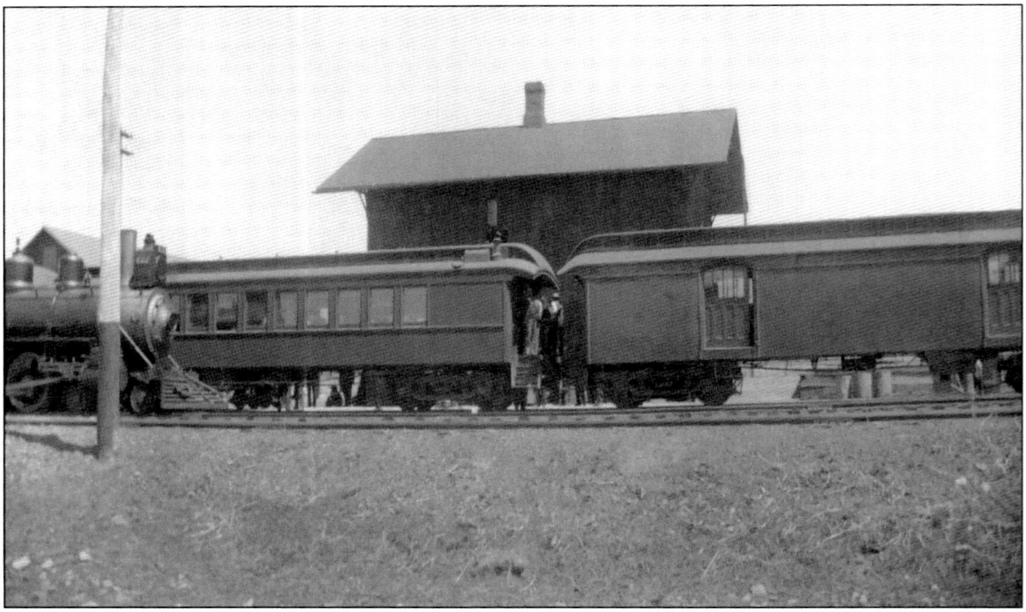

Trinidad Romero (pictured) was a member of Lew Wallace's Lincoln County Rifles. Romero was from a powerful family from Las Vegas. His father, Eugenio, had served as sheriff of San Miguel County. Trinidad's brother Cleofes also served as sheriff. His brother Secundino was a US marshal. Trinidad Romero was appointed a US marshal by Pres. Benjamin Harrison. The Rifles, captained by Juan Patron, were Hispanic riders charged with restoring peace in the Lincoln County area.

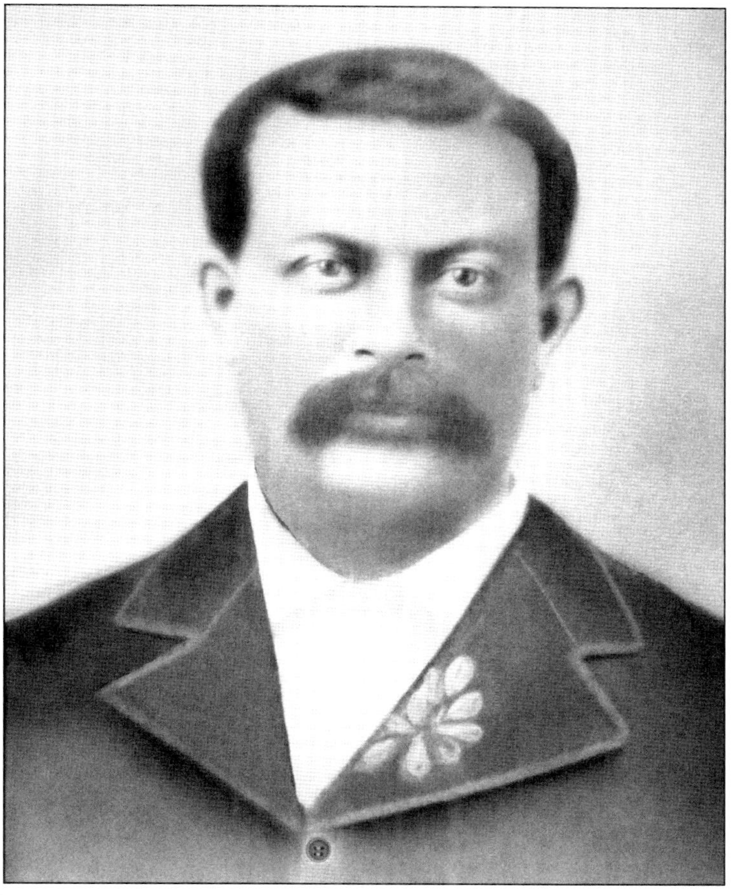

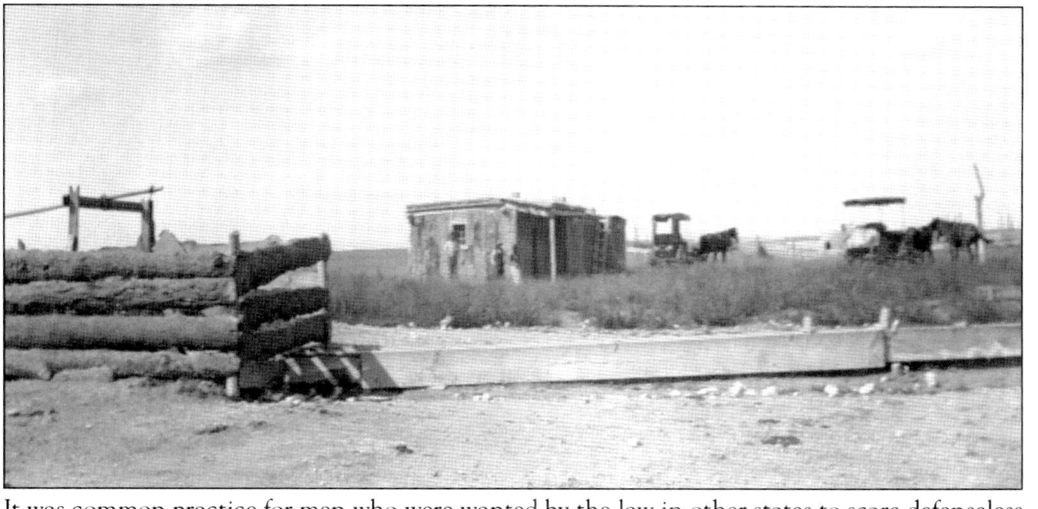

It was common practice for men who were wanted by the law in other states to scare defenseless Hispanic families from their homes, many of which looked like the one pictured here. At the point of a gun—and sometimes while burning buildings and killing men, women, and children—outlaws established a base for a ranch with stolen land and livestock.

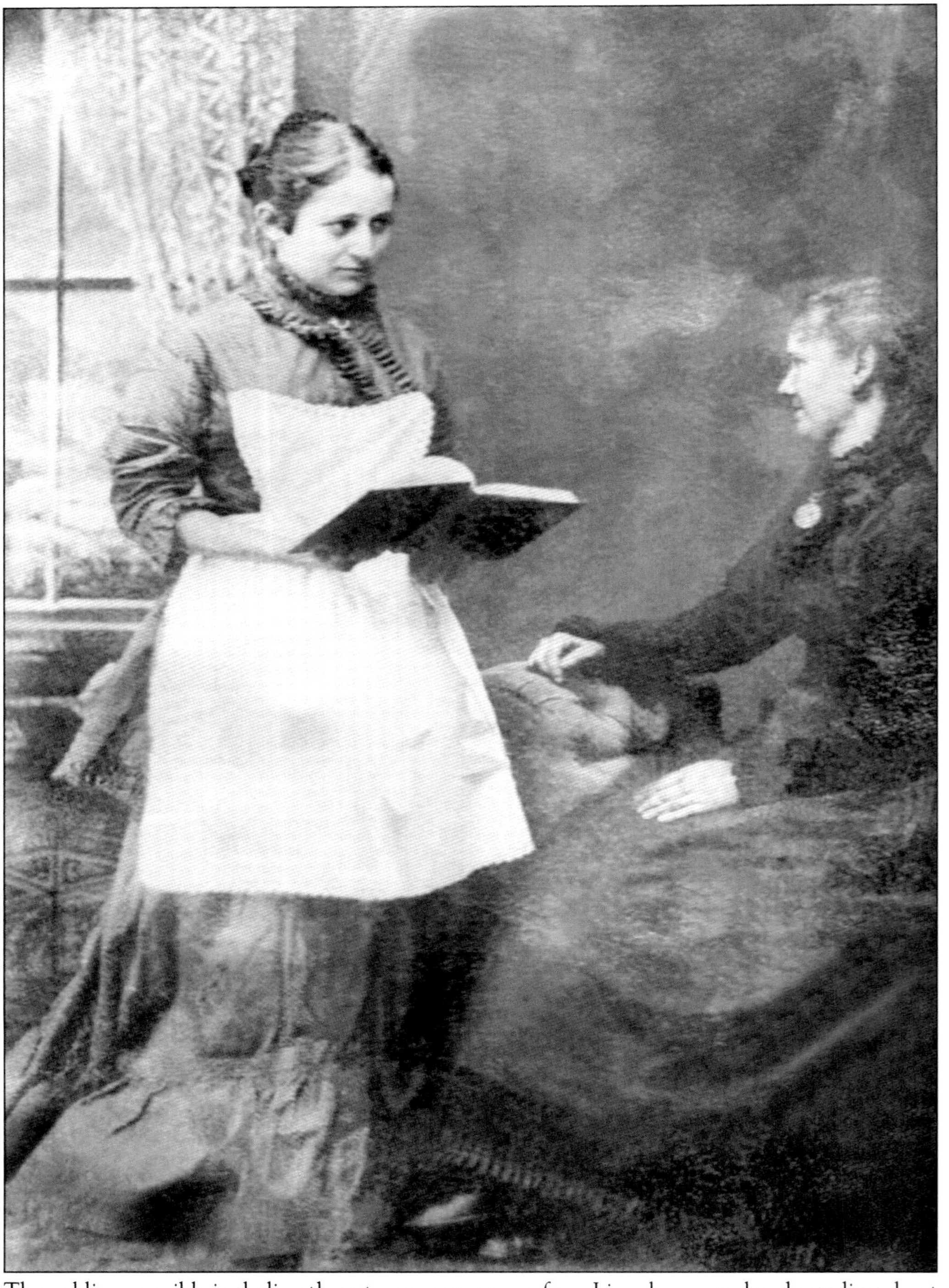

The public—possibly including these two young women from Lincoln—was already reading about the exploits of Billy the Kid in newspaper reports and serial stories before his death. Immediately after his death, the Kid rapidly became the subject of dime novels, books, poems, plays, and songs. His popularity is still intense today.

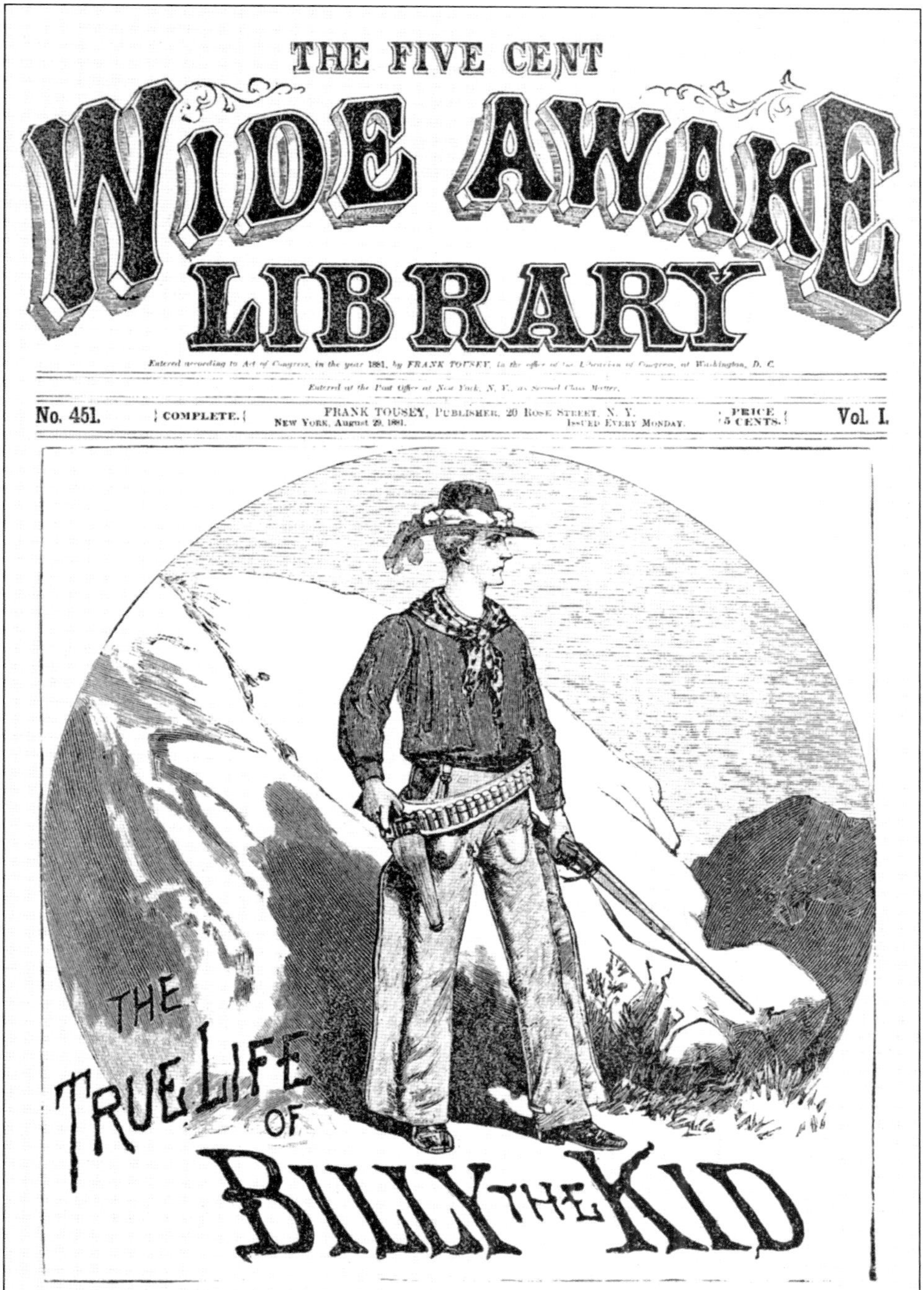
THE FIVE CENT
WIDE AWAKE LIBRARY
Entered according to Act of Congress, in the year 1881, by FRANK TOUSEY, in the office of the Librarian of Congress, at Washington, D. C.
Entered at the Post Office at New York, N. Y., as Second Class Matter.
No. 451. COMPLETE. FRANK TOUSEY, PUBLISHER, 20 ROSE STREET, N. Y. NEW YORK, August 29, 1881. ISSUED EVERY MONDAY. PRICE 5 CENTS. Vol. I.
THE TRUE LIFE OF BILLY THE KID

Frank Tousey published *The True Life of Billy the Kid* in New York on August 28, 1881. The author was Don Jenardo; it is unknown who used this pen name. The story was certainly written by someone doing research and writing prior to the Kid's death, since it was released just a few weeks after he died. The most likely candidate to be the author was Ash Upson, Pat Garrett's ghostwriter for his book, *The Authentic Life of Billy, the Kid*.

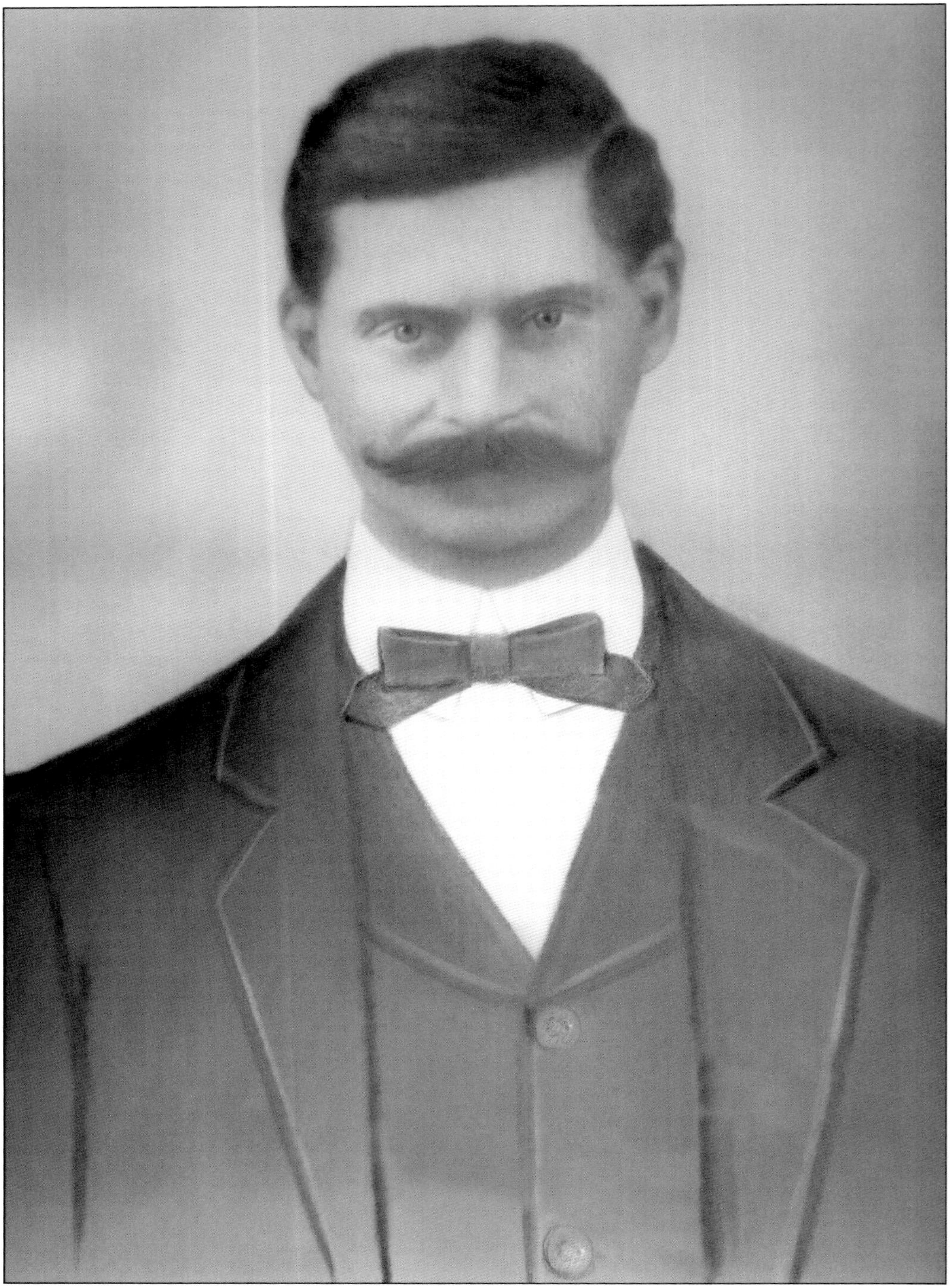

Lincoln County sheriff Patrick ("Pat") Floyd Garrett garnered fame for shooting Billy the Kid. He had a distinguished career in law enforcement and was appointed a customs collector by Pres. Theodore Roosevelt in December 1901. Garrett was shot under mysterious circumstances in 1908 just a few miles from Las Cruces, and no one was convicted of his murder.

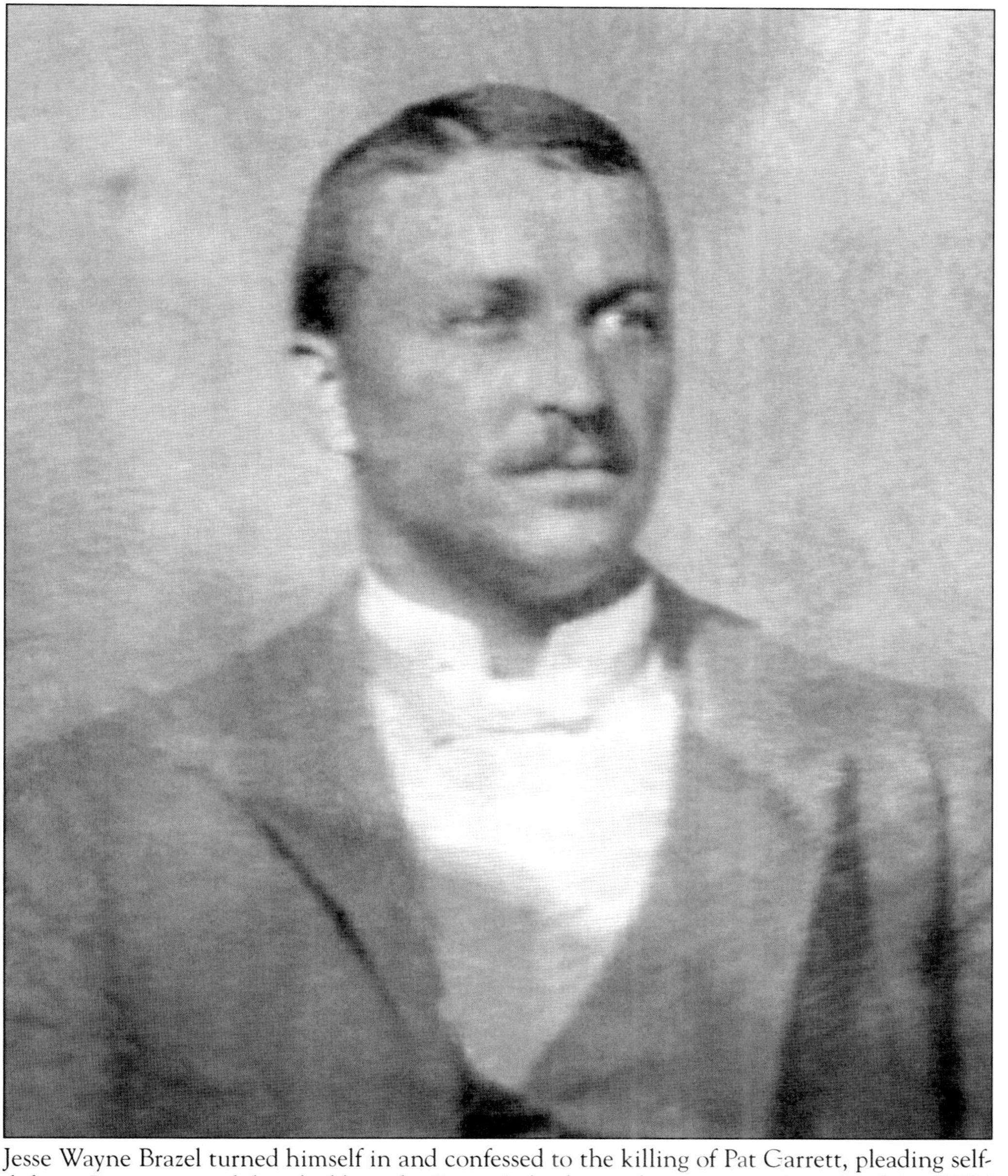

Jesse Wayne Brazel turned himself in and confessed to the killing of Pat Garrett, pleading self-defense. It was rumored that the blame for Garrett's death rested upon a conspiracy involving W.W. Cox, Oliver Lee, and possibly James Gilliland. Brazel was tried. Albert Fall served as attorney, and Brazel was found innocent after 15 minutes of jury deliberation.

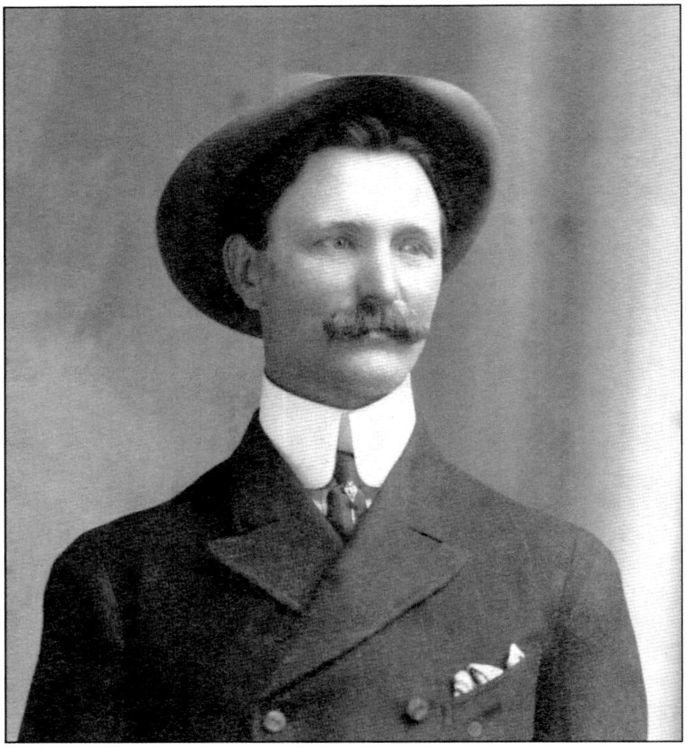

Fred Fornoff served as Albuquerque chief of police, Bernalillo County deputy sheriff, deputy US marshal, captain of the Mounted Police, and investigator for the Santa Fe Railroad. Gov. George Curry assigned Fornoff to conduct an independent investigation into the death of Sheriff Pat Garrett. His final report mysteriously disappeared.

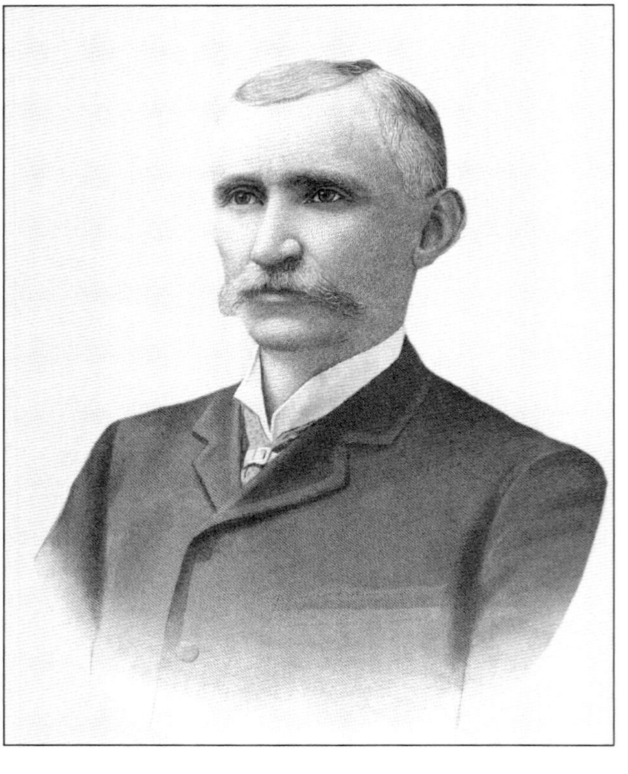

Gov. William T. "Poker Bill" Thornton served as Thomas B. Catron's law partner. Both Thornton and Catron defended Col. Nathan August Dudley at his court-martial for conduct unbecoming of an officer. Dudley was found guilty and suspended from rank and command of Fort Stanton and required to forfeit half his pay for three months. Governor Thornton hired Pat Garrett as a private detective to investigate the Fountain murders. Albert J. Fountain and his eight-year-old son Henry disappeared on February 1, 1896, and were presumed murdered.

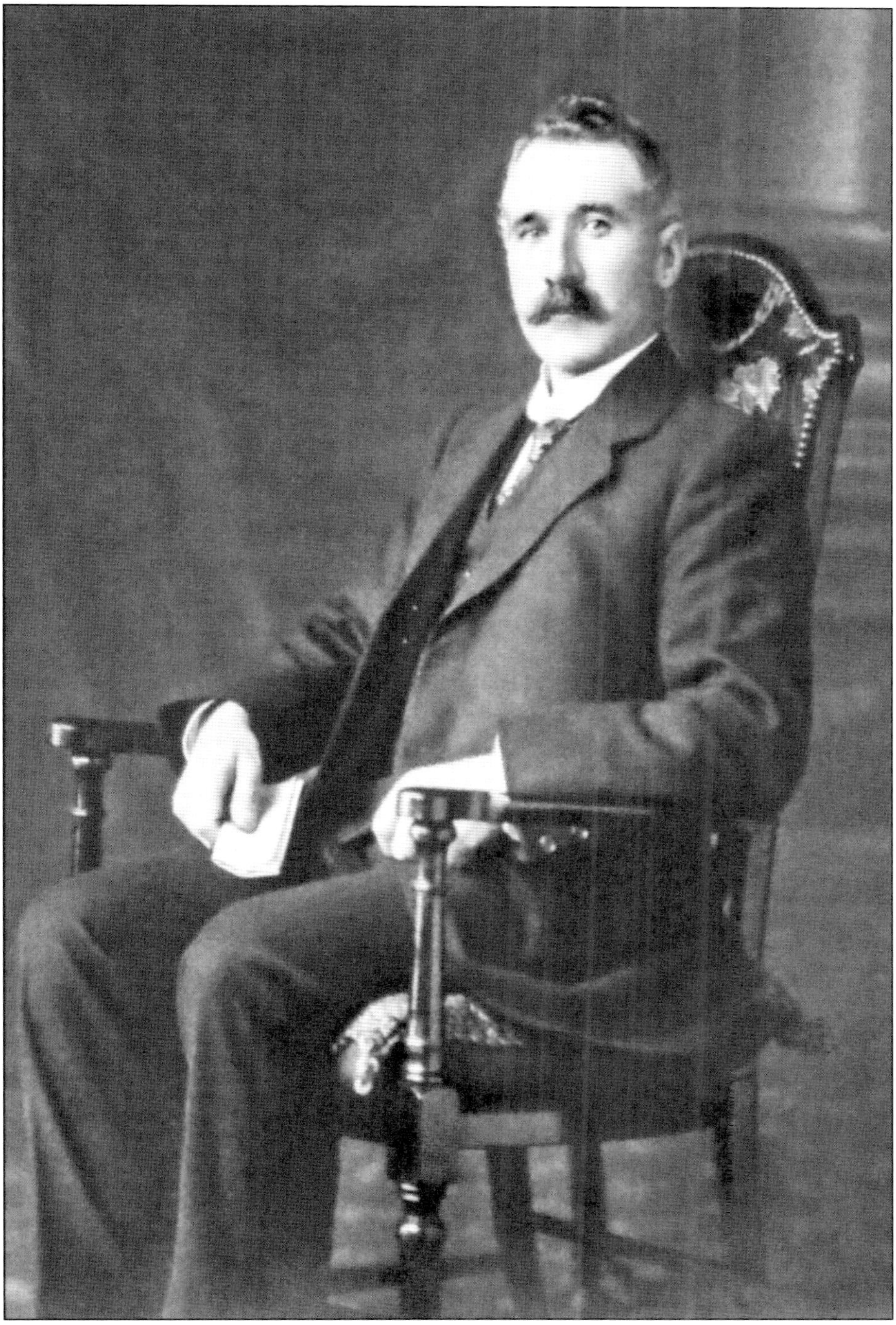

Albert Bacon Fall was a US senator from New Mexico and served as secretary of the interior under Pres. Warren Harding. He was sentenced to prison for misdemeanors in office in the affair known as the Teapot Dome scandal. Fall was a powerful member of the Santa Fe Ring. He became bitter enemies with Albert J. Fountain, who attacked the ring and James Dolan in his *Mesilla Valley Independent* newspaper columns.

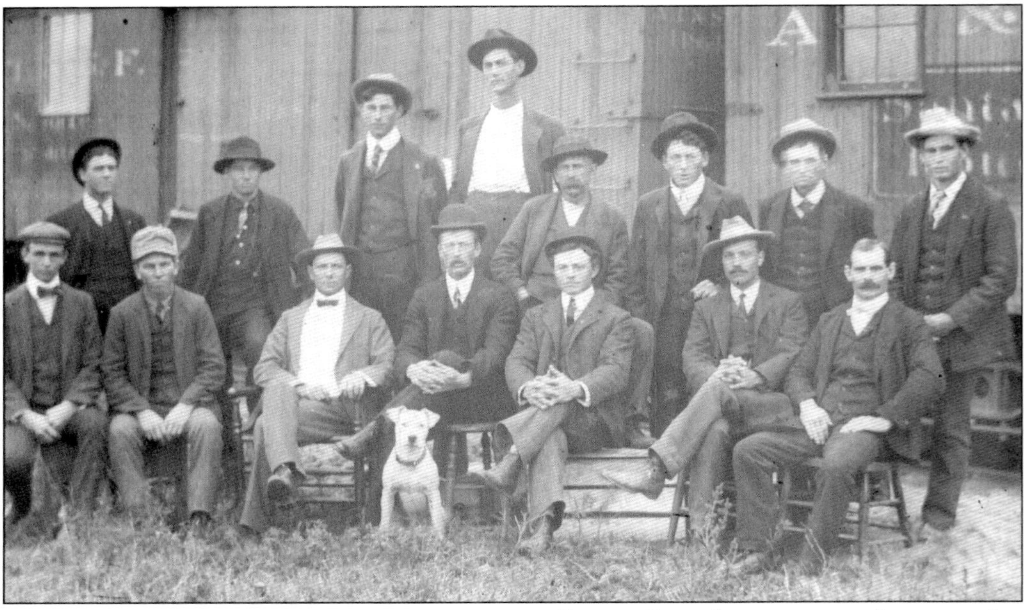

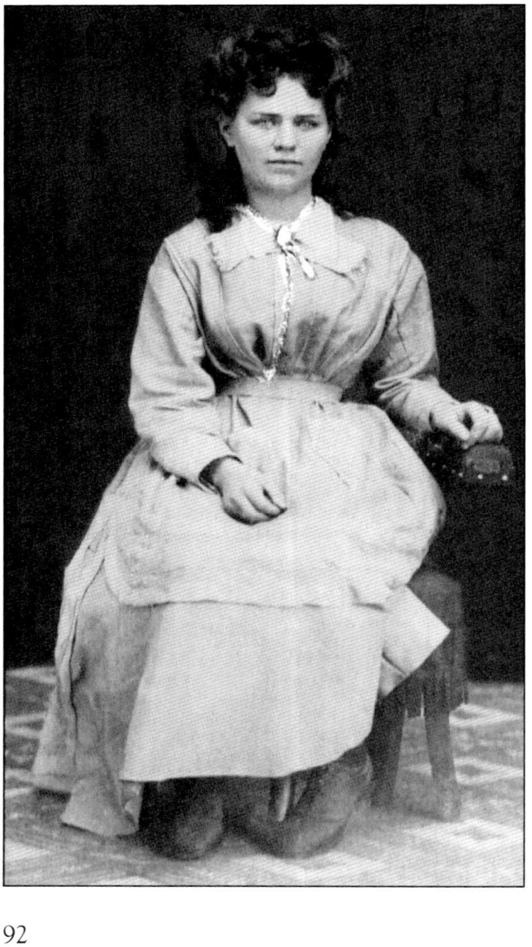

George Curry (sitting on trunk at center) was the right-of-way agent for the El Paso & Northeastern Railroad out of Tularosa, New Mexico, after serving as territorial governor. This was a short line built to connect the industrial and commercial center at El Paso, Texas, with its physical resources and the national transportation hub in Chicago. James Gilliland and Oliver Lee are sitting to the right of Curry, while W.W. Cox is sitting to the left.

This unidentified girl was professed to be one of Billy the Kid's love interests. It was claimed that the Kid had a lover in every New Mexico town, including Lincoln.

In 1882, Thomas B. Catron (pictured at right) partnered with Edgar A. Walz, his brother-in-law, and issued the following notice: "One hundred dollars will be paid any person or persons driving, trading, killing or in possession of stock in the above brands, without being counter branded." Catron, Walz, and James Dolan were, in fact, business associates. Walz managed the J.J. Dolan Co. store in Lincoln when Catron took it over due to Dolan's indebtedness. Other brands listed on the notice below include those of Emil Fritz, Pat Garrett, and William L. Rynerson.

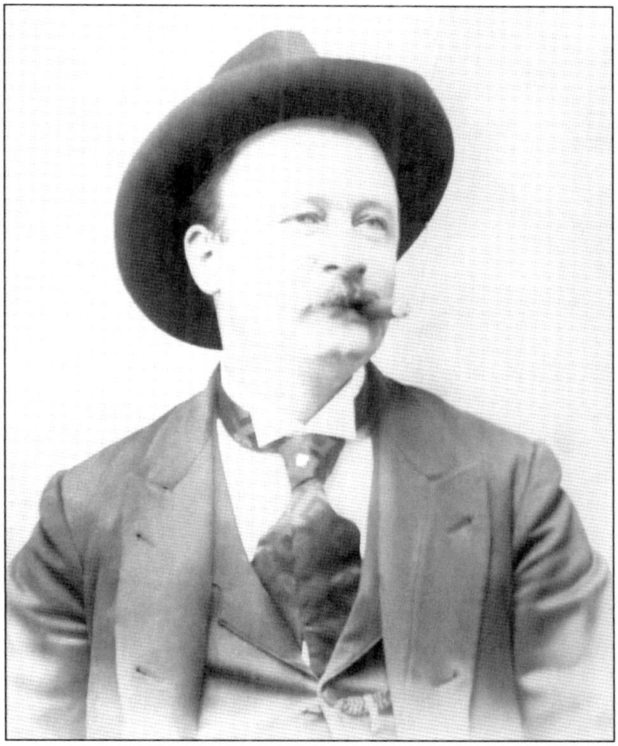

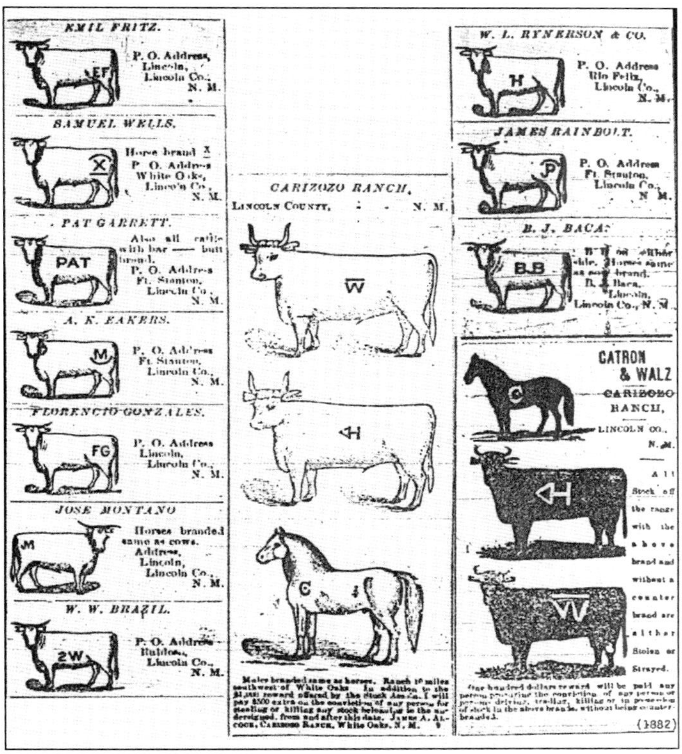

EMIL FRITZ. P. O. Address, Lincoln, Lincoln Co., N. M.

SAMUEL WELLS. Horse brand X. P. O. Address White Oaks, Lincoln Co., N. M.

PAT GARRETT. Also all cattle with bar — butt brand. P. O. Address Ft. Stanton, Lincoln Co., N. M.

A. K. EAKERS. P. O. Address Ft. Stanton, Lincoln Co., N. M.

FLORENCIO GONZALES. P. O. Address Lincoln, Lincoln Co., N. M.

JOSE MONTANO. Horses branded same as cows. Address, Lincoln, Lincoln Co., N. M.

W. W. BRAZIL. P. O. Address Bulldozer, Lincoln Co., N. M.

CARIZOZO RANCH, LINCOLN COUNTY, N. M.

Mules branded same as horses. Ranch 10 miles southwest of White Oaks. In addition to the $1,000 reward offered by the Stock Assn. I will pay $500 extra on the conviction of any person for stealing or killing any stock belonging to the undersigned, from and after this date. James A. Alcock, Carrizozo Ranch, White Oaks, N. M.

W. L. RYNERSON & CO. P. O. Address Rio Feliz, Lincoln Co., N. M.

JAMES RAINBOLT. P. O. Address Ft. Stanton, Lincoln Co., N. M.

B. J. BACA. B B on either side. Horses same as cow brand. B. J. Baca, Lincoln, Lincoln Co., N. M.

CATRON & WALZ CARIZOZO RANCH, LINCOLN CO., N. M.

All Stock off the range with the above brand and without a counter brand are either Stolen or Strayed.

One hundred dollars reward will be paid any person procuring the conviction of any person or persons driving, trading, killing or in possession of stock in the above brands, without being counter branded.

(1882)

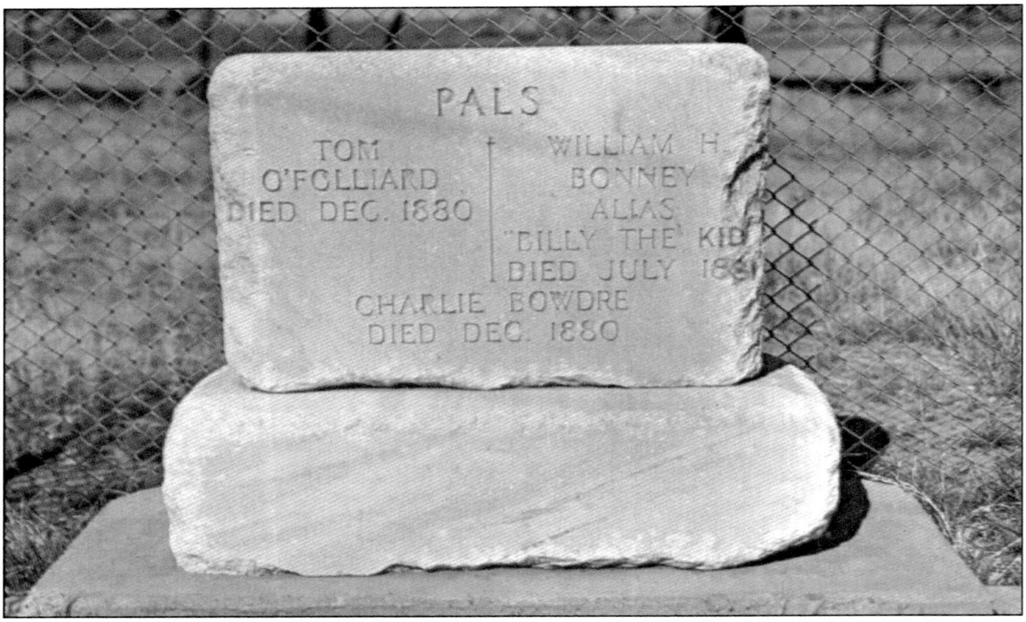

Pictured is a tombstone marking Billy the Kid's grave in Fort Sumner, New Mexico. He was buried next to Tom O'Folliard and Charlie Bowdre, who had ridden with him.

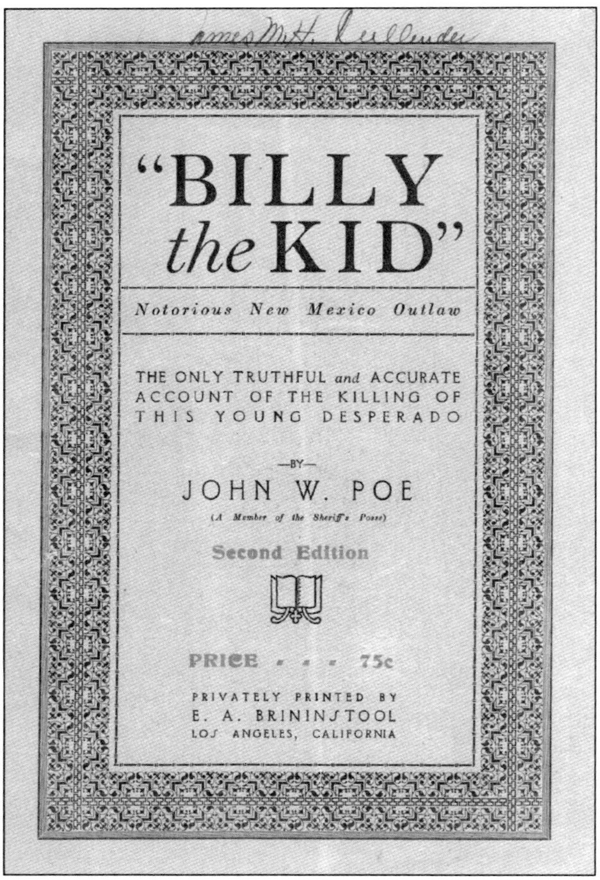

"BILLY *the* KID"

Notorious New Mexico Outlaw

THE ONLY TRUTHFUL *and* ACCURATE ACCOUNT OF THE KILLING OF THIS YOUNG DESPERADO

—BY—

JOHN W. POE

(*A Member of the Sheriff's Posse*)

Second Edition

PRICE - - - 75c

PRIVATELY PRINTED BY
E. A. BRININSTOOL
LOS ANGELES, CALIFORNIA

In 1919, *World Wide Magazine* copyrighted John W. Poe's *"Billy the Kid" Notorious New Mexico Outlaw*. Poe also wrote a book entitled *The Death of Billy the Kid*. As a member of Garrett's posse, Poe joined many others seeking to capitalize on Billy the Kid's fame. Other than Pres. Abraham Lincoln, Billy the Kid is the person most written about in American history.

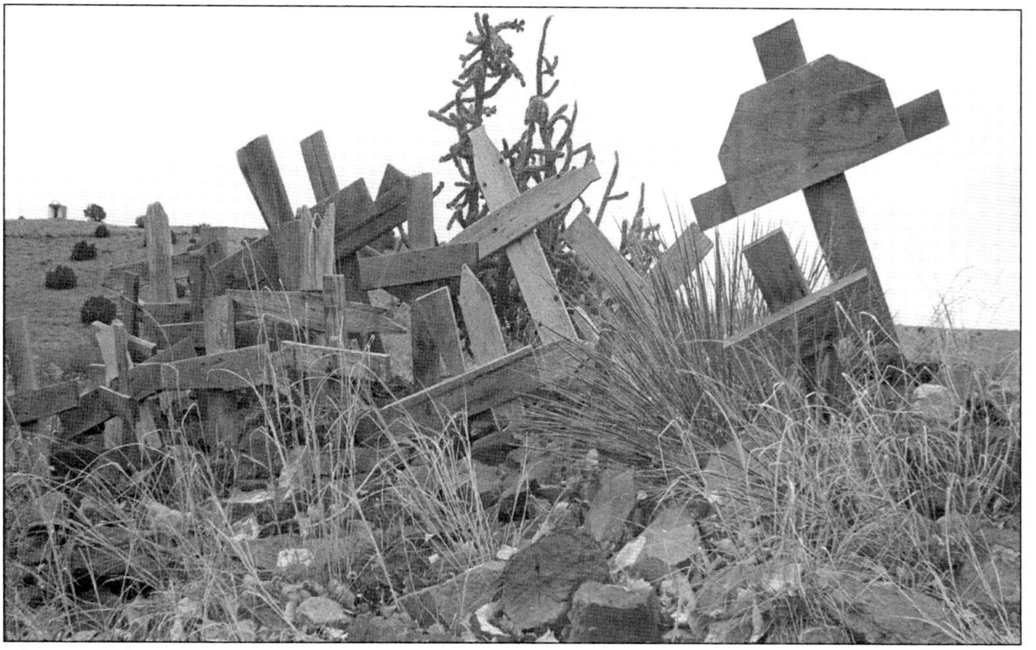

The Spanish colonial custom in New Mexico was to mark the spot where someone died with a cross, flowers, and mementos. If the person died while traveling, was killed by accident, or murdered outside of a home or building, mourners set crosses at these locations, which were called *descansos*. Lincoln and the surrounding area contained many descansos after the Lincoln County War.

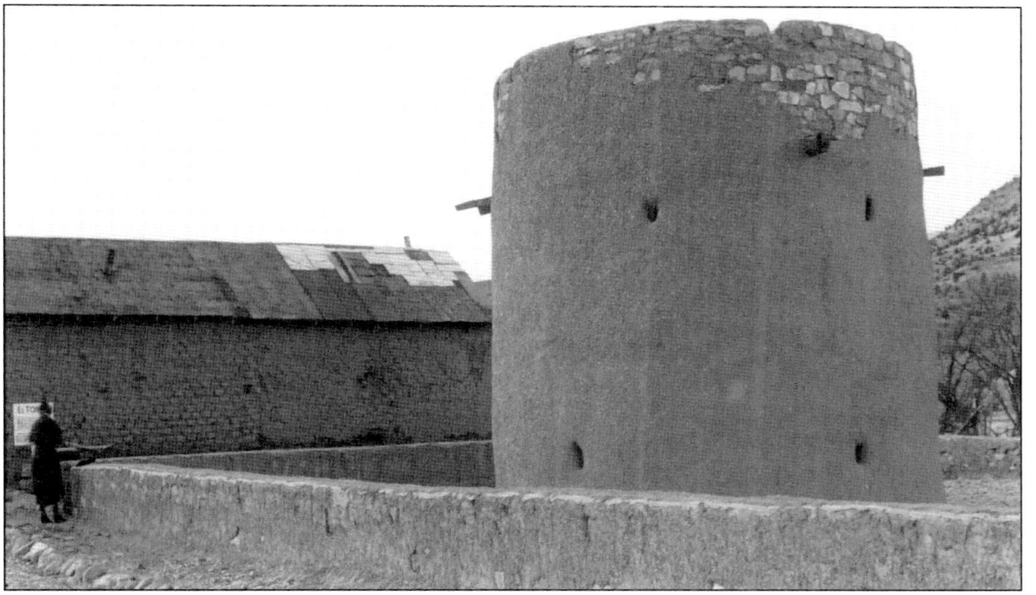

The torreon, or stone defensive tower, is a readily identifiable landmark in Lincoln. It was constructed during the 1840s by early settlers for defense against marauding Indians. During the Lincoln County War, sharpshooters posted on the roof with Winchester rifles maintained control of Lincoln's main street below. The building also served as a makeshift jail and once housed Billy the Kid.

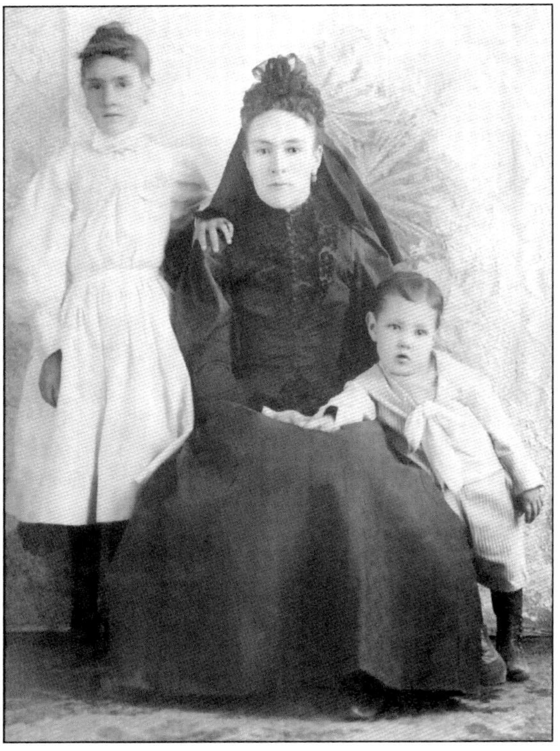

Medical care was sparse in the Old West. People relied on midwives, masseuses, and medicine women like Doña Catalina Mondragon de Valdéz, pictured here with her children. Doña Catalina treated Billy the Kid and many of the Lincoln County War participants and their families, who gave her personal photographs as keepsakes. She took baked goods to Billy the Kid while he was held in jail in Las Vegas, New Mexico, in December 1880.

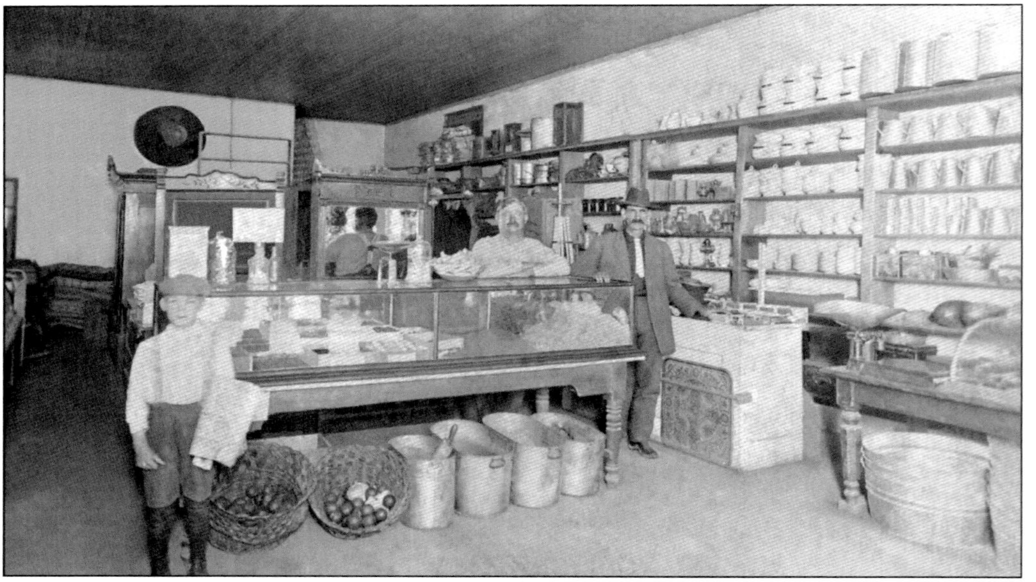

In 1912, Maximo de Aragón sold the *Optic* newspaper in Las Vegas. Max enjoyed listening to Jose Chavez y Chavez talk about his adventures. He went to Albuquerque to see Buffalo Bill Cody at the circus in 1914; finding Cody's dressing tent, he peeked underneath. Cody spotted de Aragón and invited him in for a visit. De Aragón's interest in Billy the Kid led to him amassing a collection of Lincoln County photographs. Maximo is pictured holding newspapers. In the back is storeowner Juan Vigil at left, and gambler Benedito Peralta at right.

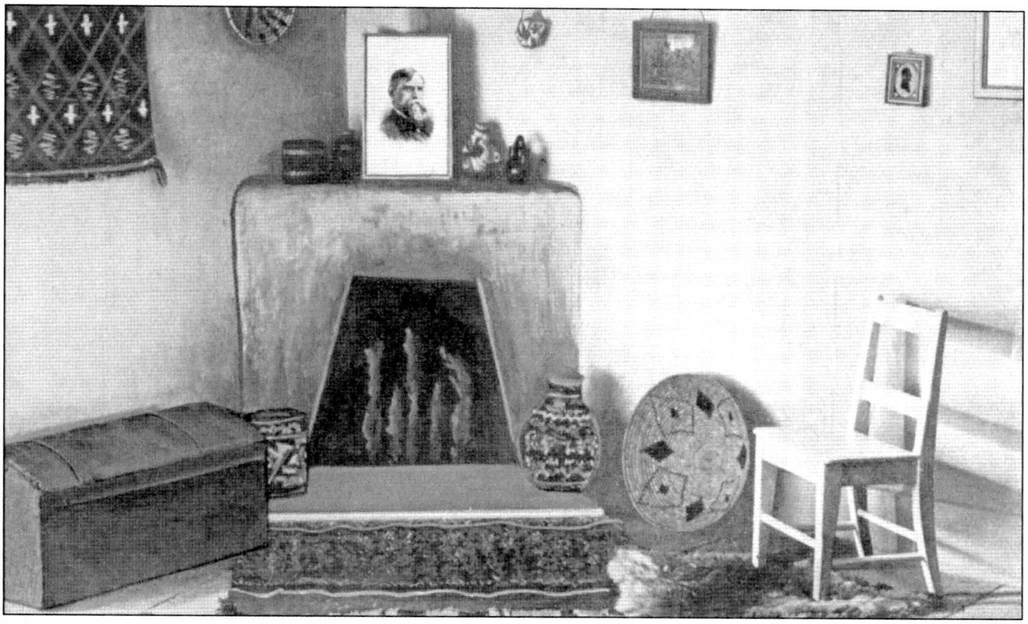

The "Ben Hur Room" at the Palace of the Governors was said to be the room where Lew Wallace wrote his famous novel while serving as governor of the New Mexico Territory. Wallace stated that he developed some of the scenes in *Ben Hur* after meeting with Billy the Kid on March 17, 1879, in Lincoln. The book's product tie-ins included Ben Hur cigars, toys, spices, and even Ben Hur baking powder.

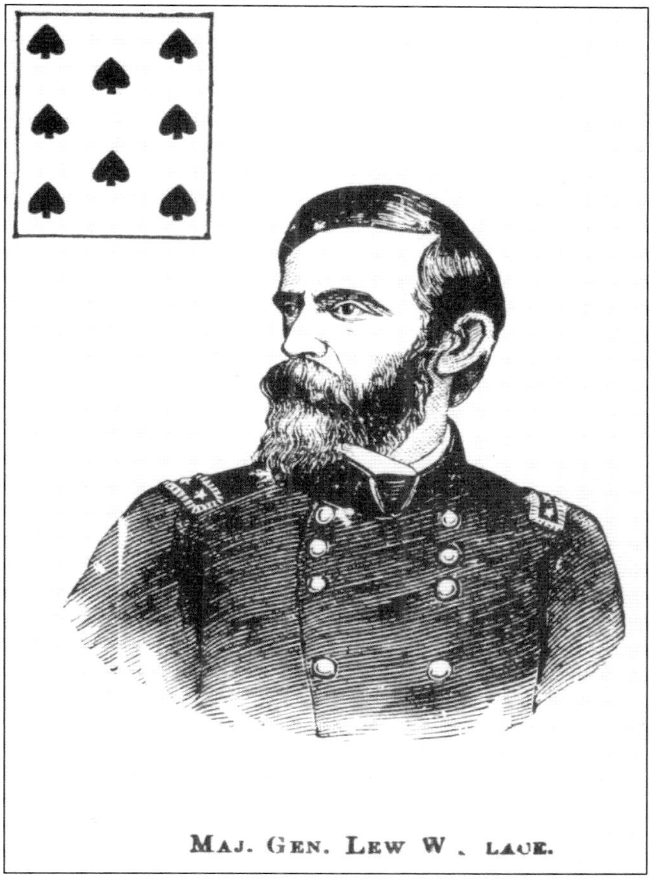

Maj. Gen. Lewis "Lew" Wallace was featured in a Union playing card deck as the eight of spades. In 1863, M. Nelson of New York published playing cards with engraved portraits of generals. Modern playing cards have featured Billy the Kid and Pat Garrett, both of whom enjoyed playing cards.

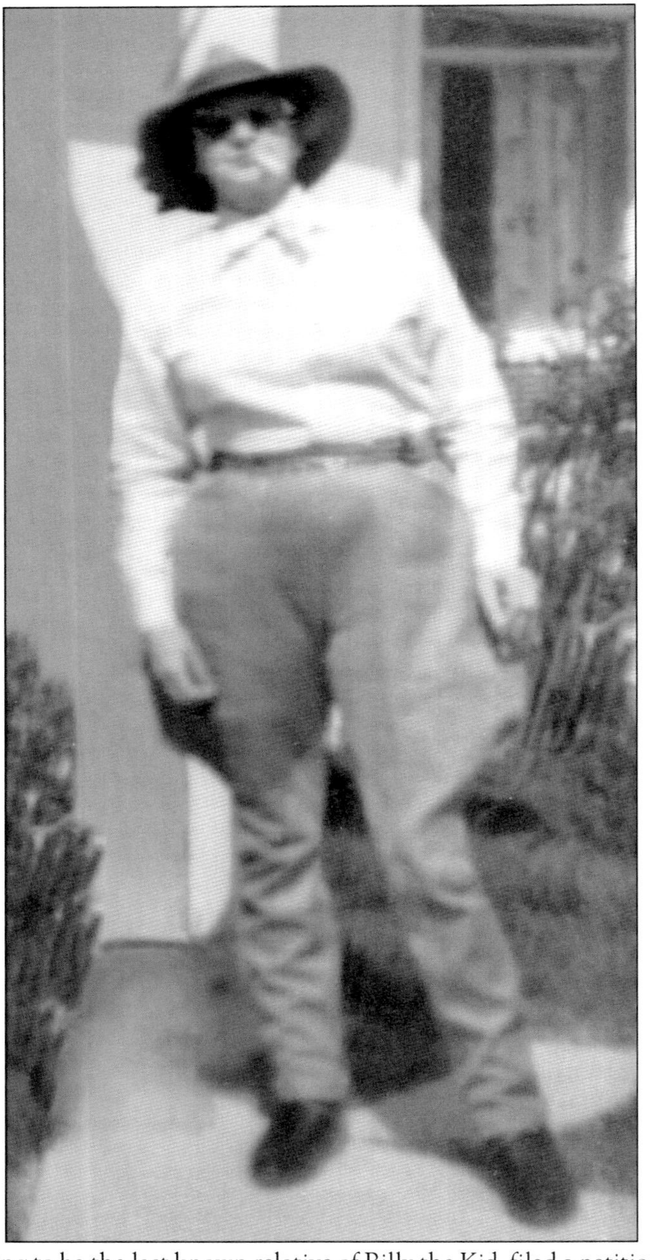

Lois Telfer, claiming to be the last known relative of Billy the Kid, filed a petition in New Mexico on June 26, 1961. She asked the courts to issue an order of exhumation to disinter the remains of William H. Bonney and move them from the Fort Sumner cemetery to the village of Lincoln cemetery. The commissioners for Lincoln County joined her on the petition. Joanna Allen, who owned the Old Fort Museum at Fort Sumner where the remains were located, and Louis Bowdre, who was a descendant of Charlie Bowdre (who was buried next to the Kid), filed a motion for dismissal. On March 13, 1962, federal district judge E.T. Hensley denied Telfor's petition, and the remains stayed in the Fort Sumner cemetery. Lincoln citizens wanted the remains moved, as they felt the tourism they would create could save the town.

Four

The Legacy of Lincoln

Each year, tourists from around the world flock to Lincoln, New Mexico, to see, feel, and touch history. They want to experience and imagine for themselves what Lincoln might have been like during the days of Billy the Kid. The aura surrounding the Kid began during his lifetime. He was already a legend in tall tales, and dime novels were circulated after his death. Newspapers across the country printed stories about the demise of Billy the Kid, and people read about it in Chicago, New York City, and London. In fact, the media has helped to perpetuate the story of Lincoln and Billy the Kid for generations. Hundreds of books have explored the subject of Billy the Kid and the Lincoln County War, and theatrical stage plays displaying this dramatic history have long captivated and thrilled audiences.

Popular actors—including Roy Rogers, Robert Taylor, Paul Newman, Val Kilmer, and Emilio Estevez—have played the role of Billy the Kid. Filmmakers featured John Wayne as cattleman John Chisum, and James Coburn, Wallace Beery, and many others have portrayed Sheriff Pat Garrett. During World War II, US troops and people back home could escape the violence of war by seeing Billy the Kid ride across the New Mexico landscape on screen. Howard Hughes featured the Kid in his movie *The Outlaw*, and Jane Russell played the Kid's girlfriend in the film. She became a famous pinup girl for the troops. The films were dubbed for foreign distribution so that people in Japan, South America, France, and many other places could enjoy seeing Billy the Kid and the town of Lincoln re-created as it was during his life and times—even if the truth was stretched for the public. The Kid and Western culture became popular in Japan due to the myth and legend of the Old West. Comic books and children's book series featuring Billy the Kid were published. Lew Wallace wrote his groundbreaking novel, *Ben Hur*, during his stint in the governor's chair in Santa Fe. The interaction between Governor Wallace and Billy the Kid is also the subject of popular culture. All of this is the legacy of the town of Lincoln, New Mexico.

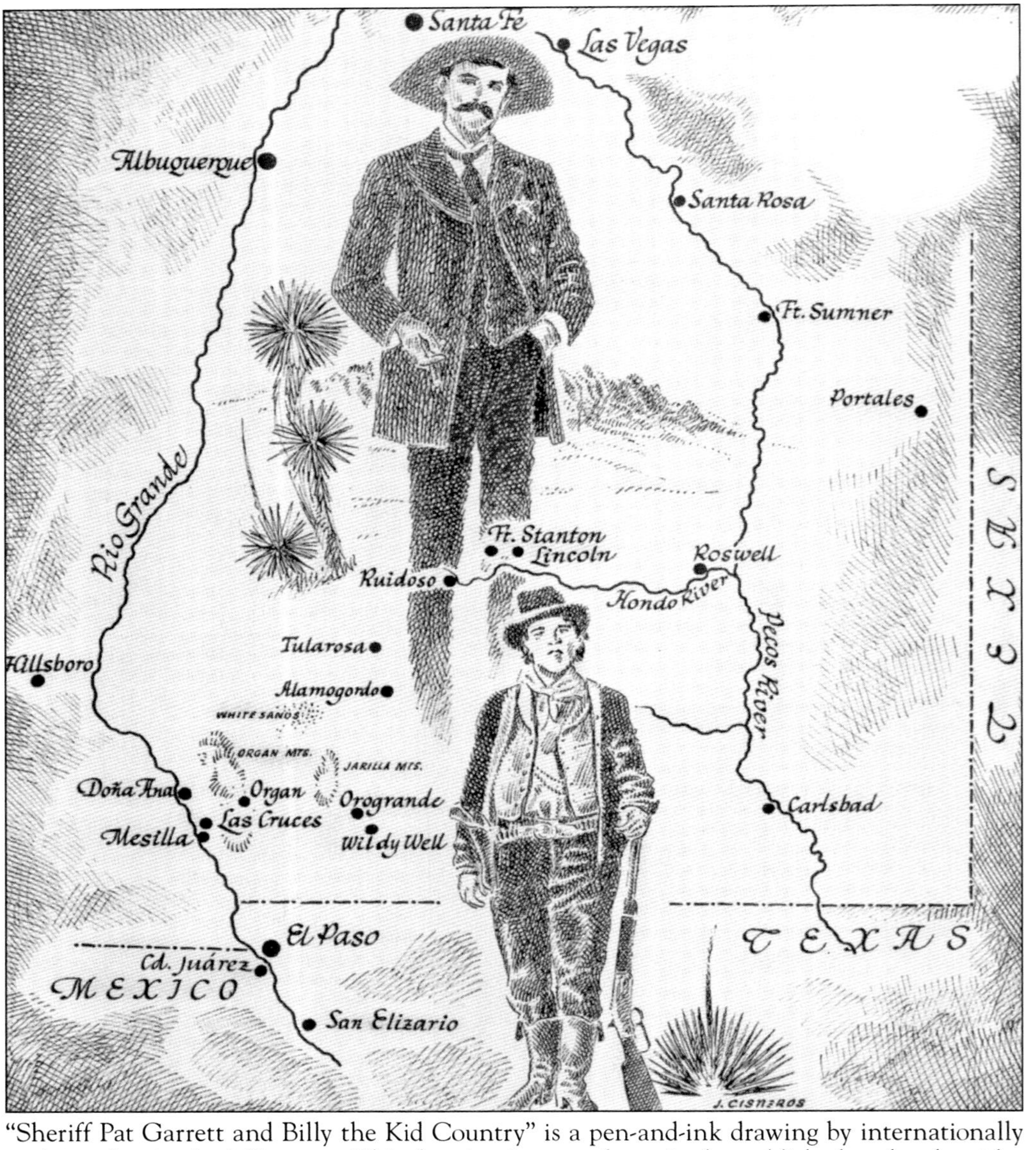

"Sheriff Pat Garrett and Billy the Kid Country" is a pen-and-ink drawing by internationally acclaimed artist José Cisneros. This drawing is part of a series he published under the titles *Riders Across the Centuries: Horsemen of the Spanish Borderlands*, and *Cisneros 2000: Faces of the Borderlands*. The New Mexico Department of Cultural Affairs and the Tourism Department have produced extensive publicity around the popular subject of Billy the Kid to draw tourists to the state. Joining the towns of Lincoln, Fort Sumner, and other cities that promote the Billy the Kid Trail, the state sees the need for a larger campaign reflecting its Western history. New Mexico museums have jumped on the bandwagon by featuring major exhibits focused on the theme of Billy the Kid. (Courtesy of José Cisneros and Leon Metz.)

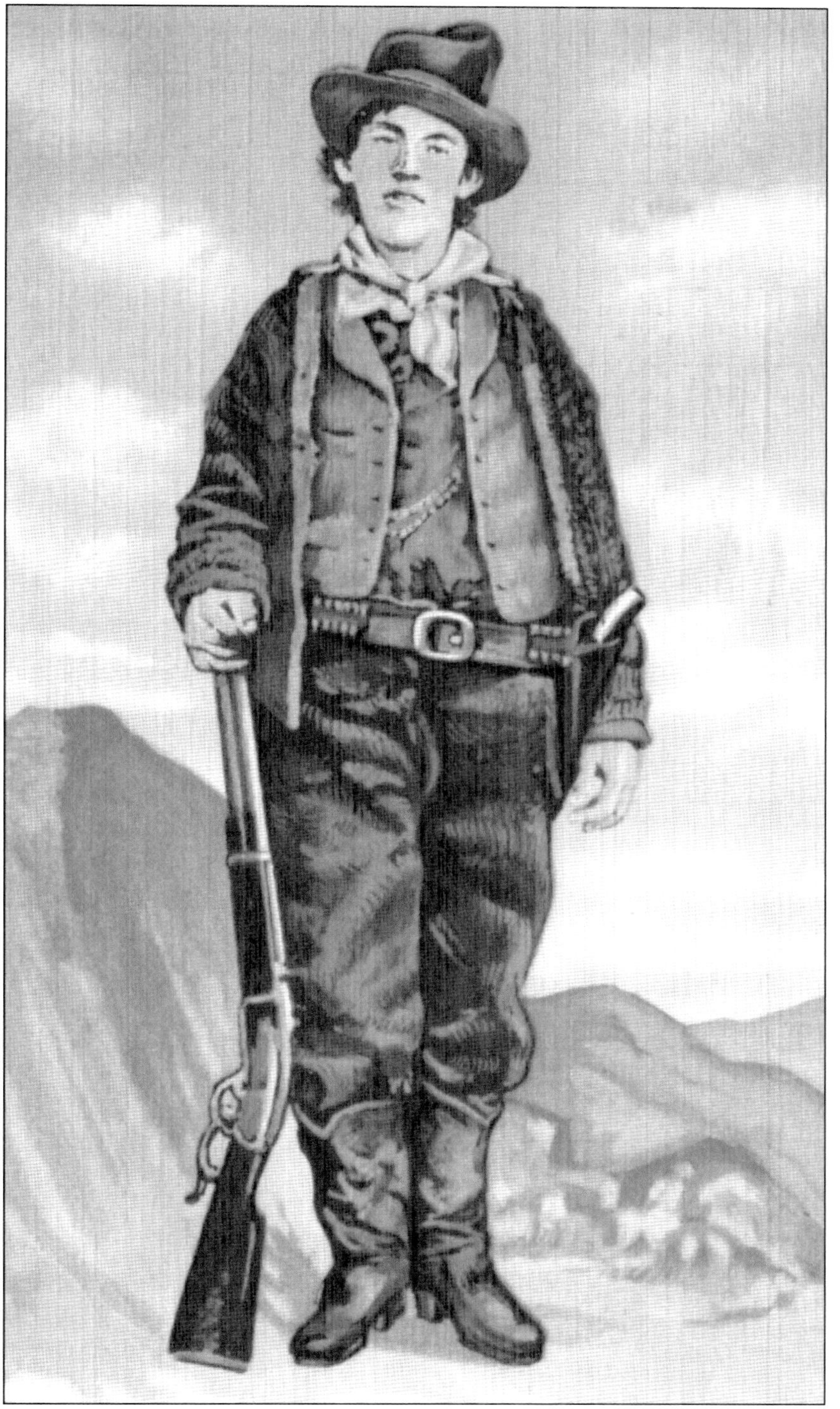

Billy the Kid and Lincoln postcards have been popular since the start of the 20th century. This card, produced by Curt Teich in Chicago in 1945, shows Billy the Kid with a New Mexico landscape in the background.

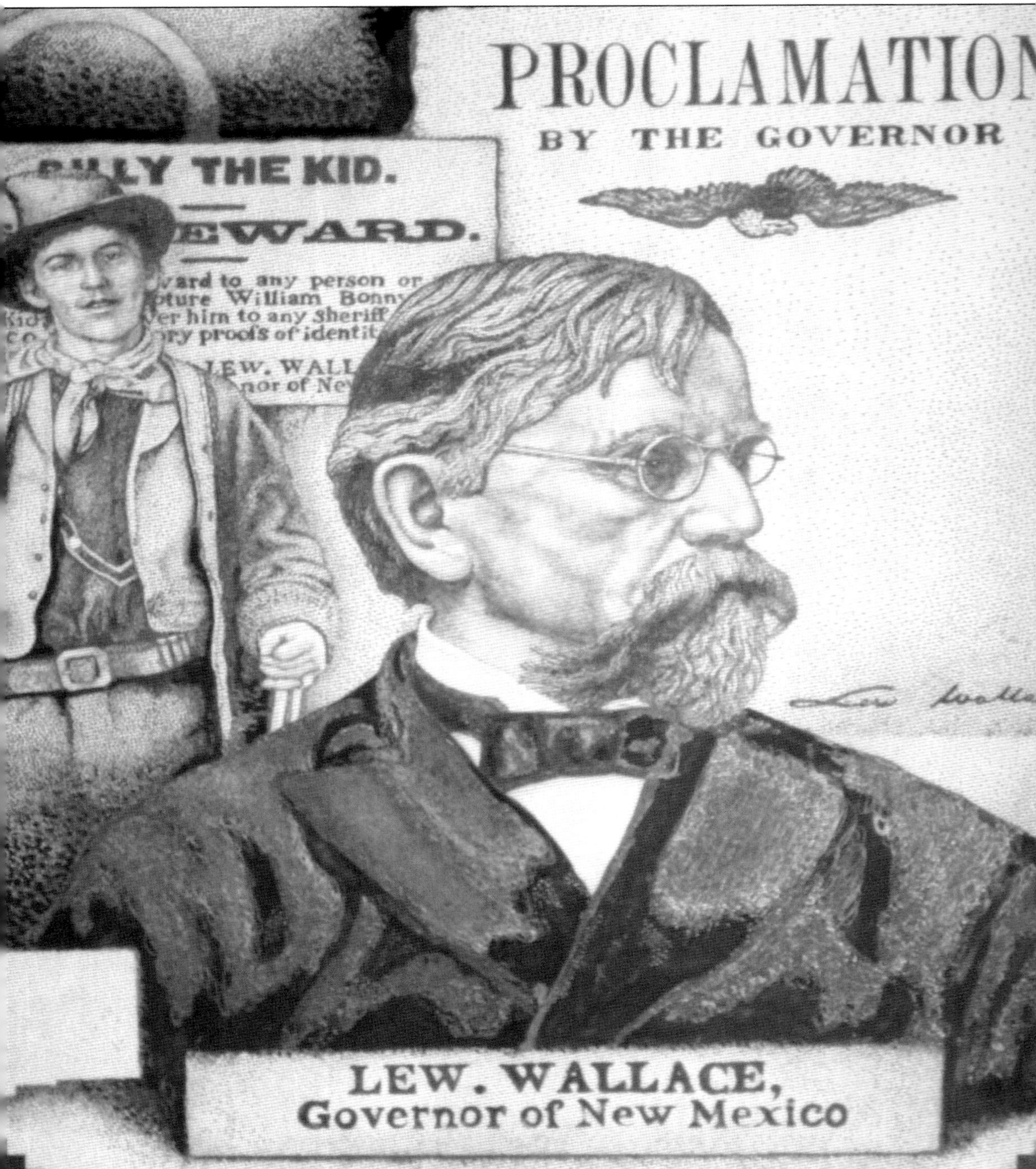

In this pen-and-ink drawing by Brent Jeffrey Thomas, the artist portrays important scenes from the story of Lincoln. Included are Billy the Kid; New Mexico territorial governor Lew Wallace, who met with the Kid at Lincoln; and the reward notice posted by Wallace for the Kid's capture.

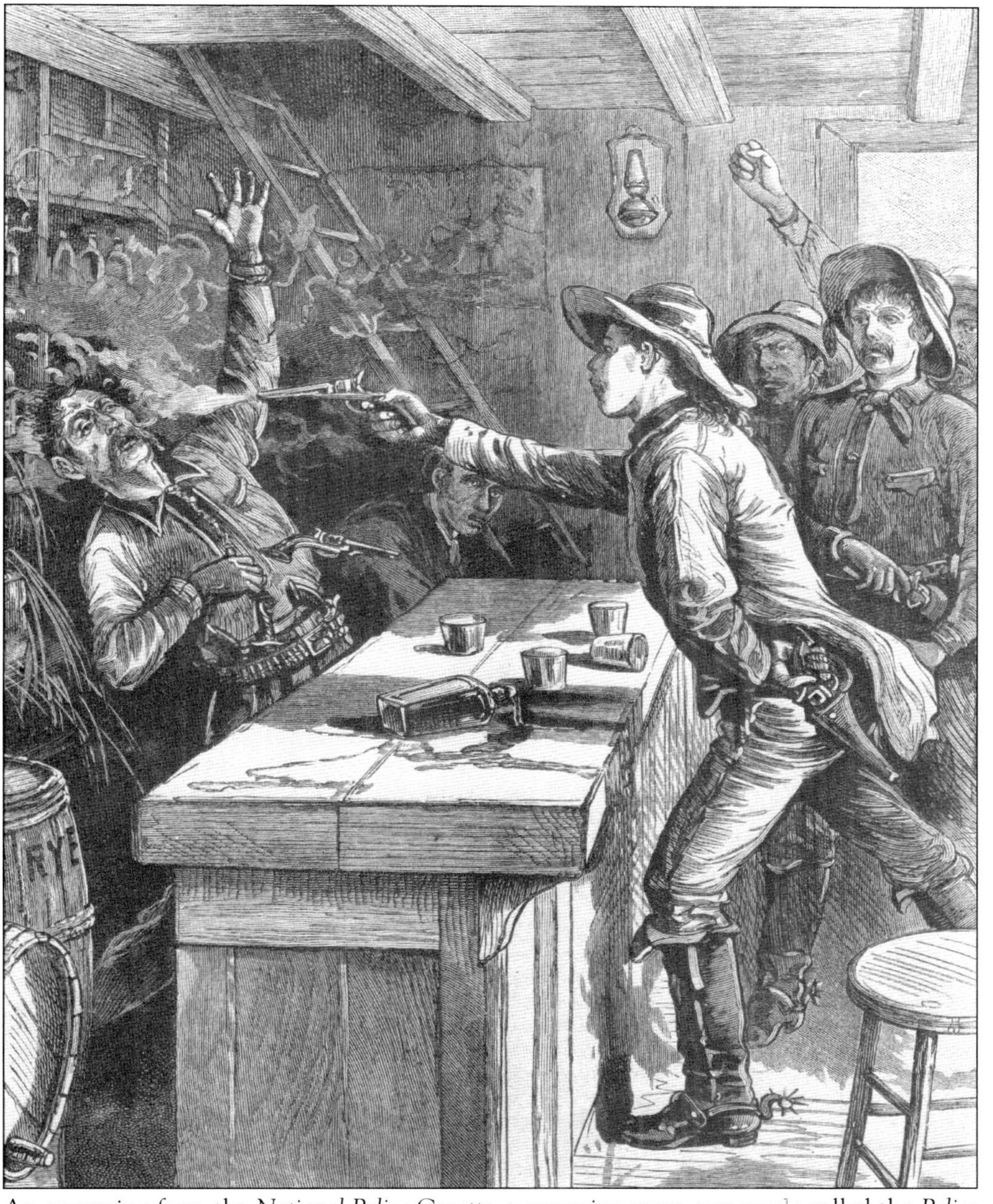

An engraving from the *National Police Gazette*, a magazine more commonly called the *Police Gazette*, shows Billy the Kid standing up to a fully armed bartender bent on shooting him and drawing a gun. William H. Bonney was popular in newspaper serials before his death and even more so in dime novels and other publications after he died.

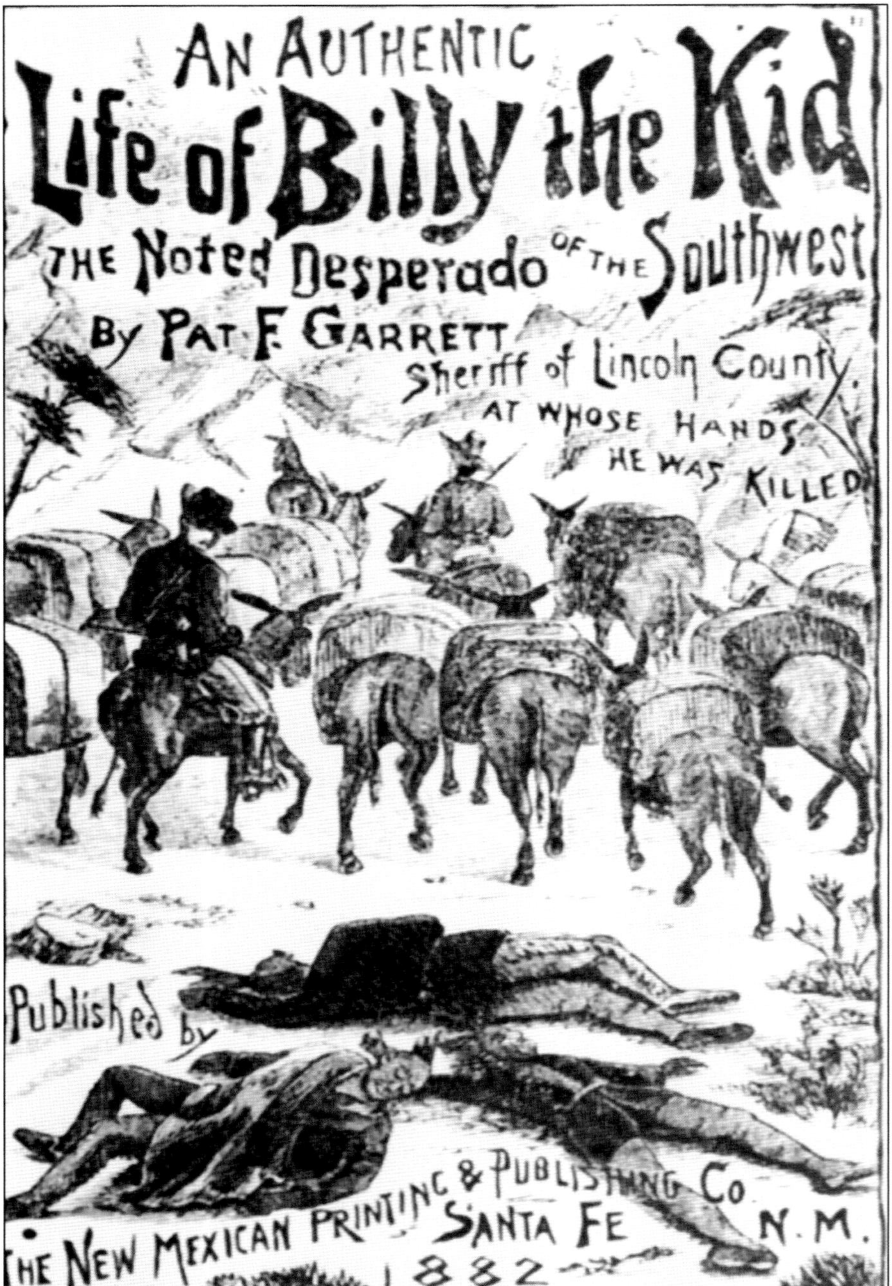

In 1882, the New Mexican Printing and Publishing Company of Santa Fe rushed to release Sheriff Pat F. Garrett's book, *An Authentic Life of Billy the Kid.* The book was illustrated with engravings produced by the Baker Company of Chicago. One engraving was done from the famous tintype of the Kid. It is known that New Mexico journalist Ash Upson served as Garrett's ghostwriter on the book. It was produced nine months after the Kid's death. Historians have questioned the inaccuracies in the book. Few copies of Garrett's book were sold and it was a financial disaster for the well-known lawman.

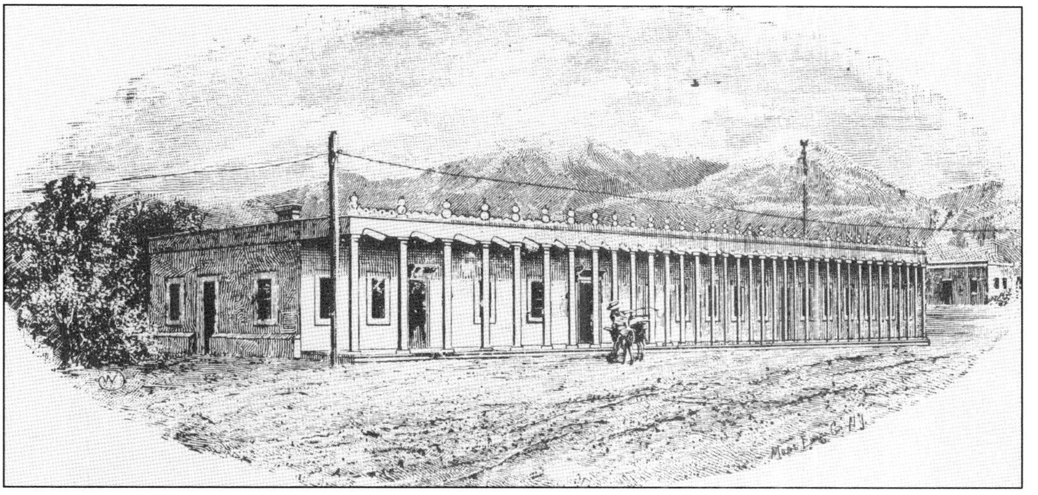

Lew Wallace's ambition as a youth was to become a celebrated artist. He spent a great deal of time sketching and painting, but he became recognized as a Civil War general and territorial governor of New Mexico. Wallace created this sketch of the governmental building in Santa Fe called the Palace of the Governors, where his office was once located.

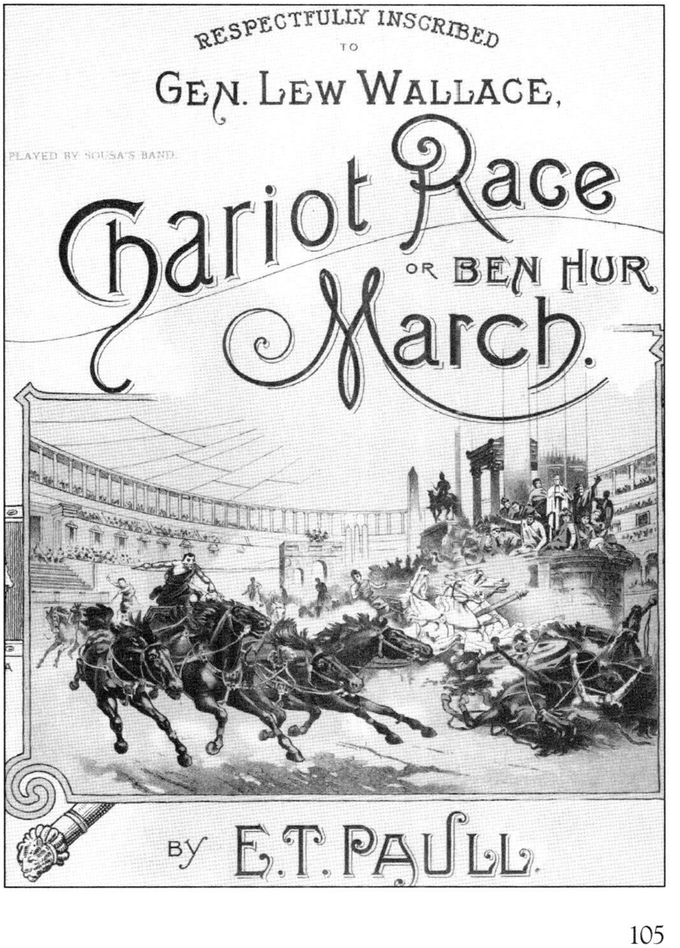

After Billy the Kid's demise and after Lew Wallace left the governor's office in Santa Fe, they both gained vast fame in the media. John Philip Sousa's band played the "Chariot Race, or Ben Hur March."

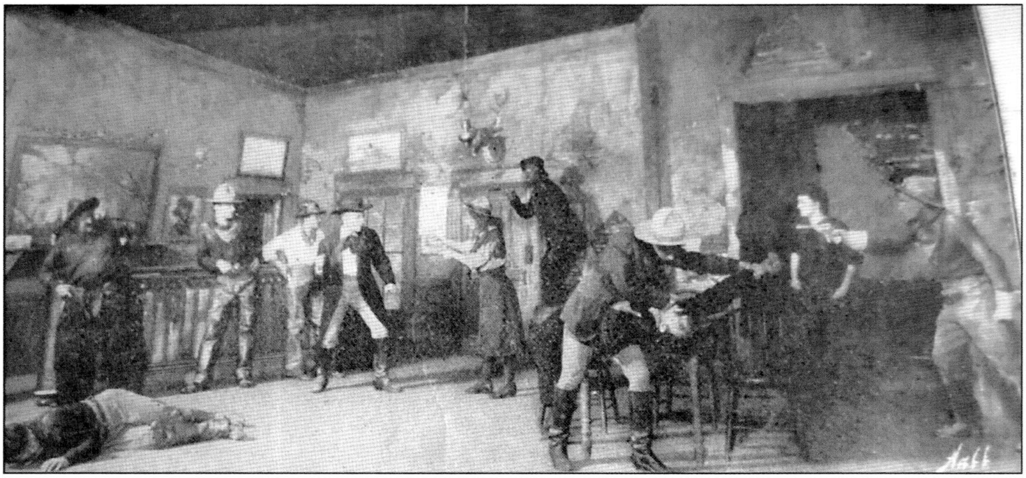

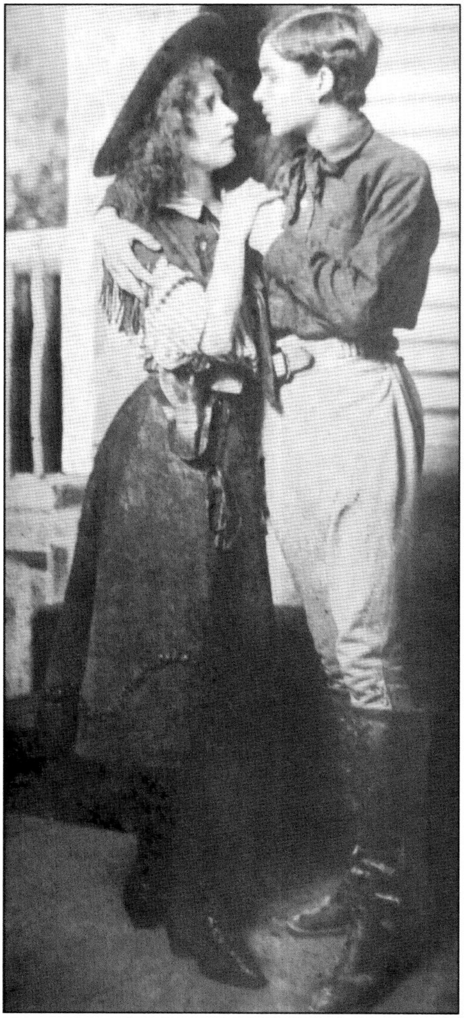

In *Billy the Kid, A Romantic Story*, a play performed in 1907 based on a book by Arda LaCroix, a group in a Lincoln saloon threatens a poor innocent girl. Billy the Kid saves the fair damsel in distress to thundering applause and cheers from the audience.

In this scene from a production of *Billy the Kid, A Romantic Story* staged in 1907, Billy the Kid has saved the day and says, "I love you Nellie, I have always loved you."

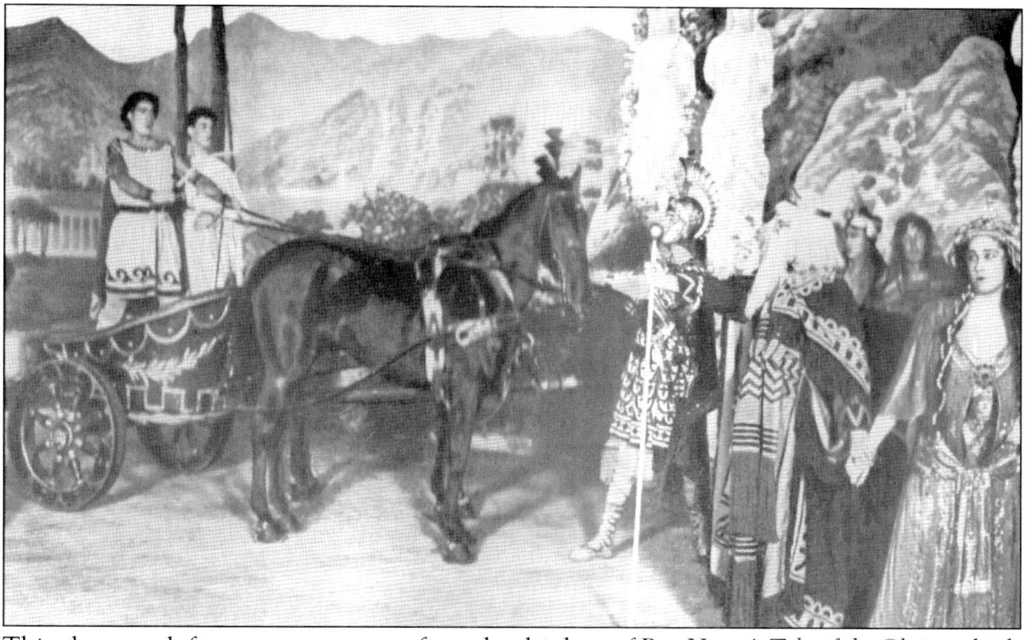

This photograph features a stage scene from the third act of *Ben Hur: A Tale of the Christ*, which was presented at the Broadway Theatre in New York on November 29, 1899. William Young dramatized the play, Edgar Stillman Kelley composed the music, and Ben Teal staged it under the direction of Joseph Brooks. Charlton Heston was the most popular actor who played Ben Hur.

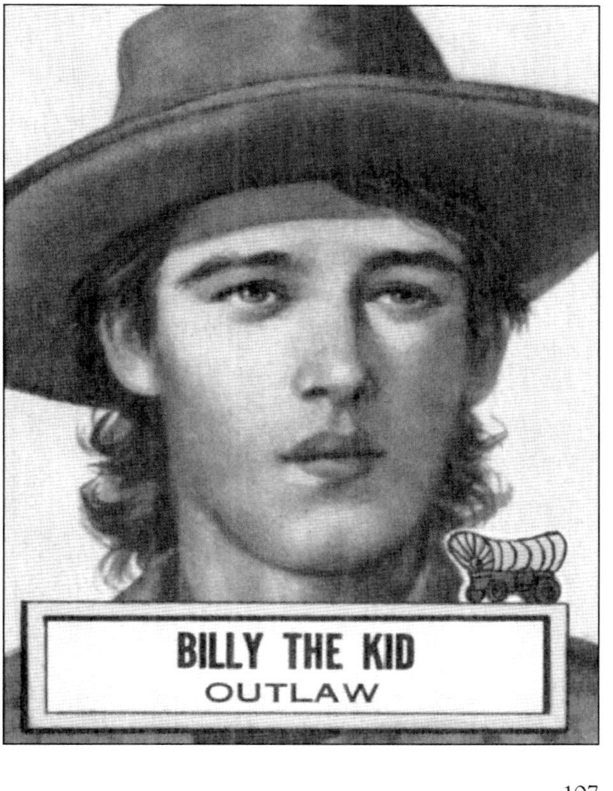

Toy manufacturers have produced frontier towns, including the town of Lincoln, as either cardboard cutouts or plastic reproductions. They have also created action figures of Billy the Kid, Regulator badges, and Billy the Kid Western clothing that was produced from the 1950s through the 1980s. This early bubblegum card was No. 6 of the Men of the West collectors' series. Children could learn about a fascinating period of US history while playing games and having fun.

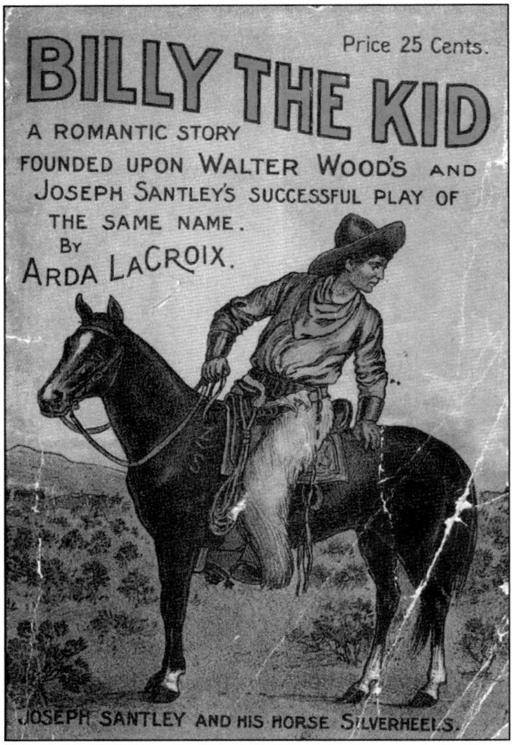

Another romantic story about Billy the Kid, again based on Walter Wood and Joseph Stanley's stage play and written by Arda LaCroix, appeared as a popular novel in 1908.

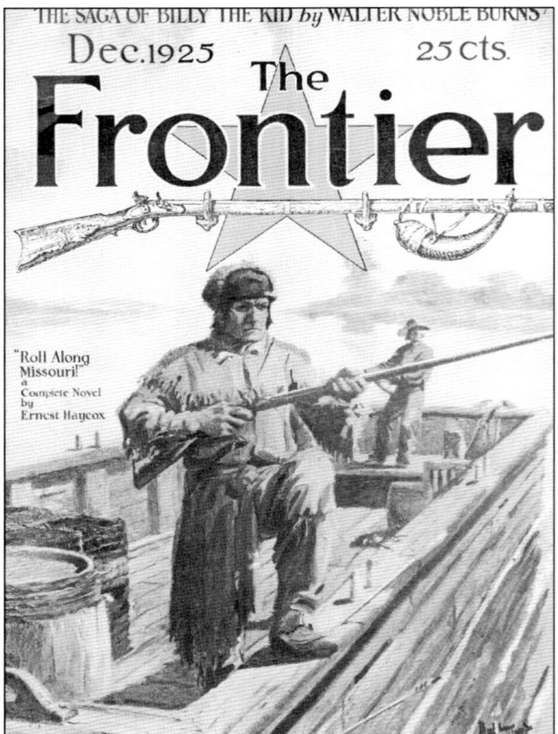

The Frontier magazine featured the Walter Noble Burns story "The Saga of Billy the Kid" in its December 1925 issue. The story did so well that Burns developed a full-length book with the same title. His book helped to transform the Kid into a popular legend.

In July 1934, *Western Round-Up*, a magazine about old gunfighter days, released its first issue with a feature story about Billy the Kid. The story, written by Buck Ringoe, was called "Billy the Kid: Outlaw King of the Killers." Touted as "The Thrilling Story of His Life and Death," Ringoe stretched the truth and filled in the blanks with fiction. For example, the Kid is shown shooting Indians and riding off with their ponies and supplies when, in fact, he never killed any Native Americans (although many others in Seven Rivers and the town of Lincoln did). This type of magazine spawned the creation of others, such as *Monster World*, released in 1966 by Warren Publishing Company, which featured "Billy the Kid vs Dracula!"

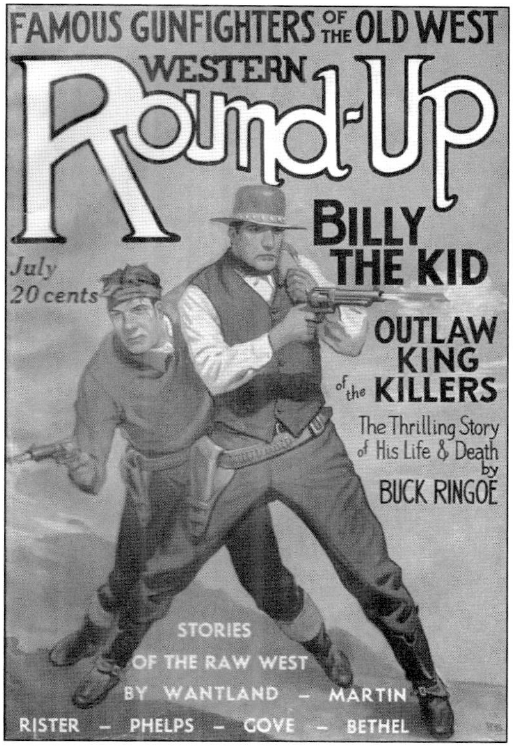

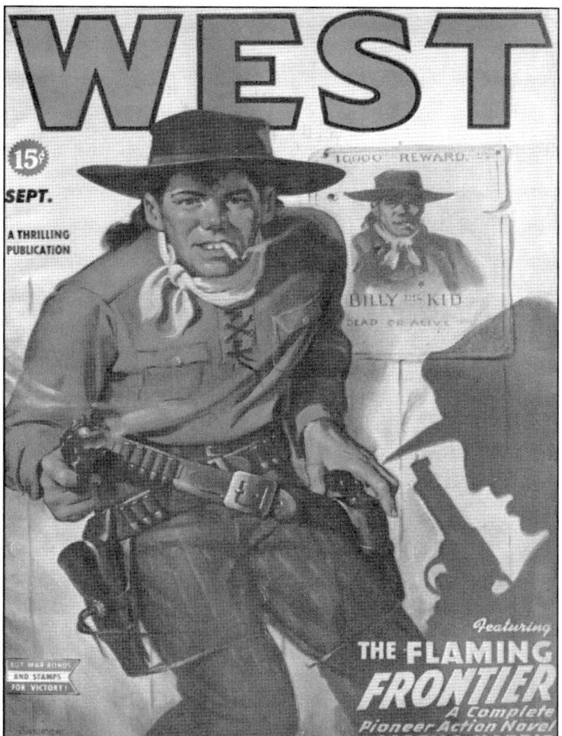

During World War II, Billy the Kid material was rolling off the presses. In this issue of *West* magazine, an advertisement for people to buy war bonds and stamps for victory was printed on the cover to help support the United States war effort against Germany and Japan. This September 1943 issue shows the Kid with guns blazing and firing along with the Regulators at Seven Rivers and James Dolan's men.

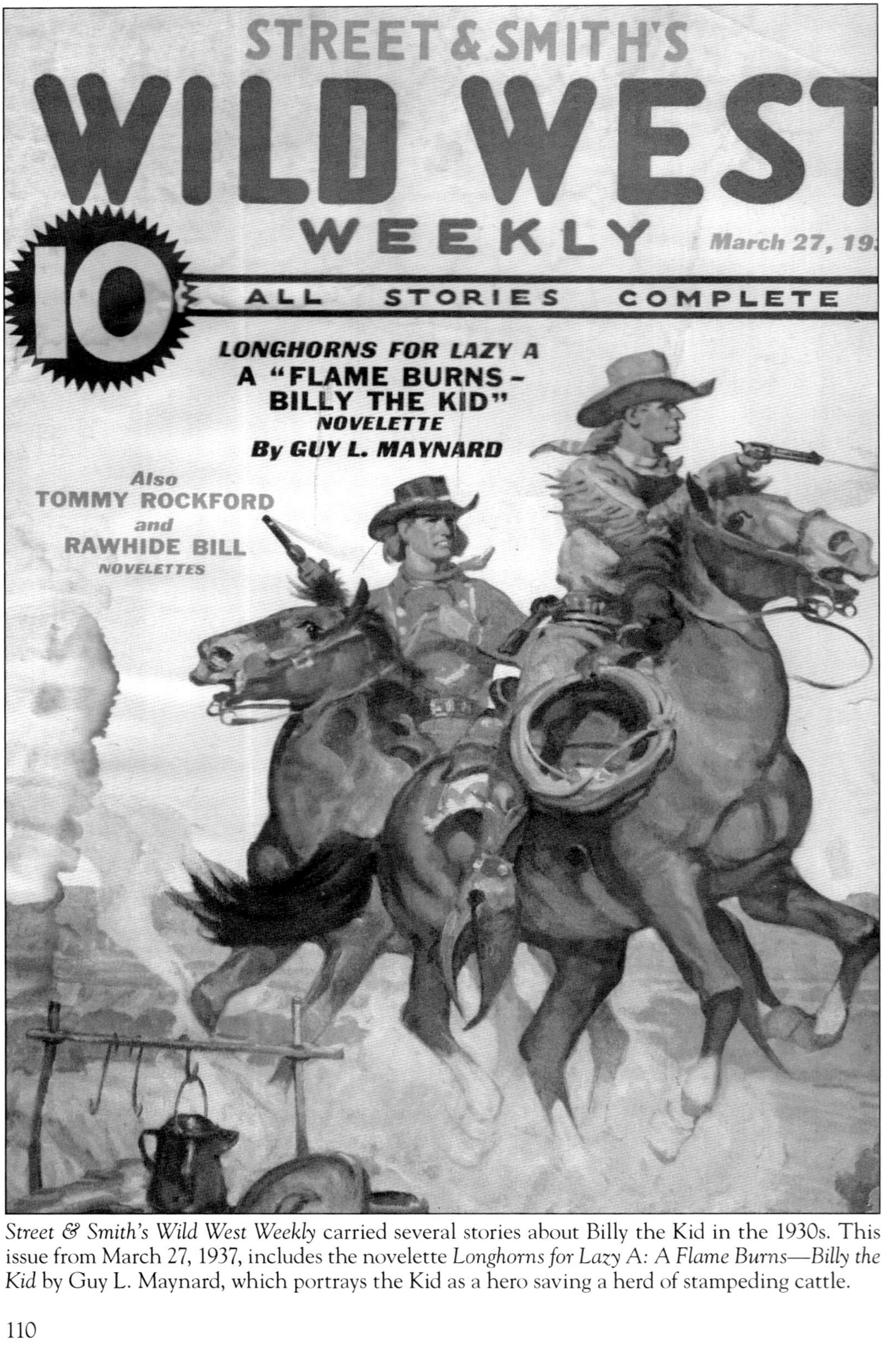

Street & Smith's Wild West Weekly carried several stories about Billy the Kid in the 1930s. This issue from March 27, 1937, includes the novelette *Longhorns for Lazy A: A Flame Burns—Billy the Kid* by Guy L. Maynard, which portrays the Kid as a hero saving a herd of stampeding cattle.

The June/July 1949 issue of DC's *All Star Comics*, published by National Comics Publications, featured the Justice Society of America battling Billy the Kid. Flash, the Green Lantern, Wonder Woman, Hawkman, Atom, Black Canary, and Dr. Mid-Nite go up against Billy the Kid and his evil minions. However, it turns out to not be the Kid at all but rather a rodeo star villain who impersonates the famous New Mexico cowboy.

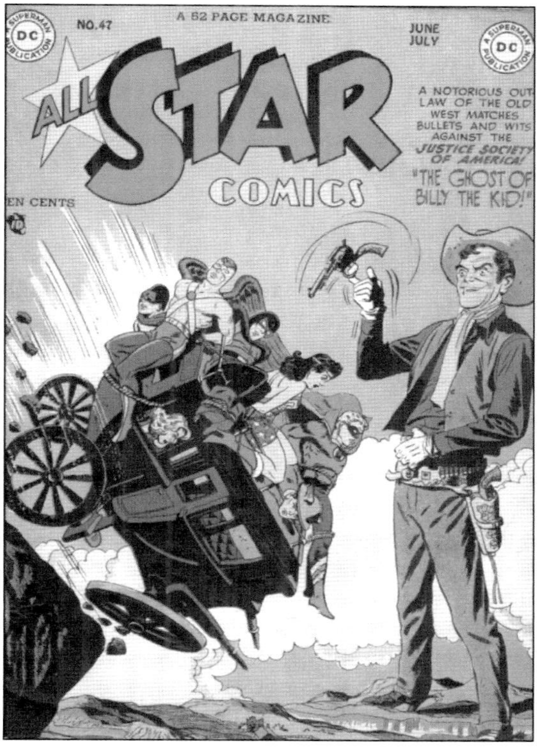

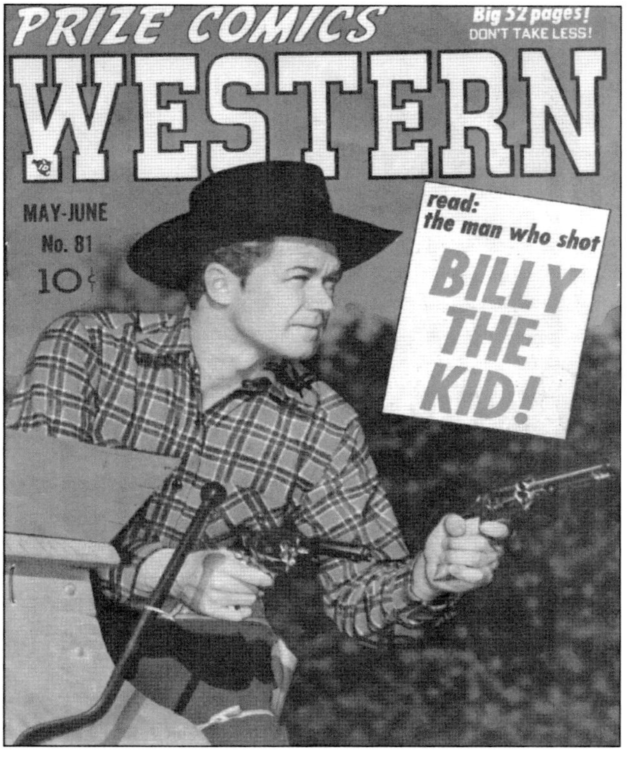

This 1950 issue of *Prize Comics Western*, sold by Feature Publications, showed Sheriff Pat Garrett as the hero of Lincoln who has a showdown with Billy the Kid. In this story, the two shoot it out on the main street of Lincoln, and Garrett wins the gunfight.

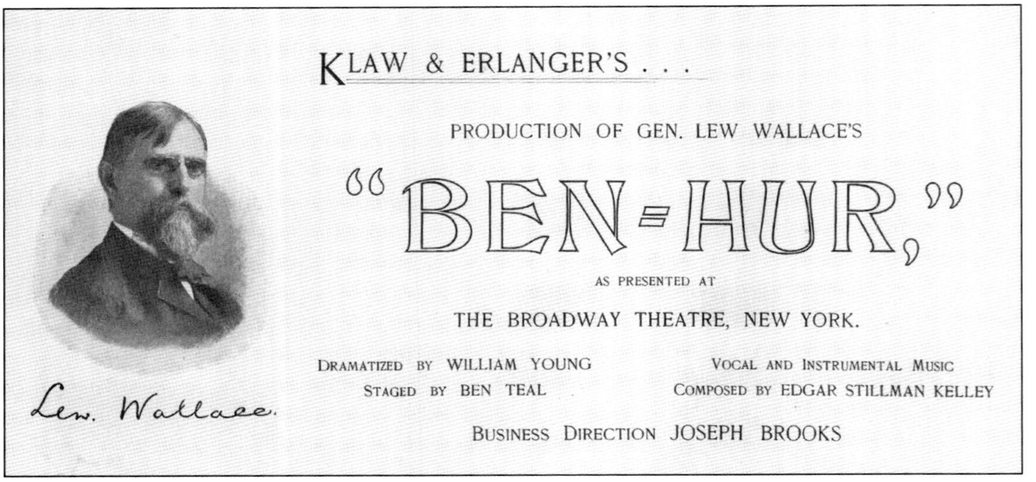
KLAW & ERLANGER'S . . .

PRODUCTION OF GEN. LEW WALLACE'S

"BEN-HUR,"

AS PRESENTED AT

THE BROADWAY THEATRE, NEW YORK.

DRAMATIZED BY WILLIAM YOUNG
STAGED BY BEN TEAL

VOCAL AND INSTRUMENTAL MUSIC
COMPOSED BY EDGAR STILLMAN KELLEY

BUSINESS DIRECTION JOSEPH BROOKS

Lew. Wallace.

After serving as governor of New Mexico Territory, Lew Wallace was stunned by the commercial success of his bestselling book, *Ben Hur.* A.L. Erlanger and Marcus Klaw produced a stage version of the book in November 1899. In 1900, Klaw & Erlanger released a set of beautiful photographic prints showing scenes from the play.

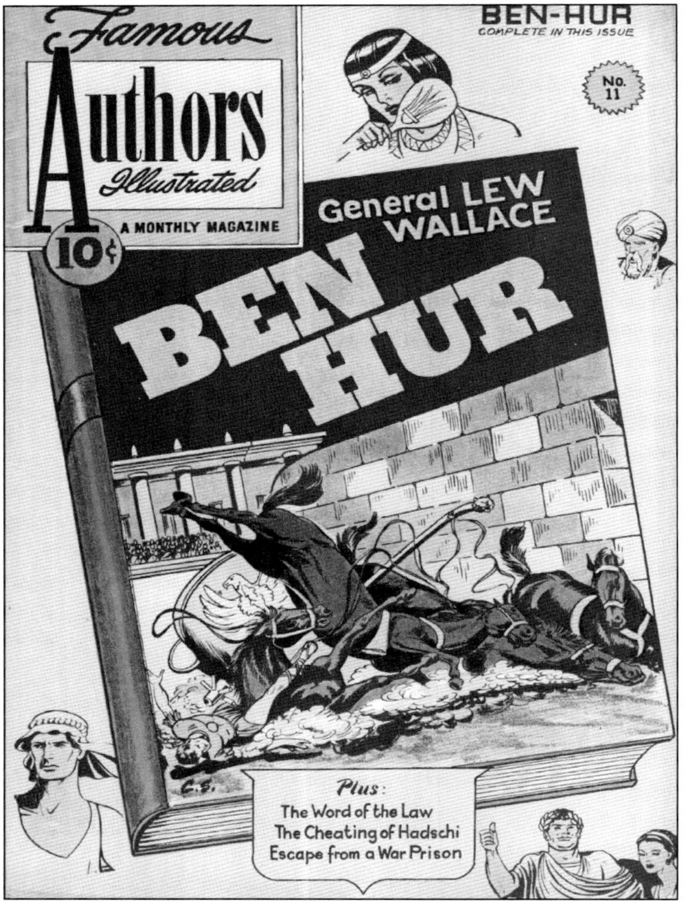

Ben Hur entered into the comic book trade in this 1951 issue of *Famous Authors Illustrated.* Ben Hur was also in a series called *Classics Illustrated*, which was widely collected by children. Comic books based on world-famous books made reading accessible to children and were immensely popular. *Don Quixote* and the works of Shakespeare and many others were published as comic books during the mid-20th century.

Many actors have played the lead role of Billy the Kid on stage and in film. In the 1949 motion picture *Son of Billy the Kid*, Lash La Rue played the Kid. In this film, directed by Ray Taylor, Billy the Kid does not die by Garrett's bullets but lives on to become a successful banker who has a son who then joins him to track down bank robbers.

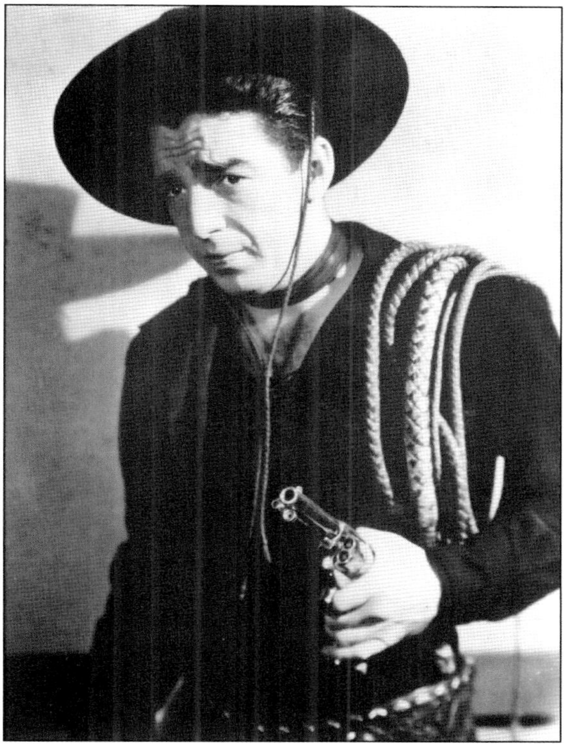

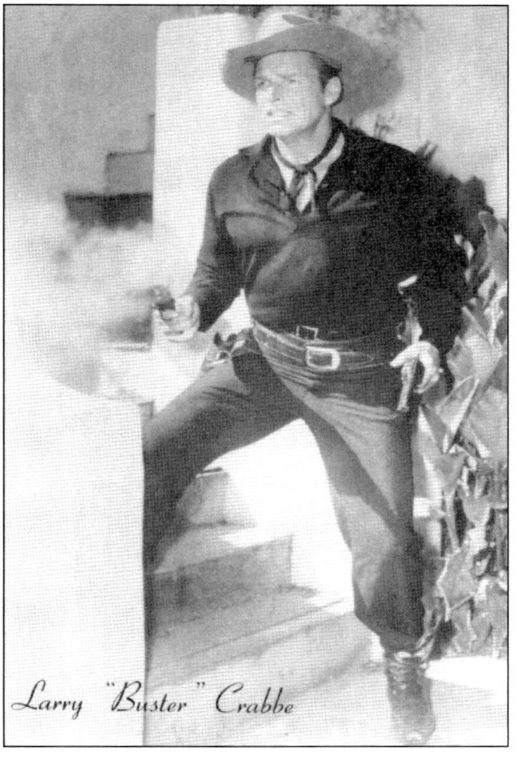

In the 1940s, Larry "Buster" Crabbe starred in several films about Billy the Kid, the first of which was *Billy the Kid Wanted*. Crabbe also starred in *Billy the Kid's Round-Up* and *Billy the Kid Trapped*.

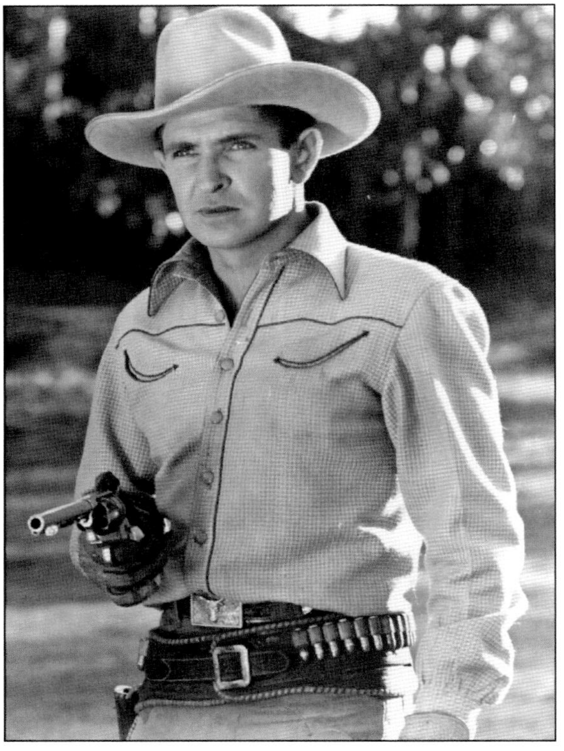

Bob Steele was one of the most popular Billy the Kid actors along with the renowned Roy Rogers. Producers Releasing Corporation cast Steele in a series of Kid films, beginning with *Billy the Kid Outlawed* in 1940. Glossy photographs of actors became popular with moviegoers and were especially in demand if the stars signed them. Fans collected the photographs and created sets such as those of Roy Rogers, who starred in the 1938 Republic film *Billy the Kid Returns*.

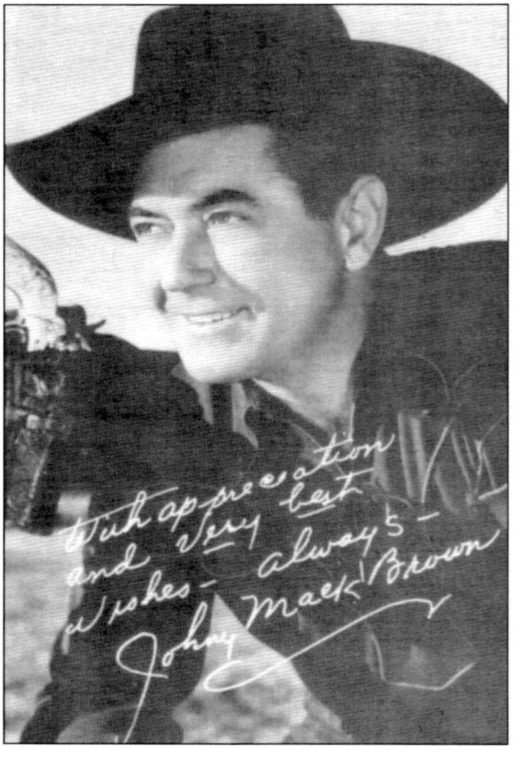

This is a signed photograph of Johnny Mack Brown, who played Billy the Kid in an MGM film from 1930. Brown was the first silver screen Kid and was cast in the character of someone who was a victim of injustice. New Mexico governor R.C. Dillon endorsed the film and was listed in the credits. The community of Lincoln was always featured in Billy the Kid movies, since the history of the Kid is inseparable from the town.

This is Bob Steele, who portrayed the Kid in the 1940 film *Billy the Kid's Gun Justice*. The Kid goes after murderous land grabbers and is blamed for countless unlawful acts across New Mexico that he did not commit. The plot is resolved when the Kid discovers who is bent on tarnishing his name and goes about trying to clear it. The story lines up with real events in the Kid's life.

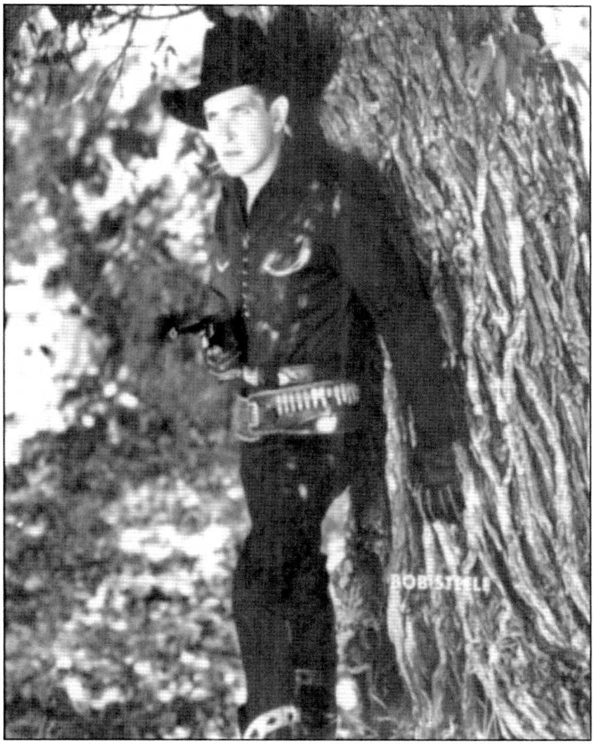

Buster Crabbe (right) is pictured here in a production still from *Billy the Kid's Round-Up*, a film from 1941 in which Billy the Kid saves a town from an evil gang. The plot thickens when an orphaned heroine whose father has been murdered desperately needs help.

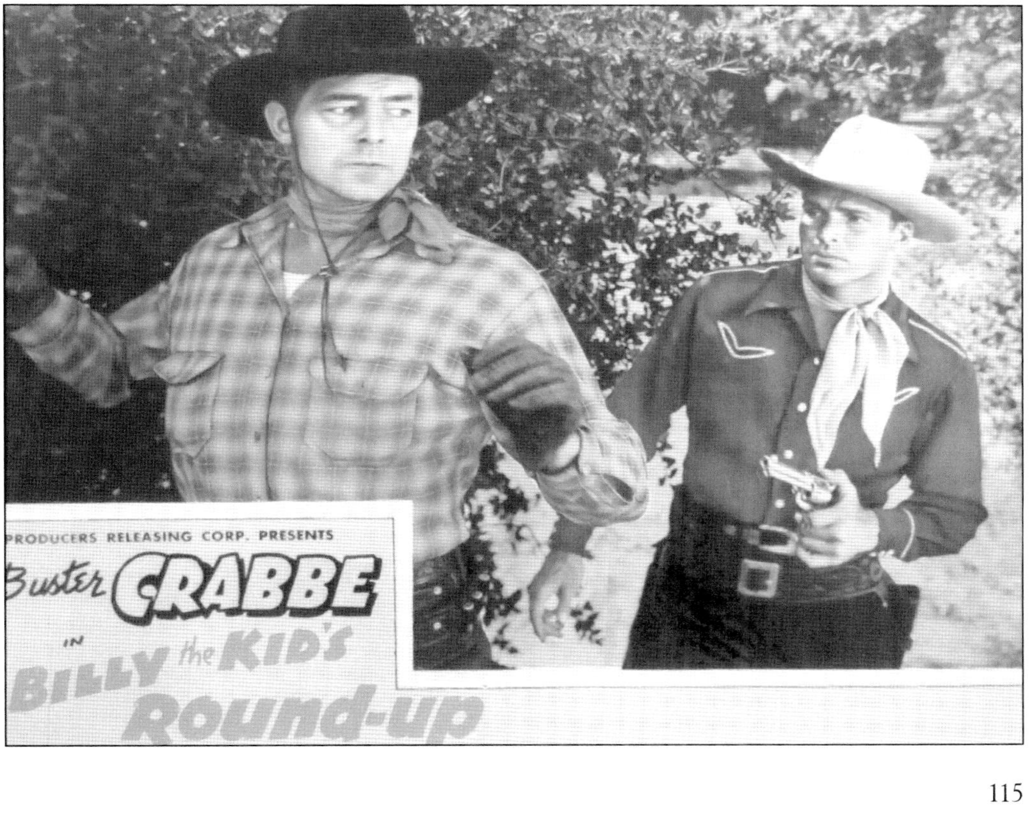

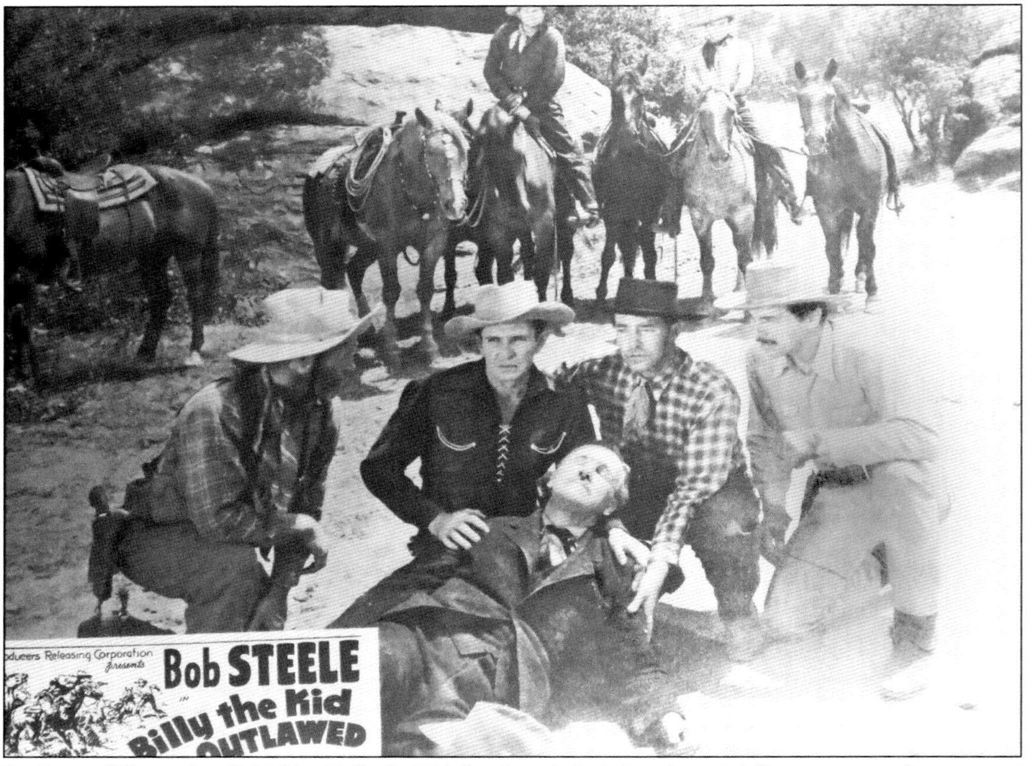

In this still from the 1940 film *Billy the Kid Outlawed*, Bob Steele and fellow actors gather around the actor playing John Henry Tunstall, who had just been murdered by a group of men sent by Sheriff William Brady. In this movie, Billy the Kid is bent on cleaning up the town of Lincoln and Lincoln County.

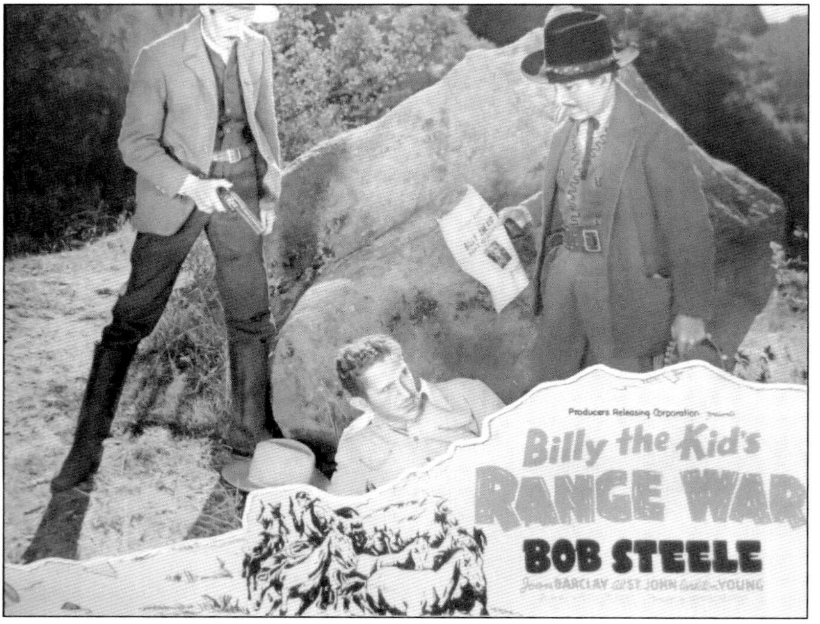

In *Billy the Kid's Range War*, released in 1941, Bob Steele sees action including fistfights, horseback chases, and gunplay.

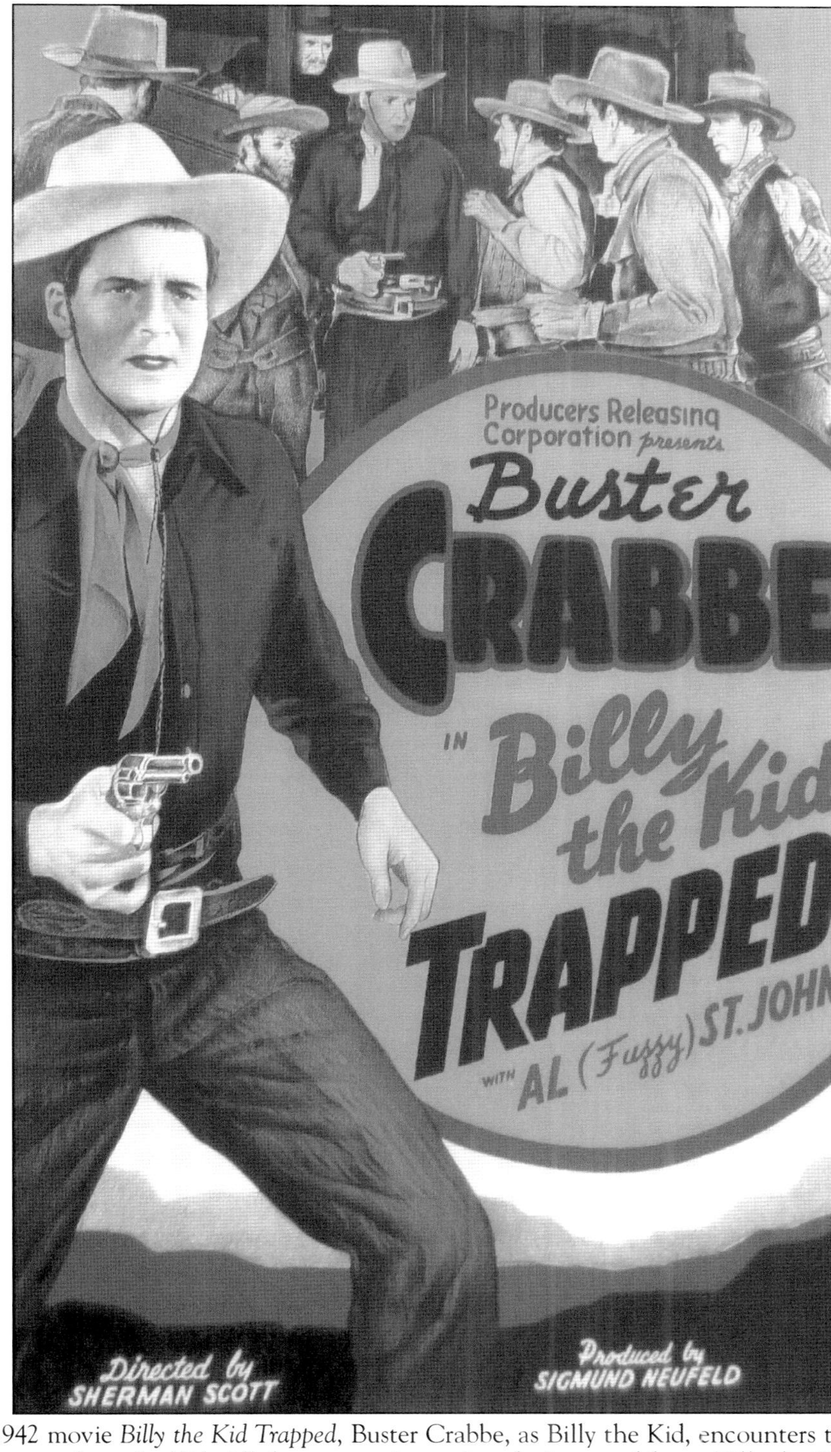

In the 1942 movie *Billy the Kid Trapped*, Buster Crabbe, as Billy the Kid, encounters three men who masquerade as the Kid. All three commit a series of crimes and frame Billy the Kid. Justice prevails when the true Kid saves an honest sheriff.

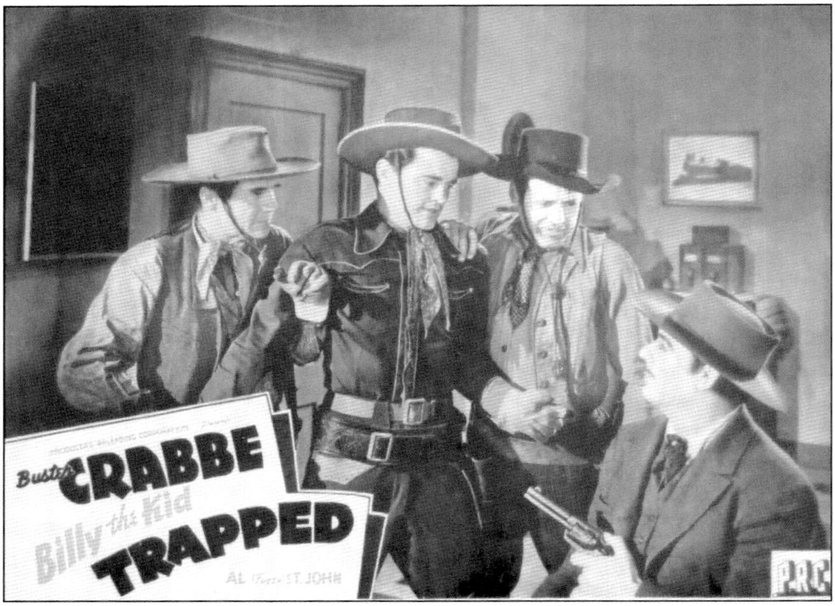

This is a lobby card from *Billy the Kid Trapped*, starring Buster Crabbe. Theatergoers were drawn to see a show via movie posters displayed outside the theater. The lobby cards often displayed scenes from the film.

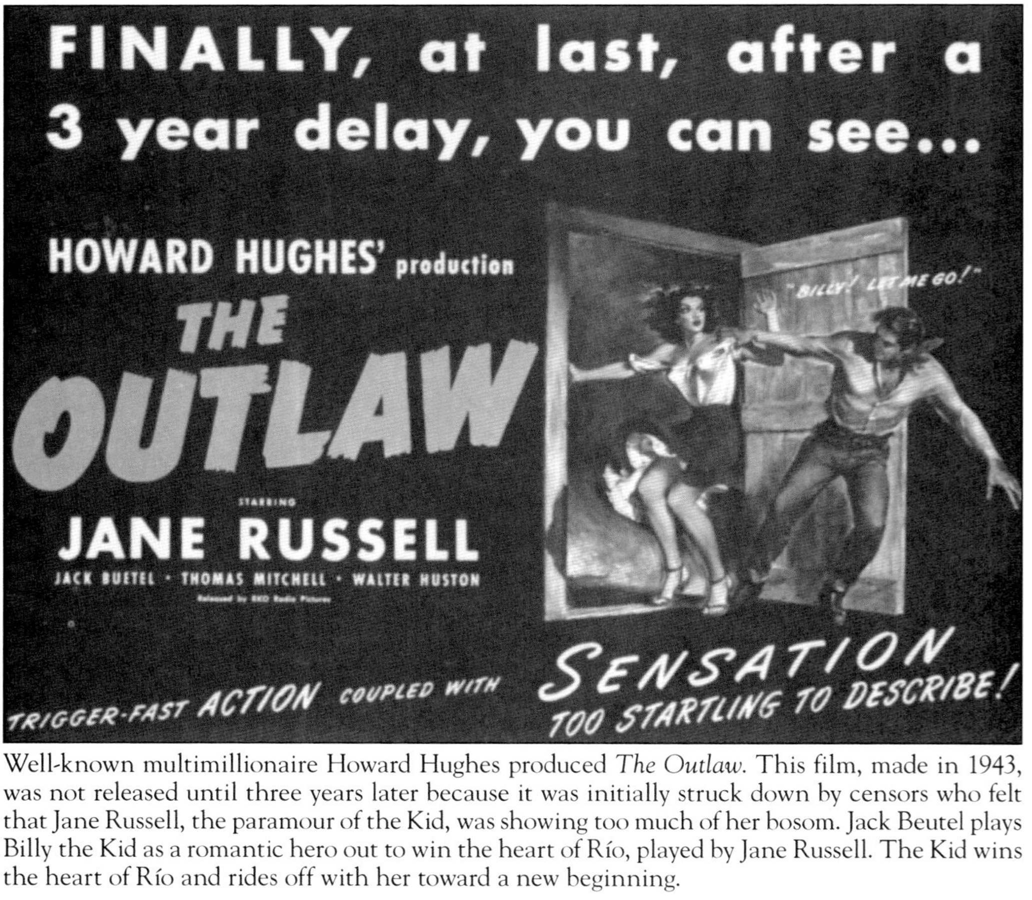

Well-known multimillionaire Howard Hughes produced *The Outlaw*. This film, made in 1943, was not released until three years later because it was initially struck down by censors who felt that Jane Russell, the paramour of the Kid, was showing too much of her bosom. Jack Beutel plays Billy the Kid as a romantic hero out to win the heart of Río, played by Jane Russell. The Kid wins the heart of Río and rides off with her toward a new beginning.

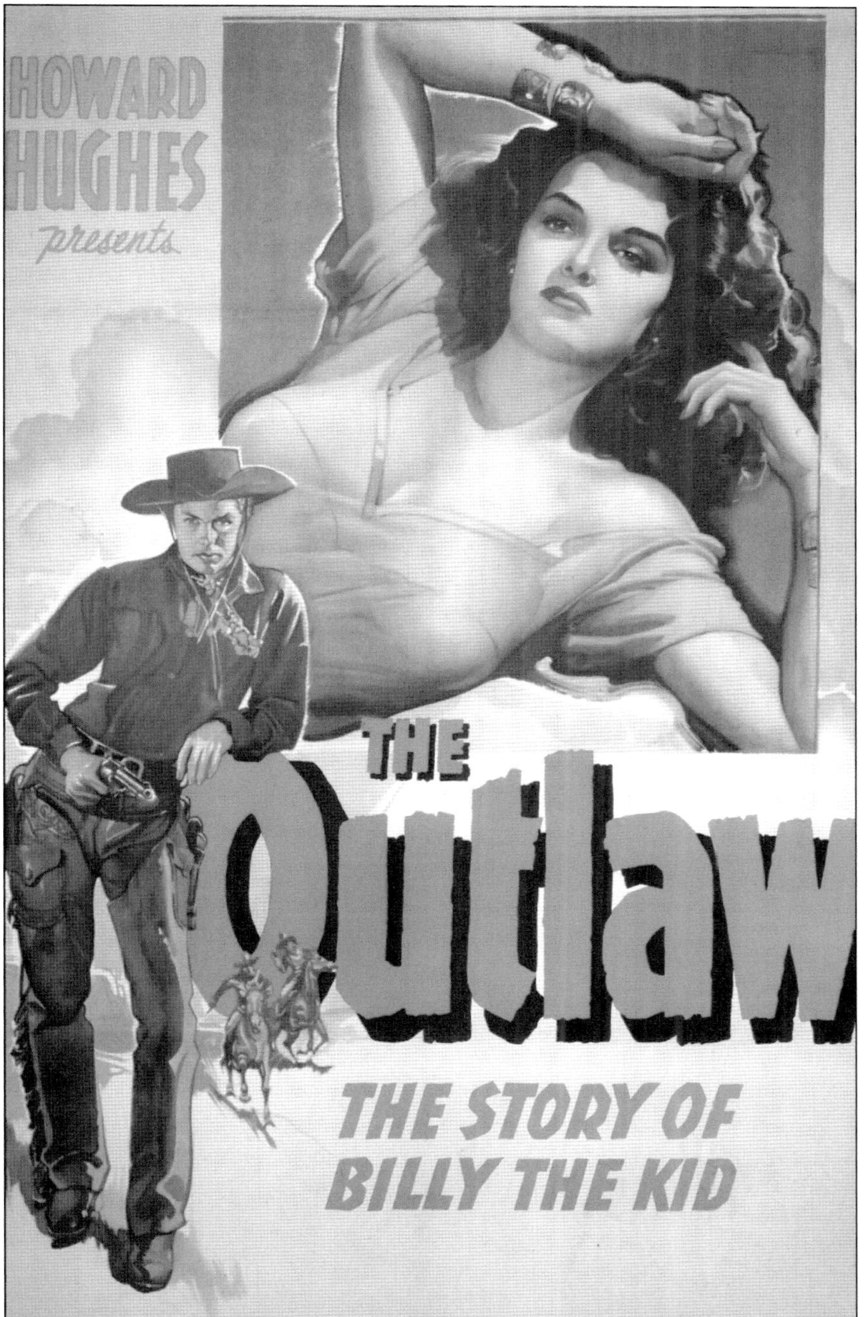

In *The Outlaw,* Jane Russell takes center stage. Russell plays a voluptuous, dark-haired, dark-eyed Hispanic beauty in her role as Río. Men are attracted to her and yearn for her. That was Howard Hughes's intent, and *The Outlaw* became one of the most famous and celebrated Billy the Kid movies. Russell became the pinup girl of American servicemen in World War II. She also starred opposite Marilyn Monroe in *Gentlemen Prefer Blondes.* Russell played many roles on film, but she captivated audiences as Río, Billy the Kid's Hispanic girl, in this movie.

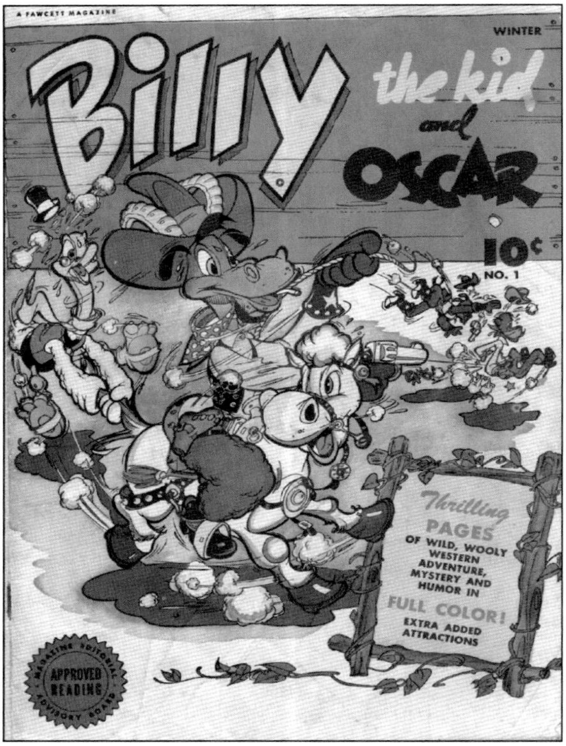

Billy the Kid and Oscar was a popular comic book series published quarterly by Fawcett Publications in 1946 and 1947. Children loved the full-color cartoon figures and were drawn in by the stories of the hero and his horse, Oscar, as they got in and out of trouble with bandits.

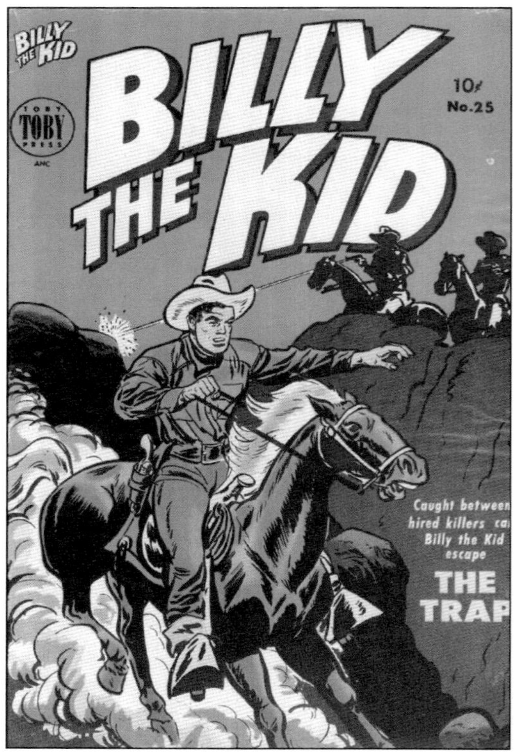

In the 1950s, several comic book publishers produced Billy the Kid comics, like this one from Toby Press of New York. Every other month, children could look forward to a new issue at newsstands to add to their collections. In issue No. 25, Billy the Kid eludes hired killers who just cannot take him down.

In issue No. 26, Billy the Kid is fearless as he takes on outlaws and cattle rustlers. Sometimes comic books featured a plot that told the factual story of Billy the Kid and his days in Lincoln.

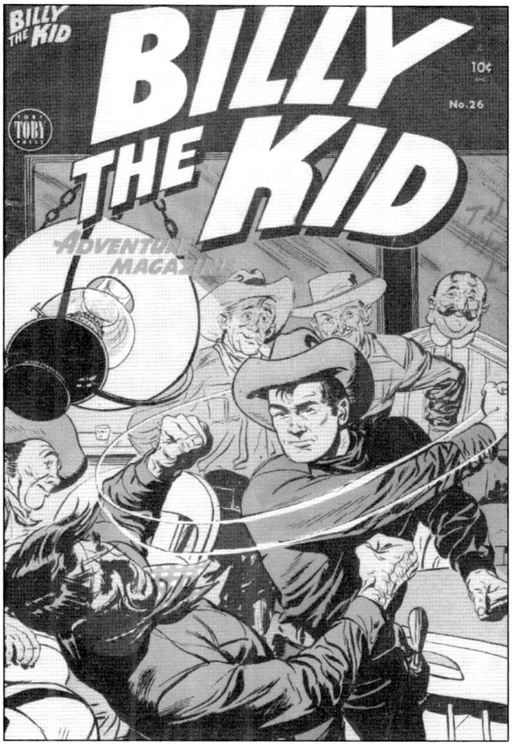

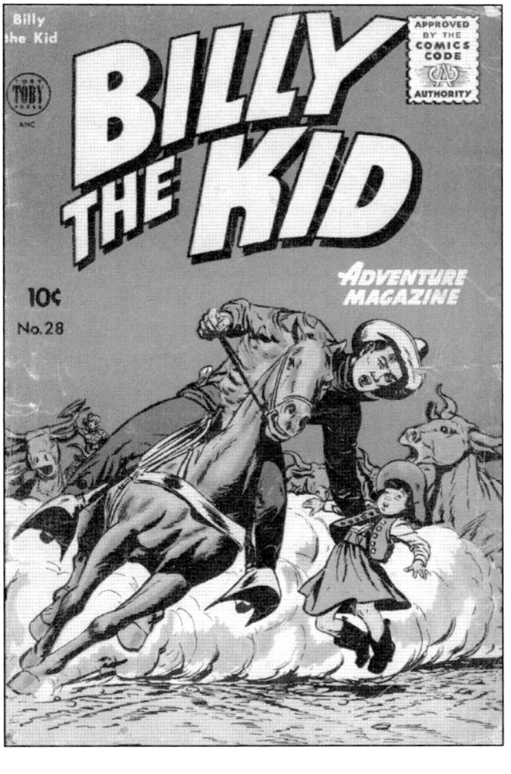

As the hero, Billy the Kid saves a little girl from a stampeding herd of cattle in issue No. 28. Charlton Comics produced nearly 200 issues of *Billy the Kid* from the 1950s to 1970s, including one called "Home Town Hero," in which Billy thwarts a plot to kill a candidate for the US Senate.

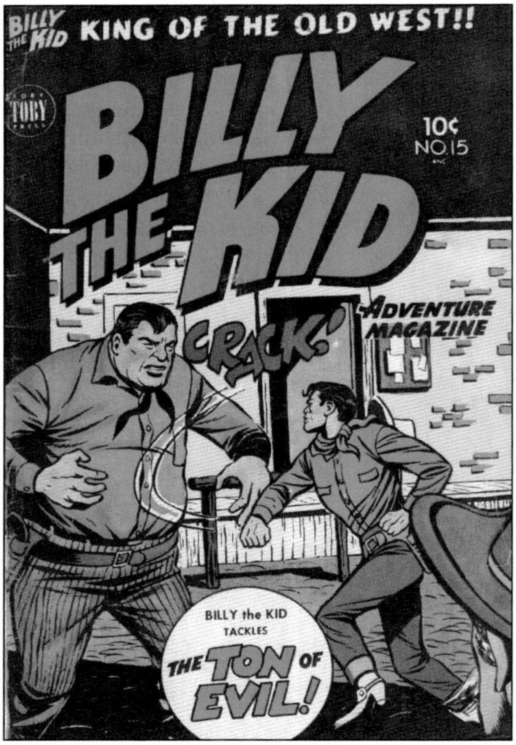

In issue No. 15, Billy the Kid fights the notorious Santa Fe Ring, represented by the Ton of Evil. The Ton cannot be stopped or killed as he destroys the town. The Ton finally gives in as the Kid relentlessly fights him.

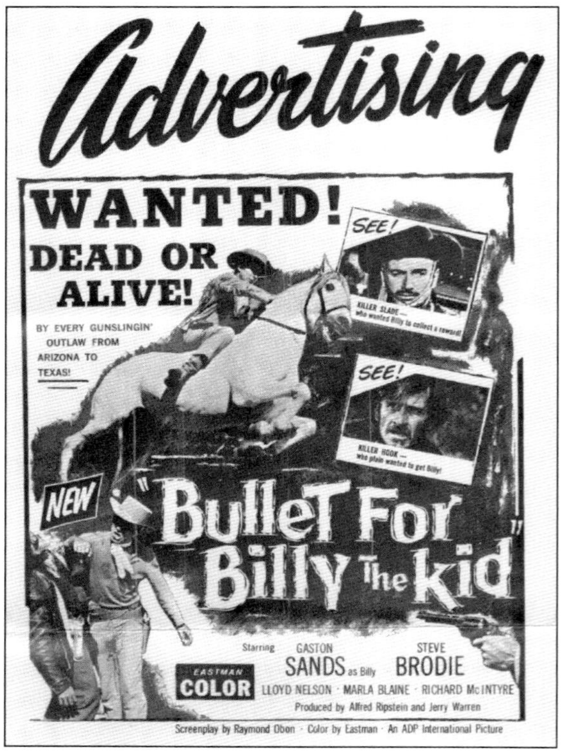

Advertising used to promote Billy the Kid movies included this poster for the film *Bullet for Billy the Kid*, starring Gaston Sands. This film is focused on gunslingers wanting to track the Kid down, but he escapes and rides off into the night.

This poster touts Lash La Rue starring in *Son of Billy the Kid*. Moviegoers in the early 1940s could see news clips that showed what was happening overseas during the war. They could also see Pres. Franklin D. Roosevelt and Winston Churchill talking about the war. Newsreels included shots of Hitler's and Mussolini's troops so Americans could know what was happening to their loved ones. After a fun cartoon, people sat back, relaxed, and enjoyed a good Billy the Kid movie.

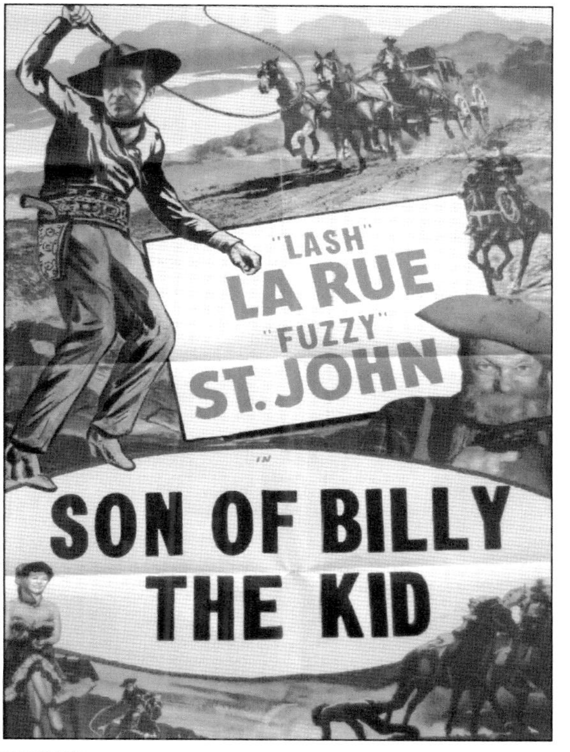

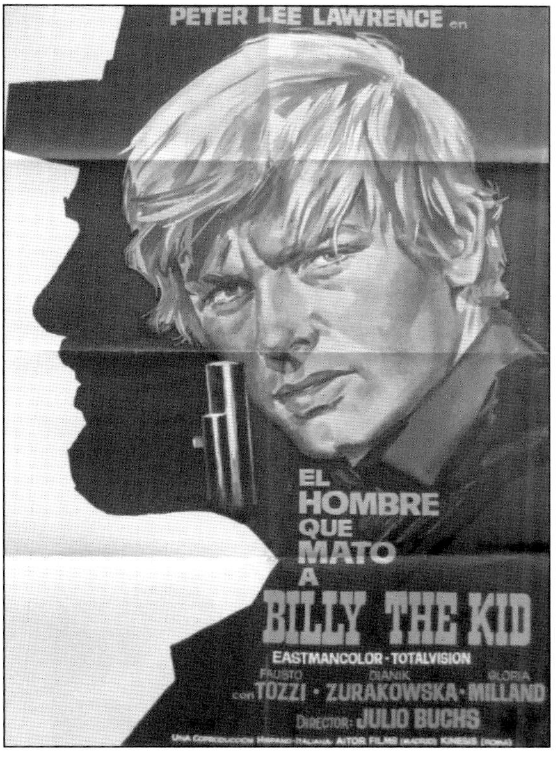

Peter Lee Lawrence was cast as the lead in *El Hombre Que Mato a Billy the Kid* (The Man who Killed Billy the Kid). In 1967, Aitor Films in Madrid and Kinesis in Rome coproduced this Hispanic-Italian production, an example of foreign-language films geared for worldwide consumption. This made Billy the Kid popular in Latin America, Italy, France, Spain, and Japan. In fact, Billy the Kid and the town of Lincoln are known throughout the world. Lincoln is now an international tourist destination for people who want to walk where Billy the Kid and Pat Garrett once trod.

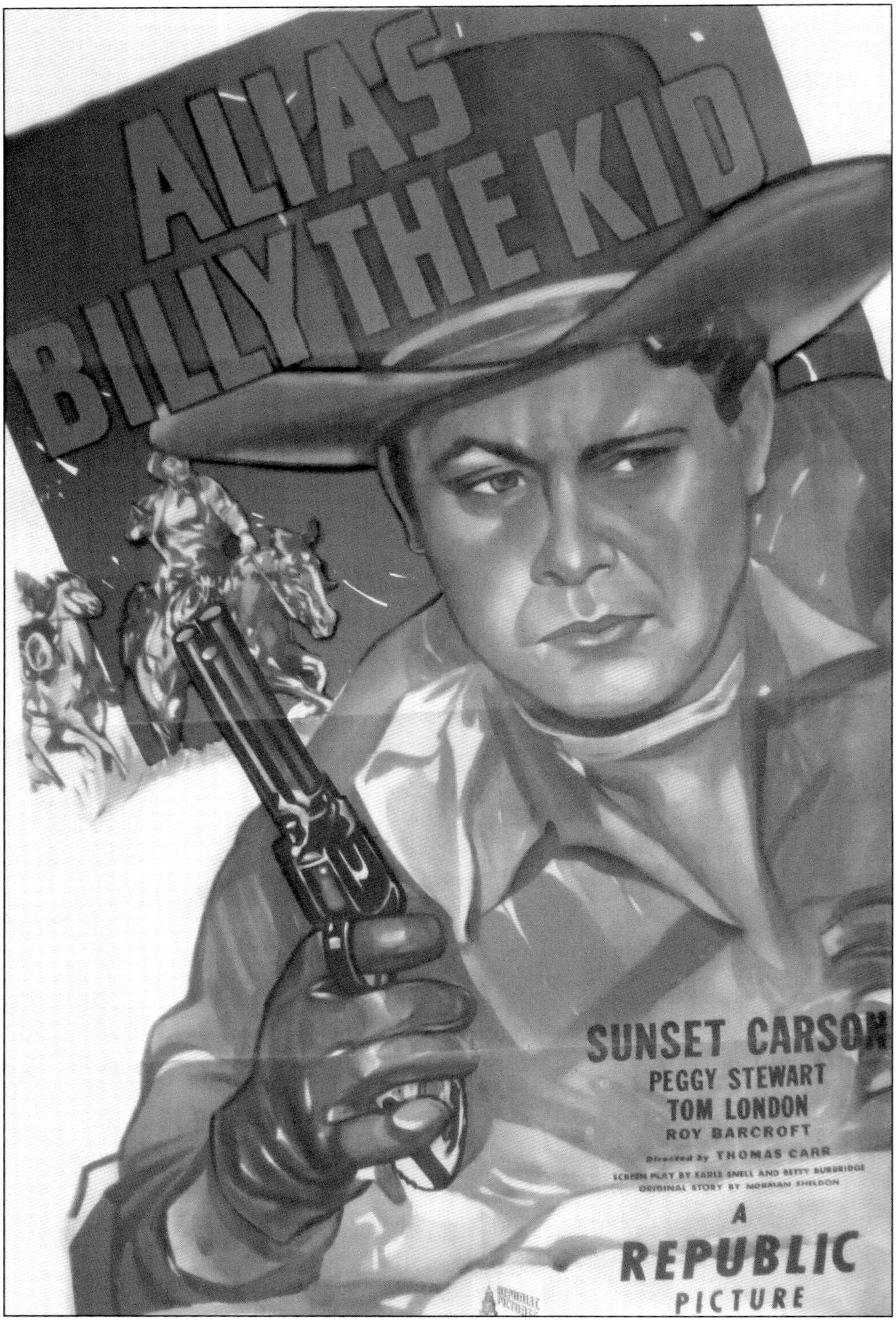

In 1946, Republic pictures produced *Alias Billy the Kid*, starring Sunset Carson. Carson joined a string of other actors playing Billy the Kid, including Audie Murphy in *The Kid from Texas* and Emilio Estevez in the first and second *Young Guns* movies. Kris Kristofferson joined the Kid's gang in *Pat Garrett and Billy the Kid* as did Marlon Brando in Paramount's 1961 *One-Eyed Jacks*, a spin off of Billy the Kid films.

Richard Romero, a fourth-grade student at Paul D. Henry Elementary School in Las Vegas, New Mexico, won the Billy the Kid drawing contest in 1983. He showed Billy the Kid standing with his favorite horse to one side and his faithful dog on the other. Upon winning the contest, Romero said that his inspiration included Jim Henson's Muppets sketches about Billy the Kid, Mickey Mouse as Billy, and other cartoon characters.

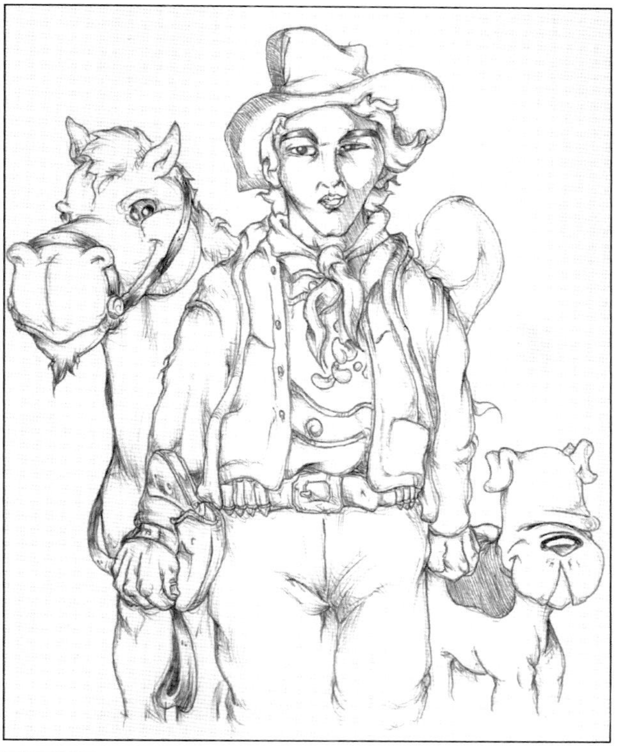

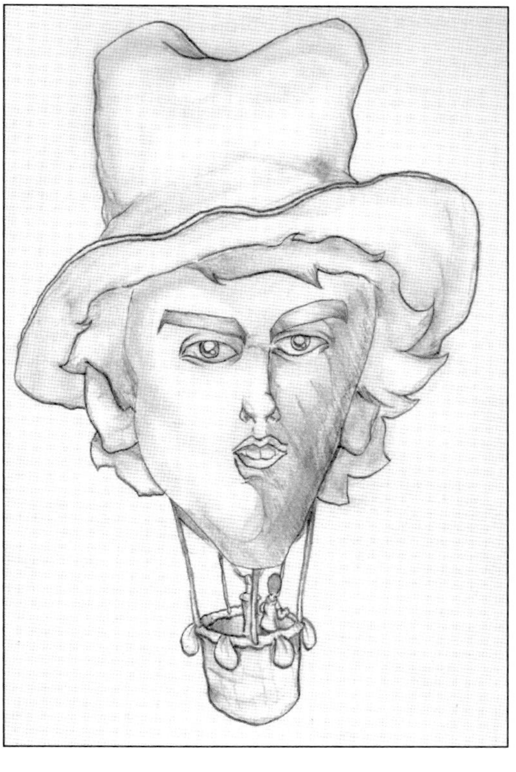

The Albuquerque International Balloon Fiesta features nearly 500 hot air balloons and special hot air balloons that have included Darth Vader and Humpty Dumpty. Fourth grader Richard Romero felt Billy the Kid should be included, so in 1983, he drew this Billy the Kid hot air balloon flying high in New Mexico's skies.

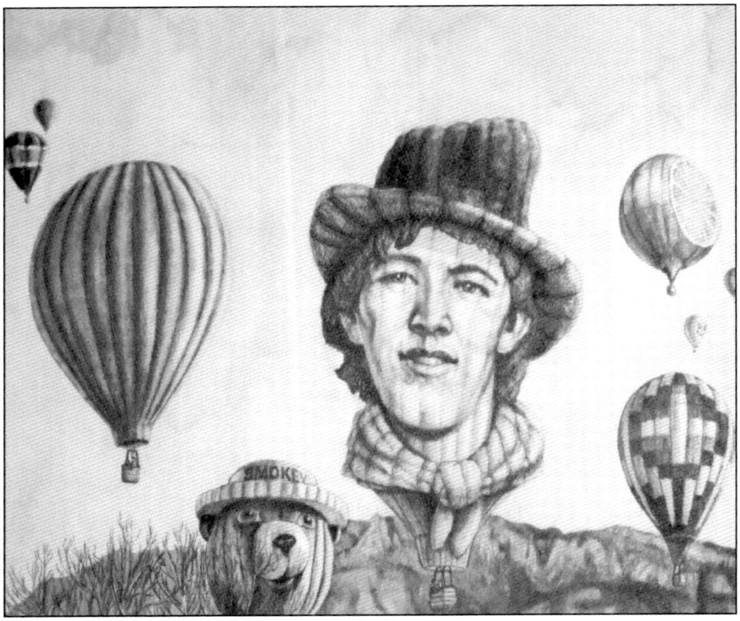

Renowned artist Brent Jeffrey Thomas drew this pencil sketch of a Billy the Kid hot air balloon rising above the Sandia Mountains next to Smokey Bear in Albuquerque. The annual Albuquerque International Balloon Fiesta attracts people from throughout the world. Hot air balloons from every corner of the Earth participate in special events and competitions capped off with massive fireworks at night.

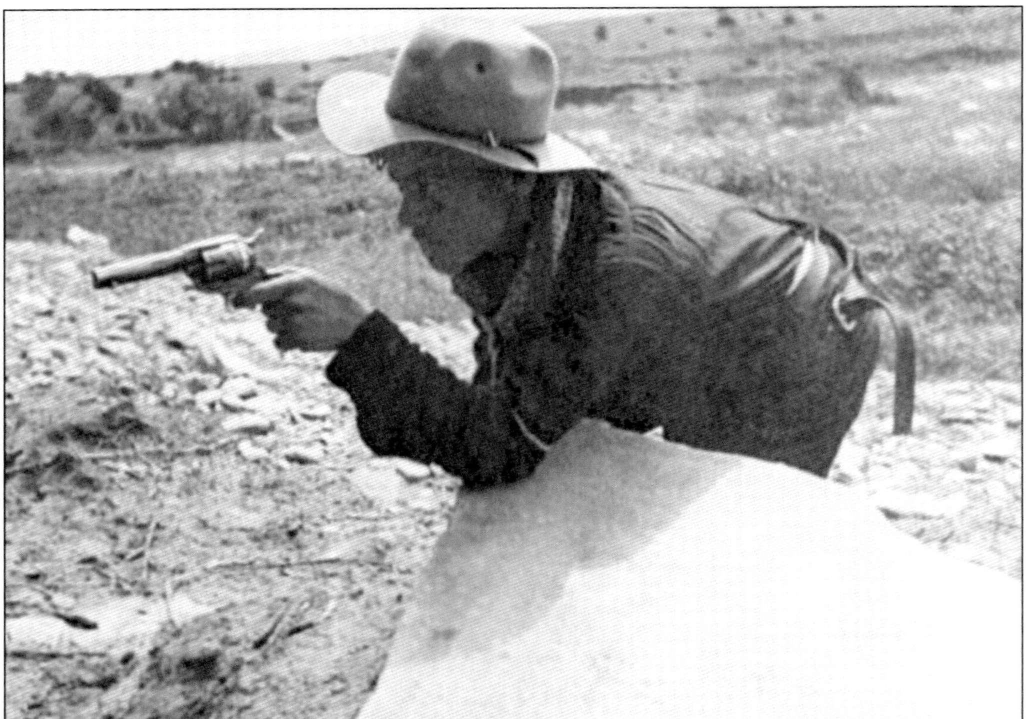

The annual Billy the Kid Pageant in Lincoln reenacts the famous escape of the renowned desperado. The pageant is the longest-running folk pageant in the United States. Local actors from Lincoln and the surrounding area portray the Kid and other principal characters involved in his famous escape from the Lincoln jail. In this c. 1950 photograph, Jesus Chavez plays Billy the Kid in the pageant.

Bibliography

Bender, Norman J. *Missionaries, Outlaws, and Indians, Taylor F. Ealy at Lincoln and Zuni, 1878–1881.* Albuquerque, NM: University of New Mexico, 1984.

Clarke, Mary Whatley. *John Chisum, Jinglebob of the Pecos.* Austin, Texas: Eakin Press, 1984.

Coe, George W. *Frontier Fighter.* Boston and New York: Houghton Mifflin Co., 1934.

Dykes, Jeff C. *Law on a Wild Frontier, Four Sheriffs of Lincoln County.* Washington, DC: The Westerners, 1969.

Fulton, Maurice G., edited by Robert N. Mullin. *History of the Lincoln County War.* Tucson, AZ: University of Arizona Press, 1968.

Kelleher, William A. *Violence in Lincoln County 1869–1881.* Albuquerque, NM: University of New Mexico, 1957.

Lavash, Donald R. *Sheriff William Brady, Tragic Hero of the Lincoln County War.* Santa Fe, NM: Sunstone Press, 1987.

Metz, Leon C. *Pat Garrett, The Story of a Western Lawman.* Norman, OK: University of Oklahoma Press, 1974.

Mullin, Robert N. *The Lincoln County War.* Tucson, AZ: University of Arizona Press, 1968.

New Mexico State Planning Office. *Lincoln New Mexico, A Plan for Preservation and Growth.* Santa Fe, NM: State Planning Office, 1974.

Noble Burns, Walter. *The Saga of Billy the Kid.* Garden City, NY: Doubleday and Co., 1927.

Stanley, F. *The Lincoln New Mexico Story.* Pep, Texas: Self-published, 1964.

———. *The Seven Rivers New Mexico Story.* Pep, Texas: Self-published, 1963.

Utley, Robert M. *Billy the Kid, A Short and Violent Life.* Lincoln, NE: University of Nebraska Press, 1989.

———. *High Noon in Lincoln, Violence on the Western Frontier.* Albuquerque, NM: University of New Mexico Press, 1987.